HARRY

JAZZ MASTERS
IN TRANSITION,
1957-69

OTHER DA CAPO TITLES BY MARTIN WILLIAMS

JAZZ MASTERS IN TRANSITION, 1957-69

by Martin Williams

A DA CAPO PAPERBACK

Library of Congress Cataloging in Publication Data

Williams, Martin T.
  Jazz masters in transition, 1957-69.

  (A Da Capo paperback)
  Collection of articles from various sources.
  Reprint. Originally published: New York:
Macmillan, 1970. (The Macmillan jazz masters
series)
    1. Jazz music—Addresses, essays, lectures.
  2. Jazz musicians—Addresses, essays, lectures.
  I. Title. II. Series: Macmillan jazz masters series.
  [ML3507.W54 1982]   785.42   82-9964
  ISBN 0-306-80175-2 (pbk.)   AACR2

First paperback printing—July, 1982
Second paperback printing—December, 1986

This Da Capo Press paperback edition of
Jazz Masters in Transition 1957-1969
is an unabridged republication of the
first edition published in new York in 1970.
It is reprinted by arrangement with Macmillan, Inc.

Published by Da Capo Press, Inc.
A Subsidiary of Plenum Publishing Corporation
233 Spring Street, New York, N.Y. 10013

Contents

Preface

A book such as this one undoubtedly needs a prefatory note of some kind. I shall try to keep it brief.

What follows are selected chronicles covering an important decade in jazz. These chronicles are the observations of a writer and of his subjects. They include reviews, interviews, brief profiles, and narratives of such events as rehearsals, recording dates, television tapings, and evenings in night clubs. All were originally written during the decade under examination, and, although I have done a bit of polishing and rewriting here and there in preparing this volume, I have tried not to indulge in too much second-guessing.

As a kind of stage setting for the book's opening section, it seemed best to backtrack a bit to the very beginnings of Thelonious Monk's rediscovery. Otherwise, you will read in these pages of newly arrived younger musicians, of musicians and groups who arrived in the 1940s and 1950s and who have continued to be active and productive, and of musicians who arrived in the 1920s and 1930s who did the same. The attempt was to make this a rounded chronicle, and at least to indicate the range of activity that went on in the music—continuing careers, new careers, and some rediscoveries, too. There are also some glances at such peripheral subjects as Bing Crosby and rock. You will read of reissued recordings, for, in addition to preserving and promoting music of the past that has lasting merit, these collections help indicate a stability and continuity for a music that has changed (or perhaps only *seemed* to change) rapidly in its first seventy years.

The chronicle is not complete of course, nor could it be, but selective. And I hope that my volume will not seem, in that book reviewer's favorite phrase, a collection of "occasional pieces," but rather a record of a time when jazz moved from one era to another, at great risk, inevitably, and with great achievement as well.

MARTIN WILLIAMS

Thelonious Monk: A Prelude to Success

The Unique Monk (Riverside RLP 12-209) has received excellent press notices. Nat Hentoff in *Down Beat* gave it four and a half stars because Monk remains "one of the insatiably, irrepressibly, and valuably individual jazzmen in our era." He "has an intense sense of drama (not melodrama) that can create a reflectively dissonant, almost hypnotic mood . . . and a sharply knifed penchant for shaping and reshaping a few key phrases into a hail of plunging aural mobiles." In the *Saturday Review*, Whitney Balliett called it "an essential record," saying, "Monk's style—loose, almost diffident dissonances, wry single-note lines, a laggard-like beat—is easily plumbed. Here he winds his way . . . keeping the melody always just below the surface and embellishing it more than reworking its chords. . . ."

One of the most immediately striking things about Monk's playing for me is that everything he says he says musically—if he has no music to make he doesn't fill out a single bar with faked blowing or rambling. All is given in terms of a musical sensibility, or it isn't given at all.

The Unique Monk is one of the most humorous jazz records ever made. The mutual agreement with which he makes him and you approach having some respectful fun with such warhorses as "Tea For Two" and "Honeysuckle Rose" is superb and is as far from mere ridicule as one could imagine. I will not attempt to describe how he does it; the effect is too subtle for the mechanics of the matter even to hint at. The delicious rubato with which he will now and then approach a perfectly ordinary chord on one of the slower numbers, as if saying he just can't find the obvious, and then delight both of you as he hits it with the joke on yourselves at how obvious it really was—or surprise you both with a delightful dissonance—is alive with human commentary. He can even have fleeting moments of what sounds like honest frivolity and

11

we accept them because this is a man we are with and men can get frivolous. "Just You, Just Me" is one of his most carefully wrought sets of variations built on and around a melody. Contrast Monk on it with his bassist Oscar Pettiford. Pettiford's solos are really excellent but he is "blowing" on chords; Monk is building a set of variations, like Brahms—like Jelly Roll Morton—with a large sense of musical form and with a constant sense of musical expression. He is not, I would say, merely "embellishing" the melody. And Monk has the artist's special capacity for involving us with him so that we seem to be working it all out together.

Record Changer, January, 1957

Monk with Blakey

I think that this collaboration of Art Blakey's group and Thelonious Monk (Atlantic LP 1278) dramatizes important events in jazz in the late 1950s for, although each man has been heard from for years, each has recently been listened to probably more attentively than ever before, and each is a man in whose work we see jazz doing what it must do as a music with an identity of its own—finding, not borrowing, its way by developing the implicit possibilities in the materials which are its substance.

Now that the "cool" conception of the early fifties has ceased to be a fad, it should be clear which of its arrangers, its instrumentalists, and its groups have been and are capable of genuine creativity within that idiom, and of exploring it further, and which are capable only of a kind of derivative hackwork. The fashion as such has passed and the real artists and craftsmen can be counted.

When the pendulum swung, it swung almost violently, and the style it swung to soon acquired a name or two: "funky" and "hard bop." Art Blakey has led groups of messengers for years, but the group he introduced in 1954 proclaimed the "funky" style. These men wanted to incorporate as much of the quality, as well as the devices, of blues and church music in their playing as they could. Inevitably, they were called regressive and even crude, but their conception was actually neither naive nor reactionary. It implied that if jazz got too far from the kind of music in its background, it might not only be in danger of a contrivance and preciosity, but of losing something essential—indeed, even of losing its identity. Such an attitude is not merely conservative, and the style not for another reason: as I have indicated above, I think it is bringing about some stylistic changes in jazz. (For a precedent, we can remember how the dominance of the almost classic ragtime conception at the turn of the century was supplanted by what has been called a "blues craze," and how a combination of elements of these two was worked out in New Orleans.)

Some of Blakey's earliest records were made with Thelonious Monk, and the two collaborate excellently. It has been said of Blakey that he took the bop style and reduced it to its elements. When such a thing happens, one had better be watching for changes.

The bop drummer both simplified his basic accompaniment and expanded it by adding to it a spontaneous series of accents and replies to the solioist's improvisations, with bass "explosions," snare, and cymbal strokes, etc.

Listen to Blakey behind Bill Hardman's trumpet solo on "I Mean You." Clearly he not only accompanies but directly leads the trumpet into ideas and motifs. It is a dangerous role for a drummer, demanding constant discretion and sympathy with the soloist. The second change is illustrated in some of Blakey's solos: probably more directly than any other drummer Blakey saw the possibility of sustaining polyrhythmic lines, and he can keep several rhythms going with an unusual kind of continuity. But the most important point for me is the one we can hear illustrated by what he does on the opening chorus of "I Mean You." He carries the accompanying 4/4 pulse, but, at the same time, he improvises a parallel percussive line which interplays with both the melody and the fundamental time; the jazz drummer becomes an improvising percussionist on a plane almost equal to that of the horns.

Rhythm is fundamental to jazz and if one develops its role soundly, one develops jazz along the way that its own nature implies that it should go. Such an obvious thing, and yet how brilliant. In the forties, Paul Bacon, probably the only American critic who understood Thelonious Monk, said of him in *The Record Changer* that he had looked at jazz, seen the gaps and, sacrificing the obvious things that everyone could do, proceeded to fill in those gaps. The same kind of thing might be said of Art Blakey.

Almost anyone knows that Monk is supposed to have been one of the founders of bop. Undoubtedly he made important contributions to the style, but it should be clear by now that what this strikingly original musician has been working on all along is something different.

Monk is a virtuoso of time, rhythm, meter, accent. He has played versions of "standards" which are little more than sets of unique rhythmic variations directly on a melodic line, with an evolving pattern of displaced accents and shifting meters—a conception at once more basic than the groups of melodic variations Jelly Roll Morton, James P. Johnson, and Fats Waller produced, and more "experimental" than the harmonic variations, which improvise new melodic lines, of the late swing and bop instrumentalists. At the same time, he may play melodic variations, and his solo here on "In Walked Bud" interplays the melodic line of that piece with contrasting motifs. And notice his rhythmic and harmonic experiments with the sparsely suggestive and obviously difficult tissue of notes that is "Evidence," both in his own solo and behind John Griffin's.

Monk's harmonies, always a part of the picture, are not innovations in themselves—it is the sequence and pattern of alteration in which he plays them that are unique. In this and in simultaneous accentual shiftings, there is an almost constant element of humor (even sarcasm) that his wonderful, deliberate dissonances often point up.

Monk also plays harmonic variations, and these may seem quite simple, even casual, on the surface. His two choruses here on "I Mean You" show the kind of inner logic they can have. The first chorus is based on a descending motif variously altered. The second on a brief and contrasting riff figure which is turned several ways, subjected to a counter-riff or two and, in the end, complemented by a descent which alludes to the first chorus and ties the two together. And, lest anyone doubt that Monk can improvise a lyric melody, let him hear the solo on "Blue Monk."

Monk's style, like Lester Young's in the late thirties, depends on surprise. It does not, like the work of earlier "stride" pianists (yes, Monk, like Count Basie, is really a member of that school) depend on the expected. He can also be one of the most exciting and original accompanists in jazz, as his work behind Bill Hardman on "I Mean You," both horns on "Rhythm-a-ning," and behind Griffin on "Purple Shades" illustrates. The latter example seems to me one of the best things I have ever heard him do on records and notice also that both his solo and his accompaniment on that piece are based on similar ideas of patterns, giving that performance a fine continuity.

I think that on the whole, Monk's compositions place him with the great jazz composers, but I will confine myself to a few points which the selections here illustrate. Whereas Ellington often leans heavily on the "show tune" tradition, Monk is more directly instrumental in his conception, even when he uses the 32-bar, A A B A popular tune form. Monk, himself, has made the point about the integration of the B, bridge, melody; notice that the bridges of "I Mean You" and of "In Walked Bud" are both developments of bits of phrases in the A melody. It is not Monk's habit to base his compositions on "standard" chord sequences, but he may; and three of the tunes here do use slight alterations of bass lines we all know. That is almost bound to be true of any 12-bar blues, of course, but notice the structure of "Blue Monk's" melody. Most blues have an open space of about three beats at the end of each four-bar unit. There are "modern" blues which deliberately fill this hole, of course, but the deceptive simplicity with which this melody unfolds makes for neither a trick nor a contrivance, but an inevitability that flows like life.

Monk does indeed "fill in the gaps."

Liner Notes to Atlantic 1278, 1957

Miles, Monk, Mulligan, Mingus, and Rollins

Since about 1949, the playing of trumpeter (sometimes flügelhornist) Miles Davis has settled into a gentle but firm lyricism, shorn of almost all his earlier attempts at virtuosity. His work has been, and is, uneven, but it is at its best a unique and beautiful experience. On "standard" songs (take "All of You" or "Bye Bye Blackbird" on Columbia CL-949) he states melody, in a sense echoing the young Armstrong or Red Allen, with a secret kind of shift of meter and accent and slight alteration of line (like a man slowly turning a crystal in a warm light) which can bring out the most unexpected beauties, then gradually alter it until he is creating something quite new out of its harmonies.

The recent *Cookin'* (Prestige 7094) is by the same quintet as the aforementioned Columbia. It has, I think, no really striking moments, but almost everyone on it plays with a consistency and unified swing. Prestige also has a collection of Davis reissues from 1954 called *Bag's Groove* (7109) in which the leader plays especially well on the first (originally released) of two versions of "But Not for Me," and which also contains work by Milt Jackson, Thelonious Monk, Sonny Rollins, Horace Silver, Kenny Clarke, and Percy Heath. It is an almost constantly eventful and representative collection, belonging in this respect with the previous *Walkin'* (Prestige 7076).

Two recent releases by pianist Thelonious Monk, *Monk Meets Mulligan* (Riverside 12-247) and *Monk's Music* (Riverside 12-242) contain, along with new compositions, new versions of some of his earlier pieces, and therefore a brief account of his work may be appropriate. His first recordings as leader were made for Blue Note from 1947-50 (now available on 1510, 1511, and most of 1509). They showed a remarkably original musician, and a man who had already learned the essential artistic lesson of discipline that so few of his contemporaries have learned: his own limitations, hence his own form and real potentialities. Monk is, to put it bluntly (and I hope not too dogmatically), with Joplin, Morton, Ellington, and, perhaps, Waller, one of the great composers of jazz. He is also, as an instrumentalist, one of the great virtuosos of rhythm, meter, and accent in all music, and a master of surprise. At least two-thirds of the Blue Note series is excellent.

Prestige has recently collected some of the Monk of the early fifties on two twelve-inch LPs. The quintet (7245) plays on six fine compositions, and the sureness with which the leader can bring out the best in his sidemen is constantly in evidence. The trios (7159) shows the economical, witty pianist at work on "standards" and his own pieces with a style at once as basic as simple blues and as soundly advanced as any in jazz.

Since 1955 Monk has recorded for Riverside. Of the previous releases in this series I shall single out only *The Unique* (12-209) and *Brilliant Corners* (12-226). The former (a good introduction to his playing, by the way) is a collection of trio performances on tunes everyone knows. It is in part among the most deeply (often sardonically) humorous jazz record ever made, and has, in "Just You, Just Me," a disciplined set of melodic variations of a kind unknown since Morton and Waller. The latter collection has work by two quintets, is complete on its own terms, and is so full of suggestions about future possibilities for jazz that one may well despair of their assimilation.

The fault with the meeting with Gerry Mulligan is Mulligan's, but is not so much that he met Monk on Monk's terms but that the Mulligan of extended solos is so often a man toying with notes and chord changes but not really making music.

Monk's Music gives further evidence of the knowledge Monk has of the musical worth of every note and phrase he writes and plays in the sound way he has expanded scores for the lines of "Well, You Needn't," "Off Minor," and "Epistrophy" for a septet. And so compellingly does his own presence guide his groups that, in a sense, it really doesn't matter that trumpeter Ray Copeland has a beautiful tone, excellent technique, but may let his lines wander a bit; that alto saxophonist Gigi Gryce (the weakest soloist) has trouble swinging; that tenor saxist John Coltrane's is an individual, harmonically provocative, constantly improving, but still undisciplined talent; that Coleman Hawkins is (as he has been for over thirty years) a master in his idiom and shows it except for a slow start on "Epistrophy." Monk himself keeps things fascinatingly alive and in motion. Present on both of these later LPs is bassist Wilbur Ware, a man whose largely unorthodox approach is, I think, potentially revolutionary.

Almost since its beginnings, jazz has been a music above the level of "folk" music, has somehow been at least *almost* a concert music. Many have tried to break the chain that has tied it to dancing and the barroom, of course, and some (Ellington excepted) have tried to do it with their own sophisticated (slightly patronizing) craftsmanship as arrangers. I am raising this question because of a recent release by virtuoso bassist Charlie Mingus and a quintet, *The Clown* (Atlantic 1260). Mingus' music has shown, I think, that he is a man determined to make jazz indisputably a music *per se*. Some of his earlier efforts, unless light, were full of good intentions. But a recent work ("Pithecanthropus Erectus" on Atlantic 1237) was astonishingly powerful. Mingus had perhaps learned that the way to produce a concert jazz was to work with and extend the things that make jazz so vital a music in the first place, for that piece is on one level as basic and direct as a "field holler" and as elementary as improvised jug band "riffs." If "Pithecanthropus" is ultimately unresolved, it shows Mingus working in a sound and promising way.

Mingus sometimes includes in his pieces shouts, cries, sounds. Of course, these things are not in themselves music and need to be transformed before they become music, but how much better to be so directly in touch with the source of music than to think that the job can be done with its skills or with borrowed musical forms. And when Mingus looks deeply into the human soul and finds terrible and wonderful things, he is willing to speak of them with enlightening directness.

There is nothing on *The Clown* which has quite such profound intentions as "Pithecanthropus." The title piece, a spoken narrative with music, is, I am afraid, an engaging novelty. But "Cuban Fight Song" and "Blue Cee" are a credit to him and to all of his musicians; they are more assimilated (the few shouts here are more an encouragement to the improvisers than an attempt to piece out the music) and again have the kind of substance that means that this is a man worth attending, whose significant intentions may well be coming to a fulfillment; jazz, of course, must find, not merely borrow, its way, and Mingus now seems to have insight into what that way will be.

Tenor saxist Sonny Rollins belongs to the line which includes Johnny Dodds, Sidney Bechet, Coleman Hawkins and Charlie Parker, not to the cooler line which includes Jimmy Noone, Johnny Hodges, and Lester Young. That he has long been a much better-than-good soloist can be heard on several of the Monk and Davis sets above, but the growing maturity and discipline which he showed on *Saxophone Colossus* (Prestige 7079) and *Way Out West* (Contemporary C-3530) were coupled with a rare power and immediacy. *The Sound of Sonny* (Riverside 12-241) is almost a portrait of a man relaxing after his triumphs. It is made up of brief performances of nine pieces with a rhythm section. One of the chief virtues of his playing on the Prestige and Contemporary sets is that it shows his willingness to meet the pressing problem of extended solos with a directness and sense of unfolding structure that few jazzmen, except certain pianists, have ever shown. Thus one might here expect statements of compactness and concentration. Instead we often do not get much past the manner (even the mannerisms) of his playing (and some of his wit) and the track is over. Certainly he is not helped by some trite piano.

Rollins' Blue Note 1558 is a better record—it would be if only for his striking solo on "Misterioso." Part of the reason seems to be the presence of Thelonious Monk on one number and for part of another. At any rate, something encourages trombonist J. J. Johnson into offering something besides the urbane fuzziness he has given us so much of lately and Rollins into showing some of his reserve strength. The piano of Horace Silver (present on five numbers, sharing one with Monk), a kind of "modern" honky-tonk, has lately seemed increasingly mannered and repetitious.

American Record Guide, January, 1958

Pee Wee Rediscovered

There is a lesson and a rediscovery for open ears in *A Portrait of Pee Wee* (Counterpoint CPST 562). Clarinetist Pee Wee Russell takes chances, dares, explores. He is never intimidated by a melody or a chord structure. Even when he uses devices that are common in his work (say, "I Used to Love You" here) he is not playing it safe, coasting, or being trite.

That almost dramatic adventurousness is disciplined by a genuine, even classic and balanced lyric-melodic gift (his solo here on "Out of Nowhere" is a very good example). And years ago that same spirit intuitively led him into the harmonic explorations far ahead of their time. Even in relative failure, he can be interesting.

He is, of course, an individual. One might almost say that he adapts music and his instrument to himself, not himself to it. But any discussion of his instrumental technique is obviously beside the point; he is thoroughly musical in the *real* meaning of that phrase.

He is not presented here as a "Dixieland" musician, which is good because he was never, I think, a good polyphonic player. He is a soloist. The arrangements, although a couple are scored in the manner one might use for a larger group, acknowledge this and acknowledge the fact that his approach is primarily melodic and not rhythmic.

Others present are playing and not resting on past achievements, either. But for this time let the report be on Pee Wee Russell.

Down Beat, August, 1958

John Coltrane:
Mainstream '58

Unfortunately *Mainstream 1958* (Savoy 12127), with John Coltrane, Wilbur Harden, and Tommy Flanagan, is a kind of ersatz Miles Davis date. And that quality goes beyond the presence of certain men and the fact that Harden is following Davis' style quite closely: "Snuffy" (Harden's tune) is a blood brother to such things as "Little Willie Leaps" and "Half Nelson" from Davis' first date as leader. But Harden deserves credit for largely getting the point of what Davis does and doing it a lot better than many others—I am thinking particularly of some of the West Coast men who play Davis' ideas but who patch them together so incongruously (even putting some climactic ones in their first eight bars) that they sound almost like a parody of the original.

In trying to decide why Coltrane's runs of short notes don't sound like double-timing, I got the idea that he may be working on a new subdivision of jazz rhythm, one which further divides the eighth-note unit of bebop into a sixteenth-note rhythmic conception. And the fact that in him this attempt is complemented by a deeper harmonic approach suggests a sound evolutionary balance of the kind that bop had. If this is so, with such a task undertaken, it is little wonder that his is still largely an exploratory style and that he has not yet arrived at a real discipline of form. Here he seems to be using that rhythmic conception more conservatively (his solo on "West 42nd St." has a commendable rhythmic development as a result), which may be the way it must be used ultimately, both for his own development as a soloist and for use in a specifically melodic playing. But such conjectures perhaps only indicate how exciting the prospects are, and patience for all may be the best thing to suggest. When the plant is growing, it doesn't do to keep pulling it up to look at the roots.

On pianist Tommy Flanagan, I can repeat what I've said before about what a real pleasure his straightforward and inventive way of playing is, especially after one has heard the way some others hoke up a style of comparable conception with obvious cocktail trickery.

The notes spoil for a fight about whether these men make "mainstream" jazz as of 1958. No arguments from here: streams flow. They aren't ponds or puddles.

Down Beat, August 21, 1958

Charles and Jackson from Below

The respect which so many young jazzmen have for pianist, singer and occasional saxophonist Ray Charles may bring about a kind of replenishment "from below" which an art often needs and which many feel that jazz constantly needs.

For Charles, in his passionately uninhibited way, reminds the jazz musician of certain basic and valuable things which his own sophistication may lead him to neglect, look down on, even scorn, and which he seems somehow unwilling to learn about from others. The great unembarrassed expressiveness and resourcefulness of musical holler, shout, and cry, of a greater use of what was once called "blue dissonance," of all sorts of neglected rhythmic devices, and of a willingness to try a thing out to see how it works—all these things can be heard in Charles's work.

If the foregoing makes Charles sound like a kind of sourcebook of ideas it is intended to because I do not think that, as an instrumentalist, he is really a finished performer, but is rather a passionate player of sometimes fascinating and effective fragments. In his vocal work, where he is tied to a lyric and its narrative or mood and is also disciplined as composer-arranger and pianist by that mood, he *is* a finished performer.

Thus on *Soul Brothers* (Atlantic 1279), a joint recital by Charles and Milt Jackson, his introduction and accompaniment on "How Long Blues" are beautifully appropriate, but in his alto solo (although it is freer than the one on "Soul Brothers") he does not get all of his obviously strong feeling into a musical expression. On that same track, Jackson, Oscar Pettiford, and (on a somewhat simpler level) Billy Mitchell all do. And on "Blue Funk," Jackson is excellent in a solo both finished and appropriate to the riff "head" or theme melody; Charles is suggestive and fragmentary.

It seems to me that Jackson's piano (which has been on records before of course) and his guitar are interesting only because he is an excellent musician and a great vibraphonist.

Thus, we have a record of isolated moments and isolated solo. Charles's best LP remains Atlantic 8006, a collection of his singles designed for the rock 'n' roll market.

Down Beat, 1958

Brubeck in Eurasia

Probably Brubeck's great popularity is not too hard to understand. His playing has a "nice guy" quality that many people would be pleased to have around the house. So, he becomes an acquaintance with a talent he handles with a warm modesty and friendliness. It would be foolishness to accuse him of any deliberate effort to cheer people up with blandness or superficial reassurance. He projects what he projects with complete honesty, and what he projects seems neither disturbing nor falsely reassuring. It is, well, it is genuinely *nice*. And it is good to hear that such niceness can be real; hearing Brubeck one can't doubt that it is real. The fact that art may have different purposes may be beside the point.

In general, and especially on this set, *Jazz Impressions of Eurasia* (Columbia CL 1251), one can't avoid the question of his swing. A lot of what he plays in person nowadays is very infectious rhythmically (yes, I agree, Joe Morello is largely responsible), but not much of what he plays here. "Nomad" has some of the counterrhythmic pounding that used to characterize so much of his work. In it, the placement, accentuation, and shading of the notes doesn't make them swing. He begins to swing on "Golden Horn" and very soon abandons. On "Marble Arch" he opens with swinging (if not very original) phrases and abandons again. There is a section later in "Arch" of apparently written, Baroque-like "fours": Desmond places his notes with swing, Brubeck doesn't. Morello and Benjamin swing no matter what happens.

But this could perfectly well be good music, swing or no swing. Is it? "Thank You" is a kind of rambling "in the style of Chopin" (with a dash of Borodin) that I believe a well-trained, vaudeville-cocktail pianist might do better and more interestingly—assuming such things are worth doing. And I think that a student of Baroque music with a talent for improvising might easily come up with a better light pastiche than "Gate." "Blues" is his best track: as light, unpretentious piano playing, one could hardly argue with it, and to point out that a "crude" ginmill blues man in 1929 might make more meaningful music would be mere churlishness. Furthermore, Brubeck is there less hampered by the unusual time signature than Desmond seems to have been. But Desmond wants to swing.

Desmond's other improvisations are another matter. Besides having his kind of swing they are musically interesting and show a melodic imagination that is rare. He is especially good on "Nomad" and his stop-time breaks on "Arch" are commendable.

Desmond seems to be able to have it both ways. If you don't listen, you might think his work is as blandly pleasant as anyone's. But very soon, without shouting, he is making you listen. Then you hear something.

Down Beat, February 5, 1959

Chet Baker, For Example

The history of the performing arts in America is certainly strewn with highly promising, immature talents which are overpraised, exploited, and often, never fulfilled. And I am convinced that one reason for what happens to a Brando, a Callas, a Chet Baker, is an almost complete lack of any real criticism in their fields in this country.

Chet Baker. Were, as some say, the similarities of his style to Miles Davis' coincidental in the beginning? Perhaps so; there is enough re-interpreted Beiderbecke-Nichols still clinging to his work to help the case along a little. But there is hardly any alternative to calling "Lights Are Low" and "Solar" on *Chet Baker in New York* (Riverside 12-281) pointless imitations—and that remark will need the hasty footnote that there is a lot of difference between effective spatial pause and fumbling or fog, and that the latent, implicit power of Miles Davis is a crucial part of his equipment.

One can call John Coltrane an effective foil to Davis, but on the quintet numbers here, Johnny Griffin's elbowing seems to clash with the atmosphere.

The atmosphere? The playing especially on the quartet tracks has an almost incredible air to it. Except when Al Haig is using some real ideas —hear "Solar" and "Hotel"—it is as if this wispy sound were constantly trying to withdraw, deny itself, disappear altogether with a faint, care-less sigh—a sigh without despair or pain, just one before a restful (and, one hopes, replenishing) sleep. Even on an up-tempo like "Hotel," phrase just follows phrase in almost desultory succession. But I suppose that keeping that up with Paul Chambers and Philly Joe Jones playing behind you represents *some* kind of achievement.

It is a very sad thing indeed to see *any* talent, of whatever potential, settling for this.

"Thoughts" and "Weather" are by Benny Golson. The latter especially is Golson reworking Golson and both, like most of his pieces, are melody tied directly to chords, a difficult thing to do well. Golson does it *very* well, but its limitations are there to be heard.

And aren't "Solar" and "Hotel" pretty close kin to be placed to-gether?

Down Beat, February 19, 1959

The Hawkins Phoenix

To be brief and maybe a little dogmatic about it, I think *The High and Mighty Hawk* (Felsted FAJ 7005) is the Hawkins record that some of us have been waiting for.

Hawkins is a phoenix: he seems to be reborn periodically as a major jazzman. (Of course, it's quite possible that it is only our ears that are reborn.) The current Hawkins was announced, I think, at Newport in '56, and was recorded on Columbia (CL 933). Since then no recording quite captured what he was doing at his best, although Riverside 12-233 came very close. This record does it; it preserves one of those rare occasions which most jazz performances necessarily only imply.

Everyone involved seems to have known it. Clayton's imagination is constant; he invents fine melodies throughout nearly every solo and executes them personally and with that taste and sense of relevance that never seems to leave him. Hank Jones, a nearly perfect complement here to the implicit lyricism and rhythmic strength of both Hawkins and Clayton, seems almost to use all the life and invention he thas been holding back over at Capitol, and shows more originality in his ideas than he has on records in some time. Sheen plays with an understanding of Hawkins' rhythmic conception that a few drummers have and it seems a release for both of them.

Hawkins has a style based on his knowledge of what notes are in chords and what notes can be added to them, of course. It is not at all strange that he is personally out of sympathy with the other major tenor school, founded by Lester Young, which approaches improvisation compositionally and, rather than opening chords, writes new melodies with a harmonic approach that is sometimes high-handed. Hawkins' way can lead to overly decorative playing, and here on "One and Only Love" I think nearly does. On the other hand, it can lead to truly cohesive and functional improvisation-on-theme, and I would be willing to use "You've Changed" as an excellent example of just how it can. His rhythms, almost always and still basically alternating heavy/weak heavy/weak, can lead to monotony but he knows how to break through the pattern and recreate it by contrast. "Bird of Prey" and "Miss G.P." show how.

But these things, like Hemmingway's short sentences or Armstrong's four-bar units, are only Hawkins' *means,* and at the right moments are only, for him, necessary ways of creating that mysterious whole we call art.

When he is being an artist, he does not seem to be using them but recreating them both as a means and a part of a new entity.

The Hawkins here of "Bird of Prey," "Miss G.P.," "You've Changed" does that and does it with ideas, a power, and sure sense of pace that could challenge anyone and enlighten us all.

(There is, by the way, a very awkward tape splice going into the last chorus of "Vignette.")

Down Beat, April, 1959

Earl Hines, 1959

Two sessions of drastically different quality and intension are put back to back on *Earl's Backroom and Cozy's Caravan* by Earl Hines and Cozy Cole (Felsted FAJ 7002).

Hines is almost brilliant; he overcomes some tepid records he has made during the last couple of years and the reputation which the apparently tired Dixieland group he currently is leading have given him. And the first thing one notices is the creative energy of his playing. One expects maturity from him but, unlike some of his younger followers from the thirties, he shows the imagination and vitality of a young man as well as the sureness of his age and experience. Maybe he can play better than ever—anyway, "Brussels," "Husite," and "Backroom at the Villa d'Este" could only have been made by a major talent.

An artist, if he is really worthy of that title, makes his own context, be it simple or complex; Hines does it immediately on "Brussels" with one of those sublimely sure entrances, sustains that, and builds on it. It is a long solo, a solo that in one respect reminds us that Hines is one of the great rhythmic virtuosi jazz has had, and throughout it there is that quality of latent power and capacity that, again, only the great ones have. The ideas come, the play and interplay of the two hands are exemplary, the hints of straying into nearby keys come and go at exactly the right moments. Even ordinary motifs are there with new twists or attack, and very much in context. The solo has a really fine curve, so well done that it begins off of earlier comping, continues into his timing for the bass solo which follows, making a whole.

On "Backroom" the integration and contrast of patching made out of chords and patches made out of single-note lines into an overall pattern could be a lesson to any player in any style. That pattern itself is obvious enough, from simple to a kind of rhythmic crescendo, but its obviousness conceals an art which for another would be mere mechanics.

If Hines' third piece, "Oooh!" fails, it fails because it is set up as a slow, introspective, even funky blues, and Hines does not seem to handle such moods well. They seem to push him into a kind of decorative playing almost in reaction.

There is little else on his side of the record but competence.

Cole's accompanists (let's call them that) seem less competent, and his side of the LP is a grandstanding display of drumming techniques. Ah, show biz!

Down Beat, April 30, 1959

Composer's Dilemma

John Benson Brooks' point of departure for his *Alabama Concerto* (Riverside 12-276) is the fine series of recordings made by Harold Courtlander, *Negro Folk Music of Alabama* (issued by Folkways). He has used them in a "concerto" (actually it might be called a symphony) in which written themes, written solos, and improvised solos alternate.

First, let it be said that the musicians involved should get high praise, particularly Art Farmer, Barry Galbraith, and that this Cannonball Adderley is the Cannonball to be heard on Gill Evans' "New Bottle, Old Wine" which, I believe, is Cannonball coming of age as an individual, purposeful, story-telling soloist.

An undertaking like this one raises a lot of questions. The most obvious one is that of the form Brooks has chosen and its appropriateness. As the progress of the MJQ from "Vendome" through the "No Sun in Venice" score clearly shows, the assimilation of a borrowed form to the point where it makes sense as jazz is not easy and certainly not a result of the will to do so. And the more "ambitious" efforts of the past ten years are strewn with failures at similar tasks. But a relationship between jazz forms and classical suites and rondos has been obvious since at least 1895 and between jazz and both polyphonic forms and the theme-and-variations form since at least 1917. The question here is whether the symphony-concerto form is (or might become) an appropriate and fruitful one for jazz to borrow.

Some kind of answer comes from a comparison of most of the third movement and of the very successful second with the first and fourth sections. The second is by far the best. Brooks has used only two themes, used them well, and he chose two for which such juxtaposition has meaning (that's never an easy matter, of course, but a matter that, say, W. C. Handy usually handled excellently). Furthermore, this is the most openly improvisational section; that is, the most jazzlike to begin with, and the playing is very good. Beside it, the first and fourth sections are apt to seem an alternately pleasant and cluttered melange of melodies, interspersed with brief variations that may get lost in a somewhat vague texture of the whole.

Another question is the way Brooks sometimes handles these themes. In no sense does he either hype them up (like the tasteless, banal Concert Hall "suite on folk themes" we are all too familiar with) nor does he patronize them. But he does seem to have "cleaned them up" a bit. The "mistakes" of a folk-performer can be a source of his greatest effectiveness and, as jazz has been showing since the beginning, such "mistakes" can be meaningfully and boldly used by a more self-conscious artist. Furthermore, Brooks' very skillful down, understated approach sometimes seems to imply more interest in the "charm" of such melodies than in the realities they impart, more respect for their "melodic" beauty than for their strength and life. The result is that, with quite opposite intentions, they may come off more as musical mood-setting than as music, more as a kind of first-rate documentary film-writing (a thing rare enough, to be sure) than as music which grasps one's attention for itself.

But one glory of the self-conscious artist is that he must take chances on just such matters. The irony is (and he knows it) that one seldom finds his attention wandering when a Mahalia Jackson is singing.

Down Beat, 1959

Writing for Whom?

The composer-arrangers are the important men behind *Cross Section Saxes* by Hal McKusick (Decca DL 9209). These men are in a peculiar position in jazz today, the position that the dramatist found himself in in the nineteenth century and that only the ballet, among the performing arts, has escaped. Just as the achievements of Henderson, Ellington, etc., were worked out originally with the specific talents of the members of organized groups in mind, so the best plays were created for continuing stock companies. Even when the dramatist later found himself cut off from such a source of inspiration, discipline, and tradition, he might write (as did the nineteenth-century concert composer) vehicles for certain virtuosi performers. One cannot be absolute about cause and effect, but one can say that when such possibilities of inspiration no longer exist for the writer or composer, his art (and even his craft) seems to suffer.

Nowadays, the jazz composer-arranger writes with little in mind but his own work and, when he is done, considers who might best interpret it. The same is true when (as was probably the case here) he is asked to write for a specific number of instruments. One of the chief virtues of Henderson and Ellington's writing is the secret kind of balance it makes among soloist, group, and total composition. In this respect, these men discovered how the heritage and identity of jazz might be both preserved *and* extended; if they had not solved that delicate problem so well, jazz might well have been carried off in a straitjacket of paper.

The best works here are George Russell's. He is, at his best, a splendid combination of sophistication and depth, of awareness of his heritage as a jazzman, and range and variety of skills. These things come together excellently on his superior blues "Stratusphunk," and the soloists, especially McKusick, respond to it. The only failure, it seems to me, is "The End of a Love Affair." It is a superior torch song, but in what I would guess was an effort to avoid its hints of melodrama, Russell came very close to cuteness.

Bill Evans, in solo and support is so much something to hear throughout that I don't want to single out his "Stratusphunk" solo. Connie Kay, whether he is playing the one after-beat out of four on finger cymbals (as assigned on Giuffre's "Yesterdays") or accompanying the blues, shows a combination of disciplined musicianship and expressiveness that jazz has rarely seen the like of. But those remarks are to neglect Charlie Persip and Art Farmer among others, and one shouldn't.

Down Beat, 1959

Two Faces of Ray Charles

Ray Charles at Newport (Atlantic 1289) comes down to this: there are four good vocals ("The Right Time," "I Got A Woman," "Talkin' Bout You," "A Fool for You"), not always well recorded and sometimes a bit too long for best effect. Besides, there are instrumental numbers which range from the Prado-like routine on "In A Little Spanish Town" to "funky" pieces like Charles's "Hot Rod" (or is it Milt Jackson's "Spirit Feel"?). Judging them as the modern jazz they usually intend to emulate, one would say that they are played warmly (although sometimes forcedly) and often not too well.

Yes, Indeed! (Atlantic 8025) is another matter. It collects Charles's rock and roll singles. Both LPs contain versions of "Talkin' Bout You," and a comparison of the two tells some of the story. On the earlier one, juke-box length and an effort to do the song the best way (and not to impress the audience) make this version far better. "It's All Right," "Lonely Avenue," and "I Want to Know" are moving chants; in versions any less concentrated or any longer, they might easily become mere rhythmic indulgences. "Get on the Right Track Baby" is a fine, witty little poem. Only "The Sun's Gonna Shine Again" approaches the self-dramatization of melodrama, and that only toward the end. "A Little Girl" clearly shows how Charles's concerted and overt emotion can override a flagging, discontinuous arrangement.

On *Yes, Indeed!* we see that Charles has taken a set of the most shockingly limited and contrived devices that any American musical fad has ever been plagued with, modified them, added to them, and with an understanding of their sources, a fine talent, and only the outwardly imposed inhibitions of length and form, created several works of delightful, honest, affirmative art. On *Ray Charles at Newport* we hear a man largely abandoning (perhaps not even knowing?) what he can do so superbly for something he does with good, even engaging intentions, but little art.

Down Beat, 1959

Rollins and the Quartet

Gunther Schuller wrote liner notes for the second volume of *The Modern Jazz Quartet at Music Inn* (Atlantic 1299) which also features Sonny Rollins on two numbers. They are the kind of notes which will make one listen with more attention and understanding (and any other kind will be either puff or pap), but therefore are also the kind that may leave a reviewer with much less to say.

The first point about the Quartet is, of course, that it began as a collection of fine players. Its forms (whatever their source) came as the best way for the group to express (and improve) itself individually and collectively. Most group forms in jazz have ultimately come from the needs and potentials of the players in them. That the Quartet's formal sense is also one of the most outstanding in jazz is a tribute to its members. No doubt the seventeenth and eighteenth centuries were Lewis' idea, but, as now transmuted by the group, they are both MJQ and Lewis, Jackson, Heath, and Kay. Has such wholesale borrowing from Europe previously produced anything but musical foolishness, between ragtime and the Quartet?

So, a record by four of the most expressive players around in a uniquely integrated and responsive group. A joy! What more to say? At least this: the beautiful distillation and rebuilding of "Yardbird Suite" is excellent, and—the difficult thing in what might have become stilted or mechanical—it is always kept in beautiful musical movement. I can quite easily do without the out-of-tempo "concert hall" paraphernalia of "Midsummer" and all it represents, or I would be able to do without it if the jazz sections of the piece weren't so good. And "Festival Sketch," granted its rhythmically interesting opening motive, seems to me lower-drawer Lewis.

Then Sonny Rollins. Schuller says he is, alternately, "whimsical and sardonic" and really creative, which is really to say that he is alternately only personal and then really artistic. Undeniably, there is a delight in hearing Rollins' own mood, more delight in hearing the coaxing conversations among the players and the confident saxophonist who implies with such little effort. But if jazz (as some contend—not Schuller) is really the art of the passing emotions of the moment, then it is either a very minor art or no art. And, despite the note of orneryness involved (Rollins clearly does not want Lewis to play a contrapuntal line back there; he wants chords and only chords), his handling of the theme melody on "Bag's Groove" shows one thing that can save an artist from the chaos of the moment and the very subjective. Like the Quartet, he has his sense of form.

The kind of form that each has evolved is different and was differently arrived at. A previous meeting on records (on Prestige 7029) is a failure. All were already very good players, but none had arrived at a sense of form. There was no basis for the meeting except perhaps the fact that both Jackson and Rollins obviously liked to blow, and that is not much of a basis. All of the differences in basic musical sensibility between Rollins and the Quartet were glaringly dramatized, and they clashed.

Here, they meet after each has achieved a maturity and sureness and meet on just that basis, and therefore their different approaches to music and musical feelings do not clash—or when they are about to, one now more mature man can modify his ways for the moment to bring them together.

There is another thing that can save from the transient and subjective, the point we began with: when real creativity simply overtakes one and dictates its own form. You have to be ready for that. Jackson was on "Night in Tunisia" and Lewis was on "Bag's Groove" and, my goodness, the results are something to hear.

The Jazz Review, October, 1959

A Letter from Lenox, Massachusetts

August 31, 1959

From the first day of this year's session of The School of Jazz there was undeniably something in the air, and it was not long before one realized exactly what it was: in its third year the school was coming of age. It was probably possible in past summers to overhear a student bull session on whether life or art is more important, but it would hardly have seemed so appropriate—and for most of the people involved this year they were really the same thing. Perhaps Jack Duffy, an auditor and classicist fresh from Tanglewood, caught it best when he said that these people seem to think and feel as one action, and that here the whole idea of work was different. He was right. Work was pleasure, thought, freedom, discipline, passion, self-discovery. One could say that of jazz itself—and in our time one can say it of few other human activities. There were several reasons for this new atmosphere at Lenox but as one reflects on them, he realizes they don't explain it all. The mysterious and natural process of growth is simply a part of it—and perhaps the mysticism of 3 is too.

The faculty has matured as a faculty; musical disagreements being granted, now most of its members seem to know better exactly what they are about and how to work at it, and the new members (Bill Evans, Gunther Schuller, Herb Pomeroy) are decidedly part of the new atmosphere. Another part of it was a generally superior student body— superior in talent, in outlook, and in experience. They were ready for a faculty generally ready for them. There were far fewer "teach me the changes and just let me wail," for whom "self-expression" is inevitably a string of hip clichés, and there were far fewer Ivy League dabblers, buying their way into a world they may secretly think they should feel superior to. The Schaeffer Brewing Company scholarships did not bring in such types from the twelve schools where they were awarded, but brought good students. And even students who do not intend to become professional jazzmen contributed to the purposeful tone and musical achievement of the school. (Let us have more lawyers and engineers in American life who know what jazz is and can play that well!) For me to add that trumpeter Al Kiger recorded with the MJQ at the end of a session is in a sense for me to slight several considerable talents. Let me put it this way: the concert at the Music Barn on August 29 was one of the best concerts I have ever heard and a credit to everyone involved. Even when nothing happened there was rare honesty, and most of the time plenty happened.

There were five small groups coaxed, cajoled, encouraged, taught, and finally led, by Jimmy Giuffre; by Max Roach and John Lewis; by Bill Evans, Connie Kay, and Jim Hall; by Gunther Schuller; and by Kenny Dorham. And there was the big band led by Herb Pomeroy. Student composer-arrangers contributed to the repertory of the small groups. Some of the results were phenomenal. For example, one ensemble had a group feeling that some professionals seldom get; Max Roach had taught one very young drummer how to drum musically in three weeks; a composer who had previously produced rather hip pop tunes discovered a real compositional talent for instruments; several who had arrived with heads full of fashionable phrases and turnarounds, learned to make real music. And certainly the donors of scholarships—BMI, the Harvey Husten Memorial Committee, United Artists Records, Associated Booking Corporation, Dizzy Gillespie, Norman Granz—can be very proud of their association with such an enterprise. But perhaps the most significant fact was the presence of Ornette Coleman and Don Cherry—on scholarships from Atlantic Records, I hasten to add. If the School of Jazz can teach them (and it did), it has surely made a significant contribution to American culture quite beyond what anyone has a right to expect of any school.

I honestly believe (not that I am alone or particularly original in believing it) that what Ornette Coleman is doing on alto will affect the whole character of jazz music profoundly and pervasively, and that the first consideration is that what he plays can be very beautiful. (I had better say that I have not heard that first recording and hear mixed reports of it as a picture of his talent.) When he stood up to solo on the blues with the big band on the first day of school, I was taken. It was as if he opened up something in one's soul and opened up the way for jazz to grow. His music makes a new sensibility for one's ears and heart and mind, all the while including the most fundamental things in jazz. It seems impossible for Ornette Coleman to talk about music without soon using the word "love," and when he plays one knows that, undeluded, it is love of man his music is talking about. As is so necessary with an innovator in the beginning he is not afraid of what his muse tells him to play: "I don't know how it's going to sound before I play it anymore than anybody else does." The step he is taking, like all great steps, seems inevitable only when someone has taken it and Coleman is taking it with a sublime stubbornness: if you put a conventional chord or rhythm under my note, you limit the number of choices I have for my next note; if you do not, my melody may move freely with far greater choice of directions.

Chaotic and a-harmonic? No. Sonny Terry is a-harmonic, but Coleman is not for he *can* work through and beyond the farthest intervals of the chords. For John Coltrane, is it not simply because he quite naturally still hears and plays off of those orderly chords that everyone uses, that, like a harassed man in an harmonic maze, he must invite the melodic disorder of running up and down scales? Somebody had to find the way out of that passionate impasse; it has fallen to Ornette Coleman to do it. When he is really creative (and inevitably he must still do plenty of mere searching), his melodies are unusual, but never jarring and one noticed at the concert, they can reach out and affect each individual in an audience.

There are problems. Musical ones: he may still have to discover and work out much of it for himself; he must find others to play with besides Don Cherry, who breathes as he breathes musically. And formal ones: it is quite true and inevitable that I don't necessarily need eight bars to develop a line that it took me eight bars to state (the blues is not a strict twelve-bar form to a Clarence Lofton or Sonny Terry), but can a group follow me? But to say that his variations sometimes do not have the usual relationships to his melodies is not to say that they have none. On "The Sphinx" his solo at one rehearsal seemed based on a constant rhythmic development of his theme.

I have said that the school taught him. When he arrived, he was (through lack of experience) no kind of large ensemble player. In the concert, with the big band and with the group of six, he had become one. And the school helped him with something about which, since he taught himself, he can learn still more: technical mastery of the saxophone. And there was a great lesson for others in his presence at the school: that music has its ultimate basis in the human soul and human feelings, not in keyboards, musical devices, or skills.

Several of the faculty justly hoped that "the critics" would not fill him full of wrong ideas about his duty to be "the next thing"—or whatever. Somehow, one has the feeling hearing him play or talk that he will simply do what he must do, not taking credit for his talent but simply feeling a duty to explore and use it, so long as he can work not deluded about "recognition," that he will play the music he hears, obey his muse, and fulfill his destiny as an artist, perhaps listening to what advice seems just and helpful but forgetting the rest, and resign himself patiently to the fate that any innovator must have. If he does that, he will be one of the very few American artists who has ever followed his talent without letting himself be somehow exploited by his "public" "or his notices." But, honestly, I really think he will.

Ornette Coleman is exceptional, but perhaps his presence at the school was not so much an exception as another evidence of the growth it has had. Watching those enlightened faces as Gunther Schuller played and analyzed the intricacies of Jelly Roll Morton's "Grandpa Spells" ("of course some of these breaks seem funny but they are also very beautiful"), I remembered John Lewis' opening speech three years ago: "We will teach you only about the jazz of the past ten years. We cannot show you how Jelly Roll Morton played because we don't know."

Marshall Stearns had played his records before, but now there was also room for a comparison of the music of Morton, Ellington, Monk, and John Lewis. And there was room for Ornette Coleman.

The Jazz Review, October, 1959

The Real Art Tatum

The ART TATUM Discoveries (20th Fox 3029) were recorded at a party and are billed as "the *other* Tatum." Reviewers have received them as such. The other Tatum is the "*real* Art Tatum" whose creativity after hours or before just the right audience is very different, we are told, from what we hear on most of his records or heard in most of his club and concert appearances. If this be so, then the other Tatum is the same Tatum, only sometimes very much more so. Tatum is for me one of the most frustrating musicians in jazz, as he is obviously one of the most brilliant. The frustration does not come because of the lack of what is usually called "strong feeling" in his work, for to expect that would be to miss the point. Nor does it come from his lack of any but the most obvious kind of melodic imagination—but to call these dazzling decorative devices melodic at all may be sheer folly. There again, one would be missing the point to expect more than one gets. And I confess that I cannot always enjoy the rapidity of mind with which these arpeggios are made, except at a primitive level of mere dazzlement.

What is frustrating is that Tatum's melodic taste is so banal. One need only look at that perpetual repertoire that included the likes of "Humoresque," "Elegie," "Dardanella," or here, "Danny Boy" and "Little Man You've Had a Busy Day." This kind of taste is reflected in the structureless haphazardry of some of his playing: the arpeggios flutter by and the thumbs drag along. Then there are the humorless interpolations—have we not had enough of "In A Country Garden" without having to be irrelevantly reminded of its prissy melody in the middle of a decorated Cole Porter ditty? And one can hope that the parade of tremolos on "Danny Boy" is intended humorously—but one can't be sure.

Then there is his technique as a pianist, a technique so much admired by concert musicians and composers that Tatum is the only jazz musician some of them will allow. They admire him for the same reasons they once admired Eddy Duchin, and they remind us that we may need to ask how much of Tatum's technique was specifically jazz technique— as one might contend that *all* of Jimmy Yancey's or Basie's or Monk's techniques are.

On the other hand, I can cite you things in these tracks, or in almost any Tatum collection, that will give me the lie: there is an interpolation from Earl Hines in "Body and Soul" that is so appropriate, so beautifully placed and integrated that one wonders at his artistry. ("Nobody Knows the Trouble I've Seen" comes in later and far less well.) And "Willow Weep For Me" is so scrupulously paced and developed that one hardly wants to speak of his final impression of "You Took Advantage" as a disarray of flourishes.

"Willow" brings us to the point, of course, for in the past (and particularly in the version on Capitol) it has been one of *the* Tatum vehicles. Tatum was a great jazzman because he had a towering harmonic imagination, and, as Dick Katz has written, only Charlie Parker's name could be mentioned near Tatum's in this respect. "Tenderly" here will prove it, excitingly and beautifully. And "Too Marvelous For Words" may convince you that Tatum knew everything there is to know or could be discovered in jazz about the European harmonic system—and it is done for once with an overt bubbling and entirely winning humor.

It is very likely that "Too Marvelous" is the greatest single Tatum performance we are fortunate enough to have. It is also, in the joyful feeling—even near-abandon—that it conveys, untypical. That almost hurts.

The Jazz Review, July, 1960

Some Achievements of a Decade

I have a friend who claims to believe that one New York record company produces its wares in a secret room where there is a file of about thirty cliché, funky tenor phrases kept on small spools of tape. The producer goes in with the currently hip chord changes in slightly different order, selects tenor phrases off of the spools to fit them, splices them together, and he has the first piece for his next LP. It wouldn't quite work literally of course, but as a comment on the current state of funk (excuse me, *soul jazz*) it is accurate enough. In the mid-fifties, the funky style seemed a salvation for jazz, then almost frozen in cool clichés. I think it was, but I think that now it has ceased to be a creative medium to all but a few of its first players and writers, and Horace Silver is certainly one of those. But I doubt if seeing a kind of battle between a gradually declining cool style and an, at first, replenishingly hot one is the best way to look at the past ten years in jazz.

The earlier revolution of the middle forties was a major one and is now a part of the jazz heritage, but by now it is over fifteen years old. If jazz is as alive and creative as we think it is, some important things should have happened, and there should have been, besides the squabbling of styles, some lasting achievements built on the innovations of Parker and Gillespie. If the past is any precedent, these achievements should have been ones of synthesis, composition and form.

If we make a list of truly great jazzmen, it should begin with Louis Armstrong and Duke Ellington, and in them already we have, as André Hodeir has suggested, a pattern of major innovation followed by larger orchestral form. Armstrong, the intuitive improviser, replenished jazz with a new musical language in the twenties; from a basis in new ideas of rhythm he revised the jazzman's ideas of melodic line and harmony as well. And by the late thirties, Ellington the composer, leader, and orchestrator was incorporating these ideas into what is probably the highest formal achievement jazz has seen. Ellington held improvisation and written part, soloist, and orchestra in delicate balance in his work, a balance in which each contributed to a total development, a whole greater than the sum of its parts.

Although I believe it is self-evident that Ellington remains a major jazzman on frequent occasion, it was very soon after his greatest period, from about 1938–42, that another major innovation in jazz took place.

If that is a good way of looking at jazz history, then perhaps we should be looking for achievements in orchestration and composition which use Parker's innovations, and perhaps looking for an Ellington. I think we do find high formal achievements in the past decade, but they have been the achievements not of one man but of several—and one of those men is not really a composer or an orchestrator but a single improvising hornman!

It is often said that the first great orchestrations in "modern" jazz were those written for the Miles Davis "nontet," the first important cool group. The group was formed a little over ten years ago, and the records that preserve its music come from 1949–50. I cannot agree that, as one man put it, the nontet summarized the whole achievement of modern jazz up to that point. It seems to me that except for some of their soloists, the nontet records miss a great deal of the import of Charlie Parker's music. The scores owe a lot to Lester Young—or for that matter to Claude Thornhill's dance band. Aside from some of Davis's phrasing and more of J. J. Johnson's, they largely miss Parker's rhythmic message, and I believe it is precisely because all of Parker's ideas were built around a strong, drastic revision in jazz rhythms that his innovations were so effective and important.

Gerry Mulligan's use of 3/4 and 2/4 time signatures in the score of "Jeru" are very welcome effects, but they are not the point. The effect of melodic rhythm on phrasing and on percussion is the point. In Mulligan's work, in Stan Getz's—even in Lennie Tristano's—even in Paul Desmond's—cool jazz seems as much an effort to work out implications of Lester Young's musical language as to deal *directly* with Charlie Parker's ideas. (And Lester Young was the most truly original jazz soloist between Armstrong and Parker, of course.) Perhaps these Miles Davis cool records are something like Don Redman's early work. The nontet charts are better, of course, but Redman wrote some of the earliest jazz arrangements for large jazz orchestra. He did them before Armstrong's revolution had really begun to take effect and he picked a set of earlier conventions within which to work.

From Redman's early writing came "big band" jazz, however, and from the Davis cool records came important things. Not the least of them is the promise of maturity in Davis himself, particularly in those splendid solos on "Move" and "Israel." That promise was finding its fulfillment beginning in 1954, I think, and was announced on records by that superb "all star" session "Walkin' " and "Blue 'n' Boogie." But also on those first cool recordings there is the presence of John Lewis as both arranger and player, and as prime mover in the organization of the group.

The Modern Jazz Quartet began as the rhythm section to Dizzy Gillespie's 1946–47 orchestra. Gillespie's was not quite the *first* effort at a big "bop" band, but it was one of the first, and in it there was plenty of effort to write scores within the new idiom and plenty of respect for Gillespie and Parker. Later the Modern Jazz Quartet was a "cooperative" unit by mutual agreement, but it was largely a vehicle for Milt

Jackson's improvising in performance. John Lewis had other, quite irrepressible and quite important ideas, however, ideas that went beyond solo and accompaniment. Lewis was concerned about compositional order and development, about relating improvising and writing, player and group.

Lewis has been criticized for his use of seventeenth- and eighteenth-century classical baroque forms. But jazzmen have always borrowed whatever they wanted from wherever they found it. The important thing is what they do with it; whether they assimilate and transmute the musical language and devices they borrow into their own jazz language, whether they renew the forms, and whether they produce a vehicle for creativity or merely a kind of quasi jazz or musical stunt. The MJQ's first fugue, "Vendome," does sound like an "exercise" as first recorded. The recent re-recording of the piece is pretty jazzy, but no more successful. But the second fugue, "Concord," is a turning point, and as British writer Max Harrison has said, there followed the specifically jazz fugues like "Versailles" and "Three Windows," which no longer remind us of Bach or the practice room but are vehicles for creative collective jazz improvising. When they have made such achievements as those later fugues, we should not mind being patient with such things as the Quartet's rather fussy and extrinsic baroque introduction to "Softly, As In A Morning Sunrise."

That recording of "Sunrise" shows another aspect of John Lewis's innately formal inclinations and, again, it is polyphonic. As an accompanist Lewis does not "comp" on the chord changes. Frequently he will elaborate conventional background riff patterns from the thirties into countermelodies to Milt Jackson's improvised lines. It is a great pleasure to listen for such things, of course, and they are important. Lewis can make his backgrounds complements to Jackson's lines and not interferences. He can also use them to give the ensemble a texture so sadly lacking in most groups today.

Most important, he can use them to give a performance continuity and cohesiveness—keep it from sounding like a mere string of vaguely related episodes by various soloists. On a piece like "Ralph's New Blues," Lewis uses the rather Monk-ish device of accompanying Jackson's solo with a version of the theme itself, then gradually departing from it into an improvised countermelody as Jackson builds his solo.

Lewis's best compositions have memorable and deceptively simple melodies. He has also tried several "extended" works and suites. I believe that the one unquestionably successful long work by Lewis—

perhaps the longest truly sustained work in jazz—is "Django." There couldn't be any better evidence of its compositional and formal strength than the fact that on the two recordings they have made of it, the members of the Quartet give it very different interpretations, yet the compositional design and character of "Django" remain strongly evident.

"Django" is made of a theme-melody and a brief phrase or motif used as a kind of countermelody. The two are brilliantly juxtaposed. The gentle theme seems very simple, yet it manages to suggest a great many things: a funeral, reverence at death, the French gypsy guitarist-turned-jazzman for whom it is named, impressionist music, jazz and the jazz heritage. The countermotif is a simple, swinging blues bass figure, and a very old one—as a matter of fact it appears on one of King Oliver's early records. Between these two melodies there is a wonderful tension, and the range and refinement of feeling that "Django" encompasses makes it a unique emotional achievement in jazz. It begins with a reverent and delicate sadness. That mood is soon transmuted into a redeeming joy by the improvising and by the reiterated bass figure. Finally, there is a return to introspective pensiveness. The debt to the jazz tradition of New Orleans funerals is obvious.

"Django" is also worked out for the specific talents of the members of the Modern Jazz Quartet, and perhaps the essential point with the Quartet is that it *began* as a collection of first-rate, improvising jazzmen, and then went further. Approaching form from the other direction often produces a stilted and merely formalistic music—form, but no content. But at the same time that the MJQ has developed its music partly in terms of the talents of its members, those members have explored and extended their own ranges and resourcefulness as its forms have evolved.

The next time someone complains that the music of the MJQ "inhibits" Milt Jackson, he might remember not only how much its music *does* depend on just letting Jackson go, but also how much Jackson's ability has grown in range and technique in the past seven years.

But I do not mean to suggest that the only recent achievement in the balancing of improvisation with compositional development belongs to John Lewis and the Modern Jazz Quartet. There is the work of Charlie Mingus and his groups. In attempting a *collective, simultaneous* improvising among several players, he has clearly surpassed Tristano and Mulligan, I think; it is almost as if he was the successor to Morton and Oliver in using an improvised polyphony. As a virtuoso bass player, Mingus can maintain a rhythmic center for the group and at the same time lay down an effective melody of his own. But that is only one aspect of the wonderful dense group textures Mingus achieves.

Perhaps one reason his achievements are not even higher is that Mingus does not work permanently with the same musicians. If Mingus could keep his groups together (or is it *would* keep?—at any rate *did* keep) . . . "Pithecanthropus Erectus," "Cuban Fight Song, "Blue Cee" are powerful recordings, even if we do complain that they are emotionally unresolved. Mingus' is not a conservative talent like John Lewis' and at the same time that he seeks a group music, he also seeks (sometimes to an extreme) to do something really new and, as he puts it, "stop copying Bird." A few years ago, that sort of desire led him to associations with some musicians who were dubious jazzmen and who had rather academic approaches to atonality, but such indiscretions are probably past for Mingus.

Thelonious Monk has managed to fulfill the role of major composer and still expand the jazz language. Monk's technique is all jazz technique; he has no other kind. There are many important aspects to Monk's talent, and his rediscovery by jazzmen a few years ago (an event most fans have now caught up to) was undoubtedly a significant event. By 1951, he had written many of his best pieces, by which I mean things like "Off Minor"; "Straight, No Chaser"; "Misterioso"; "Four In One"; "Eronel"; "Criss Cross"; "Evidence"; "Skippy." They are all excellent, logically developed, instrumentally conceived compositions—not "tunes" or "numbers." Even Charlie Parker's best melodies are "lines" which serve only to set up a harmonic framework for improvising. But with most of Monk's pieces you have to know the melody *and* Monk's harmony, how they fit together, and use both in making variations. There is nothing "difficult" or forbidding about this; if a listener can follow a melody, he can grasp this use of a theme, and doing it with Monk's music is one of the great pleasures in jazz.

I recently heard a famous jazzman playing Monk's "Bemsha Swing" with the wrong harmonic voicings. The piece sounded like a fairly trivial little ditty; when it is played properly it is a first-rate jazz work.

We listen to Monk naturally waiting for the expected. But if he does the expected, he does it in the most unexpected way. Yet a delay in rhythm, or slight alteration of phrase, satisfies us completely once we have heard it. Monk himself sees to it that the performances of his groups have a continuity and wholeness, frequently, as we can hear, by using the theme melody itself in accompaniment and in his solos. Monk will fragment it, reduce it to a single basic idea, rebuild, elaborate it.

He does the same sort of thing in playing "standards" and he frequently recomposes such "tunes," with new harmony, into real, two-handed, piano compositions.

In his sets of variations on "Just You, Just Me" or his high comic version of "Tea for Two," the choruses are good in themselves, but Monk goes quite beyond a mere chorus by chorus approach to variation, and the over-all patterns and developments of the performances are exceptionally satisfying. The individual variations often depend on Monk's unique, teasing, and virtuoso sense of rhythm, accent, and time, and his effective use of space, rest, and silence. In his rhythms and in his wide harmonic intervals, Monk shows that he is also an advanced jazzman, as well as a composer with a more conservative interest in form.

An improvised blues like Monk's solo "Functional" is a *tour de force* of elaborating a brief, traditional, one-bar blues phrase into a beautifully sustained performance of nine minutes! But probably most ingenious and delightful of all as an example of logically improvised form is his solo on "Bag's Groove" (*take 1*) on the Miles Davis "all star" recording. For all its originality, the form of his improvisation becomes an easy delight to follow if you have a few hints.

Monk takes one phrase at the beginning of his solo and uses it as the basis of all that follows. He turns it, adds to it, briefly contrasts it with another phrase, subtracts from it, opens it up, condenses it, reduces it almost to a single note, with the most ingenious, varied, and far-reaching use of rhythmic phrasing and accent of all his recorded solos. He is making this long solo all-of-a-piece and in his rhythms, he is quite original. It is this same interest in form *and* in new discoveries that led Monk to write "Brilliant Corners," a piece which shifts back and forth between two tempos without losing its momentum or having any aspects of a trick.

But as important as Monk's music is, he is not the first pianist to have such a "classic" interest in form and development—indeed some sort of larger designs from pianists are as old as jazz, or at least as old as Jelly Roll Morton. A unique event of the past few years is the fact that a hornman has shown such an interest and shown it brilliantly. There were times a few years ago when Sonny Rollins seemed to be taking over the roles of composer, orchestrator, self-accompanist as well as improvising horn soloist—all for himself.

Admittedly, one of his basic points of inspiration were Monk's ideas about using the theme itself in improvising rather than totally abandoning it, after an opening statement, and improvising only on a set of chords. And surely if Rollins has not been a very good jazz improviser to begin with, no formal achievement on his part would mean anything. Everything that Rollins plays on his recording of "Blue 7" is perceptively and melodically related to its theme, and its eleven minutes hang together in a way that few other recordings in jazz do. (And that cohesiveness even includes a thematic *drum* solo by Max Roach!) Actually, "Blue 7" would be an exceptional record if it were only for Rollins' use of variety in dynamics and his sometimes sardonically humorous way of dissecting the melodic line. But there is much more.

Rollins has another way of structuring his solos which is more traditional and which has been only hinted at on his recordings. It involves gradually disintegrating a melody, departing from it into a free variation based on the chords which is at first kept simple by short lines, few notes, and regular rhythms. Rollins would then build this improvising by making longer, unbroken lines of shorter, rapid, virtuosic notes, and more complex rhythms, to a peak of melodic complexity. From this he would then reverse his order, revert to simpler lines, easier notes, and gradually rebuild and restore his theme melody. The whole is again greater than the sum of its parts. And this achievement came at a time when most hornmen seemed to be trying only to keep going as long as possible without repeating themselves. Many of them still do, of course, and many of them are using memorized Rollins phrases to do it.

I realize that I have not mentioned Clifford Brown and the way he rallied jazzmen to return to the warmer aspect of their heritage when cool seemed to dominate all. Nor have I spoken of Art Blakey who, besides being an important drummer, has been a very valuable jazzman in several other respects during the past six years. Nor have I discussed Max Roach's expansion of the percussionist role he asserted so well on "Klactoveedsedsteen" in 1947. I have praised Horace Silver but I haven't really talked about his music. Nor Getz's. Nor Mulligan's. Nor have I said anything about the exciting potential in the John Coltrane of two or three years ago. Nor have I said anything here about what is now being called "third stream" music, combining classical music and jazz.

Nor, for that matter, have I said much about the continuing creativity of, say, Buck Clayton, Vic Dickenson, Coleman Hawkins, Ben Webster, or Earl Hines, all of whom seem to me to have done excellent work during the past few years. But, then, I don't intend this to be a complete history or survey of the fifties.

As I imply above, periods of important achievement in composition and form have been followed by striking reactions and renewals of the jazz language—in Armstrong, and in the way Parker's innovations followed Ellington's synthesis. Perhaps on the basis of what the MJQ, Mingus, Monk, and Rollins have done during the past ten years, we should now be looking for another innovation. I believe we hear it— potentially at least—in Ornette Coleman.

But that is another subject. Meanwhile, I think that, from the fifties, the best of John Lewis, of Charlie Mingus, of Thelonious Monk and of Sonny Rollins—like the best of Armstrong, the best of Ellington and the best of Parker—will endure.

Metronome, January, 1961

Monk and Coltrane: Echos of 1957

Thelonious Monk with John Coltrane (Jazzland LP 46) contains some alternate takes of pieces already issued and some entirely new material. To spell out the contents for a bit, "Functional" is a remarkable, unaccompanied piano solo. It is an alternate version to the one included on *Thelonious Himself* (Riverside 235) and so different from the original that I think it should have been given a different title.

"Off Minor" and "Epistrophy" are alternate, less sure, and briefer versions from the septet date that produced *Monk's Music* (Riverside 242). The former has very good solos by Hawkins, Copeland, and Monk; the latter solos by Coltrane and Copeland.

"Nutty," "Rubby," and "Trinkle, Tinkle" are by Monk, Coltrane, Ware, and Wilson—the quartet that had an almost legendary stay at the Five Spot in New York during the summer of 1957, a prelude to Monk's rediscovery as a major jazzman and to his current popularity, and surely one of the most important (and exhilarating) events in jazz in recent years.

These three selections were recorded and the tapes were labeled "for posterity" and set aside until contractual conflicts had been resolved, permitting their release now. They are strong experiences, and if they are not as good as the performances one heard those summer nights at the Five Spot, they are nevertheless exceptional jazz.

Each member of that quartet played with great enthusiasm and at the peak of his own abilities, and through Monk's music each man was discovering and expanding his potential almost nightly.

Monk and Coltrane had exceptional emotional rapport. Technically, on the other hand, they were superb contrasts. Coltrane's techniques are obvious, Monk's more subtle. At the same time that Coltrane, with his showers of notes and his "sheets of sound," seemed to want to shatter jazz rhythms into an evenly spaced and constant array of short notes, Monk seemed to want to break them up subtly and phrase with a new freedom. Monk is a melodist; his playing is linear and horizontal. Coltrane is an arpeggio player; his approach is vertical. He is a kind of latter-day Coleman Hawkins.

But even Coltrane's earlier solo on "Epistrophy" shows that he found enormous harmonic stimulation in Monk's music—he seemed to know not only where Monk *was* but where he was headed, as very few players did. But again, as the quartet tracks show (particularly "Ruby"), Coltrane also knew that Monk's melodies are very strong and important and that it isn't enough merely to run their changes. Over and over again here, Monk's materials discipline Coltrane and order his explorations in a way that no material he has since dealt with seems to have done.

Ware is, like Monk, a melodist, and he also finds surprise twists even in the most traditional approach. Wilson, whose early work had the smooth evenness of a Jo Jones, responds to Monk's hints with enthusiastic and appropriate polyrhythmic patterns.

Monk also got a remarkable variety of textures from this group—by playing with Coltrane, by playing contrapuntally *against* Coltrane, by laying out and leaving Coltrane to Ware and Wilson, sometimes predominately to one of them, sometimes to both equally.

Some details: On "Nutty," after Coltrane has strayed further and further into elaborate harmonic implications of the piece, Monk enters for his solo with, as usual, a simple and eloquent reestablishment of the theme in paraphrase. He does the same on "Trinkle," with an even more subtle recasting of that intricate melody.

"Ruby" is a knowingly embellished version of a lovely piece. The end of Coltrane's opening solo has a particularly beautiful (and

Monkish) effect of suspension, and Monk's decision to begin his solo with lightly implied double-timing was a near master-stroke of meaningful contrast.

The best quartet performance is "Trinkle." The one flaw is that the line itself, unlike most of Monk's melodies, is a bit pianistic in conception to be fully effective on saxophone. But the spontaneous interplay between Monk and Coltrane in "Trinkle" is quite wonderful, as is Monk's intuitive logic in knowing just when to stop it and let Coltrane stroll along against Ware and Wilson. Ware's solo is good (and I'm afraid makes one long for those evenings when he would spin several effortless choruses in each piece).

As I said, this solo "Functional" is quite different from the previous version. On the earlier releases, Monk manages to play variations on one of the simplest and most percussive of all blues phrases in a nine-minute tour de force of cohesive imaginative invention. Here we hear nearly ten minutes of Monk playing the blues in a dramatic yet lyric curve of melody.

Other delights: the interplay of Ware behind Monk on "Off Minor." Copeland's solo on the same piece; in his way he knows the relationship of parts of Monk's music, of melody to harmony, as well as Coltrane does.

Nostalgia can corrupt memory, of course, but even allowing for that, I don't think these quartet performances are up to the level one heard at the Five Spot from this group. However, "Trinkle" very nearly is. The other two are fine performances. I think that in this way "Epistrophy" is excellent, too. And "Functional" is a near masterpiece.

Down Beat, 1961

Rex Stewart
Post-Ellington

Rather like Miles Davis by the late fifties, Rex Stewart had by the late thirties developed a unique, expressive, and important solo voice, partly by the very fact of accepting his limitations as an instrumentalist and making ingenious use of them in developing his own style. I've often wondered if he was not something of an inspiration for Miles Davis in this respect. Admittedly Stewart was an inspiration to Dizzy Gillespie in the way that he extended the technical and emotional range of his horn as an instrument of color and fiery effect. Stewart did all this, of course, directly under the influence and encouragement of Ellington.

The 1940 sessions, to be heard on Riverside 144 ("Bugle Call Rag," "Solid Rock," "Cherry," and "Diga Diga Do"), find him still directly under that influence, and also find him an improvising, inventive jazz soloist, using standard materials as his vehicle. A real soloist he is there, and an outstanding one. By contrast, Barney Bigard does not solo at all one might say, but, as Ellington taught him to do, uses his choruses as vehicles for patterns of clarinet color and sound, never really making them improvised melodic episodes that intend to carry their own weight.

I particularly enjoy Stewart's beautiful blues coda on "Solid Rock," but probably his best improvising is on "Cherry" where he plays a succession of apparently unrelated melodic fragments which gradually and unobtrusively build a larger design of ingenious and unexpected wholeness. Stewart could have got hints about how to do this from King Oliver's work and from Bix Beiderbecke's, of course, and again I found myself thinking of how often Miles Davis does the same kind of thing today. Then there is Stewart's casual way of playing almost *against* the time in his solo on "Diga Diga Do," and the way he suddenly contrasts that approach with very orderly and regular use of the beat in the bridge of the same piece.

49

The second four titles on the same LP represent a 1946 date and Stewart, now out of the Ellington band, is not so much the jazz improvisor on them, as he is a man being his own Ellington, being his own leader-composer. "Flim-Flam," "Blues Kicks the Bucket," and "Madeline" are all compositionally performed with far less variation, and the compositions are very Dukish. Those three stand up well, but "Loopin' Loba" is a vaguely executed, virtuosic piece, sometimes apparently intended to suggest be-bop, sometimes Eldridge or Shavers-ish.

The two final tracks led by pianist Jimmy Jones complete the LP with a pop song ("A Woman's Got a Right to Change Her Mind") played fairly straight by Harry Carney and Lawrence Brown, and "Departure from Dixie," a piece which the notes call reminiscent of early bop, which isn't, but which has very good solos by Carney and Brown, and good briefer ones by Hardwick and Thomas. How well they know their styles, and with what sureness they do what they do!

The first four titles are especially rewarding jazz for Stewart. They are also for Brown, especially on "Diga" where, as usual, he takes those chords and writes what amounts to an elegant blues line on them. There is also Dave Tough's drumming, which helps a bit to cover for Fleagle's rather stodgy guitar.

Something should also be said about what an interesting and exploratory player Billy Kyle was in those days, but for now let a simple assertion say it.

Metronome, April, 1961

L, H, & R

I'm sure that no one could doubt that Jon Hendricks is a clever, perhaps even ingenious man, and that the vocal group Lambert, Hendricks, and Ross, heard with certain ears, can be a very entertaining act. Their popularity should puzzle no one.

However, they are supposed to be jazz singers, some say. A jazz singer, like a jazz player, is supposed to improvise—or at least be able to improvise—and the very limitations within which L, H, & R work obviously discount improvisation. And it seems to me that the very task of setting words strictly to previously recorded, semiimprovised music has enough obstacles strewn in its path so that the results, however clever and ingenious, cannot in the true sense of the word be *creative.*

It is not Jon Hendricks' fault that people have called him a poet, certainly, but several people have, and one man has even written a rather scholarly *explication de texte* of his lines. It seems to me that if Jon Hendricks is a poet, then Cole Porter and Ira Gershwin are both probably poetic geniuses. (I know of several blues singers I would call poets.) Hendricks' verses from the LP on which the group sings Ellington (Columbia CL 1510) include "In tails or in tatters/This is all that matters," and "This is so exciting./You are so inviting./Here is this oasis/My heart knows where its place is." * Poetry?

Setting words to Ellington records can be a very different thing from setting words to Basie records (or Horace Silver records), tasks which Hendricks previously set himself. In the old Basie band we listen for swing, group spirit, and solos by Lester Young, Buck Clayton, Harry Edison, etc., that were almost ends in themselves. Ellington's achievements are quite another matter, for Ellington is the great composer-orchestrator who can make even the most brilliant soloist an integrated part of a grand design.

I have been told that L, H, & R make jazz seem "fun." I wonder if they don't sometimes make it seem pretty light stuff. At any rate, if some of those lines that Hendricks has set to Lester Young's solos really represent the kind of thing Prez was talking about musically, then I must have been living in a fool's paradise all these years for admiring Prez's depth so much.

In "Main Stem," Ellington effortlessly conducted Rex Stewart, Johnny Hodges, Ray Nance, Barney Bigard, Joe Nanton, Ben Webster, and Lawrence Brown through a fast orchestrated blues that comes off not as a clutter or string of solos but as a whole experience. Hendricks' version by contrast seems a tense monotony of phrases about "winkin' and blinkin'" lights. I wonder what the point is. And when I compare Ellington's magnificent contrapuntal orchestration of "I Don't Know What Kind of Blues I've Got" with this version, I continue to wonder. And Ellington's "Rocks in My Bed" takes a traditional lament and

* "Caravan" copyright 1937 by American Academy of Music, Inc. Copyright renewed 1965.

cheerily makes fun of it as if it were feeling sorry for itself. L, H, & R takes Ellington's irony and make it . . . well, to me, trivial. And "Cottontail?" Do you know what that's about? It's about a naughty rabbit, caught in a farmer's yard, who runs away.

I've spoken of tenseness. Part of it comes because the task the singers set for themselves sometimes inherently strains the vocal equipment of each of them. "All Too Soon" begins too low for Dave Lambert's small range and ends too high. The very slow tempo of "Midnight Indigo" soon has almost everybody's pitch wobbling. "What Am I Here For?" is again too low for Lambert and ends too high for Hendricks. (It seems to me that such things are quite a different matter from the natural use of falsetto *whoops* that blues singers use every day.) Finally, toward the end of "In A Mellow Tone," the combination of Johnny Hodges' virtuosity and Jon Hendricks' verbal ingenuity set Dave Lambert a vocal obstacle course that any singer might have trouble with.

Jon Hendricks has said that the title of a piece gives him the idea for his lyric. Is that why he didn't mess with "T. T. on Toast," "Are You Stickin'?" or "Dinah's In a Jam"?

Metronome, April, 1961

MJQ In Europe

European Concert (Atlantic 2-603, $9.98; S2-603, $11.98) is a two-record set by the Modern Jazz Quartet of performances taped in Sweden. The playing is on the whole so very nearly perfect that one almost wonders what this exceptional group of musicians can possibly find to do next. It is a kind of anniversary set in that the Quartet—John Lewis, piano and musical director; Milt Jackson, vibraphone; Percy Heath, bass; Connie Kay, drums—was formed nearly ten years ago at a recording session for which its four original members were gathered. They discovered that they enjoyed playing together very much and they decided to continue. They did so, intermittently at first and, finally permanently. The remarkable fact is that they continue to play with the same life and commitment to improvisation that they had in the beginning, and with an enormous increase in expressive range and sensitive group interplay as well.

They are lucky, too, for on the surface everything the Quartet does *seems* cool and almost controlled, and anyone who wants to take their work as a sort of pleasant but lively background sound can apparently do so. But anyone is a bit more receptive to the music will discover that under the surface there is a musical vitality and range that very few jazz groups have ever achieved.

"Bluesology," in the present set, can probably stand for the depth, breadth, and delight of their achievement. The piece has been in their repertory since the beginning and it is written in the simplest of all jazz forms, the twelve-bar blues. It still inspires them to sublime melodic improvising—individually, collectively, and, in the spontaneous and captivating response between Jackson and Lewis, contrapuntally. Similarly, there is John Lewis' "Django," memorial to the French gypsy guitarist-turned-jazzman Django Rinehardt, and surely one of the major compositions of modern jazz. The Quartet has been playing it for more than six years—in fact, this is their third recording of "Django"— yet they continue to find something fresh in it, and they manage to convey its wide emotional range, from reverent solemnity to a redeeming joy, with deepening insight.

There are other delights: the superb Lewis piano solo on the Duke Ellington piece called "It Don't Mean a Thing"; he is momentarily suspended, abandoned by all accompaniment and left with only his own extended melodic lines to propel him, until, at a moment when the tension is almost unbearable, Heath and Kay quietly reenter behind him. There is also the exploration, chiefly by Jackson, of the ballad "I Should Care," and of Thelonious Monk's remarkable, brooding " 'Round Midnight."

One does have reservations: "Vendome" still seems to me rather forced and academic compared to the group's later efforts at jazz fugues, and, although I grant it is an exhilarating work-out, I still wonder if one can do justice to such a superior popular song as "I'll Remember April" at such a fast pace. However, in the light of what this set does achieve, I wonder if such reservations may not amount to mere carping.

FM/Stereo Guide, December, 1961

Rehearsing with Ornette

Ornette Coleman was holding a rehearsal in a room at the new Atlantic Records studios off Columbus Circle. (It was in a recording studio on Columbus Circle that Fletcher Henderson met Don Redman in the early twenties!) Past the double doors of the sound-proofed rehearsal room were Coleman, his new trumpeter, Bobby Bradford; C. M. Moffett, the stocky drummer Bradford had recommended and brought along with him from Texas; and bassist Jimmy Garrison. There was also the group's manager, Mildred Fields (on the telephone, of course); and a couple of visitors were in and out briefly. In a corner of the room—quiet, constantly listening, but with the expression on his face as relaxed as the rest of him—was John Coltrane and of all the people interested in Coleman's music, Coltrane has become one of the most interested. The room was small but there was no feeling of confinement. There was a piano against one wall, and Ornette Coleman used it from time to time to make points, but used it sparingly.

The group had finished running through the ensemble of a new piece as written out on a slip of manuscript paper. Coleman, sitting at the piano, said over his shoulder to Jimmy Garrison, "I'm going to write out the bass line on this one. Use these notes on the piece, but don't make it sound like one note going into the other."

"Can I do that without using the bow?" asked Garrison.

"*Can* you? That's what I'm asking!" They both laughed. Ornette turned to the group. "This time just play the melody for the *emotion*. Just play it as quarternotes for the emotion." They ran through the theme again, phrasing it strangely while concentrating on feeling. At the end, Coleman said quickly, "Okay—let's try it a little faster," as he sat down on the piano bench, playing his alto to the back of the group.

At the end of another try, Coleman suddenly turned to Garrison. "Yeah! You dig that? You almost did it! Play that same thought out.

54

Don't play it like bass notes—don't get that kind of sound like you're walking behind someone. This is a musical phrase." Then he played the bass line on his saxophone, after a false start. "Don't read it as a *time* phrase."

They were now into the piece again with bassist Garrison now beginning to make a complex pattern of rhythms instead of accompanying as the group went into the final part of the tune. When they finished, Coleman turned to Moffett. "Can you make a five stroke roll under him at the end of that phrase, at the same time he is doing that?" As Moffett consented he turned again to the whole group, "Then we go into the playing," smiling, "I mean the . . . uumm . . . improvising."

Garrison: "I'll find out how many different notes I can play against that E that you guys hold at the end of the ensemble."

Coleman: "Yes! That's it, that's it!" They did the number again, with brief solos from Coleman and Bobby Bradford. At the end, the leader again turned to the bassist. "You know," he said as if he had just realized it himself (perhaps he had), "you can go down in fourths behind us on that piece if you want to." Then to the room in general, "I can't find the tempo to make the notes sound right on this one," running over the theme on his alto at a new speed.

The occasion had certainly taken on a character of its own—perhaps a revealing one about Ornette Coleman's music. There was discussion of techniques, and there was technical language being used (some of it conventional, some of it almost homemade), but the meaning behind the language was usually quite evident. And it was not the sort of discussion one would ordinarily hear at a rehearsal—not all of it, anyway. Complex and subtle things—points of phrasing a melody and unison playing—were simply understood and executed without a thought. During the whole afternoon, for instance, no one ever signaled a tempo or even gave an obvious downbeat! Yet everyone started together and stayed together. But some comparatively simple things had to be emphasized—you *can* play descending fourths on this piece, although in this music some other basic practices of tonality might not work; an unaccented five-stroke drum roll might be phrased slightly differently; forget the time-keeping in the rhythm (nobody will get lost) and play everything, including the percussion, as musical phrases. And perhaps some of these things were even discovered during the rehearsing on that very afternoon.

(The occasion was also quite a contrast to the first rehearsal Ornette Coleman had held in New York over two years ago—a hurried, nervous affair [nearly panicky for a couple of the players] on the bandstand at the Five Spot, sandwiched between a trip to the police for cabaret cards and an opening night, complete with invited press, that very evening.)

They were playing again. During Bobby Bradford's solo, a visitor touched his ear-lobe and nodded toward the trumpeter, smiling, in indication of how well the young trumpeter was continuing to get with the melodic freedom of his music, and to playing with few guides but his own imagination. At the end of the piece, Coleman said to Moffett, "Yeah. But when you repeat the drum patterns you see they don't come around the same way everytime."

"So when you're lost," Bradford cracked from across the room, "you're always lost at a different place!"

"Sure," smiled Ornette over the laughter. "So Bobby will keep track of where we are."

"See, Jimmy," Bradford continued to banter, "this is where he wants us to stop." He played a trumpet phrase. "In other words, take it phrase by phrase, but stop in the middle of the phrase." When the laughter had subsided again, "Seriously, Ornette, if we stop there we change the whole tune."

Coleman: "I guess that was a Sears-Roebuck stop. Let's find a Macy's stop." Turning to Moffett, "The rhythm you're playing now sounds like you're playing the piece. Play *against* the piece."

"I see. Counterpoint."

They ran through it again, and at the end Coleman turned again to Moffett, "That was good, but you ought to get another pattern to use in that piece too. And in that last little phrase you were still playing the melody. I don't even *want* it to sound like we're playing an arrangement."

Moffett: "Okay. On the turn-back, I'll play something different."

Coleman: "Aaaahhhhh!"

Moffett: "I know, I did it just half way in counterpoint that time. Let's try it again."

They began once more, still together, and still with no downbeat to be seen.

At the end, Coleman again turned to Moffett, "You hear that phrase you played at the end there? It implies another note. Your mind just fills it out even if you don't play that note. And don't think about the time at all, just about the accents."

Suddenly becoming very formal, and all but losing his Texas accent, Ornette Coleman turned to the room in general and said, "I wish it were possible to maintain the swing without making an obvious beat. I confess I don't know how to do it."

They were about to begin a new piece now when Coleman, had announced by running off the first phrase, a sort of stop-and-go pattern. ("Wait till you hear this one!" whispered Mildred Fields.) "Will you please put some *names* to those things," pleaded Garrison, "so I can play them with you sometimes on my bass instead of waiting till you guys are halfway through the ensemble before I know what you're playing?"

Bradford laughed, "You know what he tells me? He turns his head and says, 'Let's play *la-de-do-doo-da* or *lee-doo-doe-doe-dum*,' and I say, 'Yeah!' "

Ornette: "Let's put numbers to them. C. M. can keep the numbers."

They all laughed. "That won't work! You will have to ask him for the number to *la-de-dah-do*, and it's the same thing all over again."

"There's *one* with a title we know," said Garrison, "Let's play the one you call "The Idiot." He hums.

Bradford: "Is *that* the name of that one?"

Coleman: "Yeah. I named it for the movie—of the Russian novel, you know. I thought the melody was the way the hero was."

Garrison: "Ornette, we ought to change the title to 'Simple' or something like that. Suppose there are some idiots out here. They might not like it."

Coleman: "Suppose there are some on the bandstand!" laughing.

Bradford: "Well, *I* don't feel a draft!"

Metronome, December, 1961

The Strange Alliances of Jazz

During the late 1950s jazz began to form some striking alliances with older and time-honored arts: jazz and poetry, jazz and ballet, jazz and theater, jazz and symphonic music. And it has formed some with at least one younger art: background music on a number of television shows and in several movies.

Such activities have been greeted by some people as signs of a growing prestige for the music. I am not so sure. I am inclined to ask, what
is the price of such prestige?

Well, it may not do jazz any credit for it to underline a mugging on
a TV thriller, you may answer, but what about jazz accompanying the
New York City Center ballet company? That is surely prestige, is it not?

Perhaps, but such things are not so simple as they seem for a well-
done, authentic TV score actually may do jazz more good than its presence as a diversion during an evening of ballet. It ain't just what you
do but how you do it.

Most of the world's music is but a functional part of other things.
Think about it. Most music is for dancing, marching, worship, or merely
to help provide a congenial social atmosphere. Western concert music—
the music of Bach, Mozart, Beethoven—is the only music in the world
that is developed and independent, that asks to be listened to for its own
sake.

It is also true that only about three or four movie scores are worth
hearing on their own, and that even some ballet scores find their way
into the concert hall only as throwaways. And no one thought the lyre-
strumming with which an ancient poet like Homer accompanied his recitations was even worth describing; we don't know what the music
sounded like, but the *Iliad* and *Odyssey* survive and are still read.

Jazz has been a folk music always at least *about* to become an art
music, and most of its partisans have insisted it should be listened to
for its own sake at least since the 1920s.

They flocked around the bandstands and collected records in the thirties. And by the mid-forties, jazz clubs had no dancing, and jazz concerts were almost commonplace. Now jazz apparently can buy prestige
by becoming "functional" again as a part of recitations, movies, TV,
and the rest.

JAZZ AND POETRY

The curious phenomenon of jazz and poetry apparently has died out,
at least in its most publicized form.

It seems to have begun in San Francisco in the spring of 1957. There,
the members of the local artistic (or is it beat?) community who (like
many of their ilk in other big cities) had long had an almost fan-ish interest in jazz, began getting into the act.

In a small night club called the Cellar poets and would-be poets began reciting verses and rolling their abdomens while the musician-owners played something more or less like jazz in the background.

One leader in this activity was Kenneth Rexroth, who has written about jazz ("he may have known Charlie Parker, but I doubt if Bird knew him," commented one musician) and who was getting a second wind as a kind of father-overseer to several younger writers who have come to be known as "voices of the beat generation."

Somebody said, not without certain mystical implications, that the idea for his activity came from declamatory British poet Dylan Thomas. (Nobody mentioned Vachel Lindsey's "jazz" poetry from the 1920s, which was often publicly read to music.)

Soon, poetry nights found the small cellar (capacity 150) jammed with patrons attired by everyone from Capezio to Scaparelli, Sweet Orr to J. Press. Bruce Lippencott was leading his men through backgrounds for Rexroth, Laurence Ferlinghetti, Kenneth Ford, and (a real poet who could also read well) Kenneth Patchen.

Certain jazz journalists, tossing around terms like "art" and "new form" with a not-unusual abandon, began pounding out accounts of the activity for the magazines, and recordings were made.

The next fall, the Half Note, a small and then recently opened jazz club in lower Greenwich Village, began holding a weekly poetry-night competition with prizes awarded. During these meetings the devoted young artists began arguing hotly enough among themselves to bring fears of open brawls, and one of the clubs young managers was angrily confused because, as he put it, "they are criticizing American life!" It wasn't long before the Half Note had found it wise to settle for a weekly appearance by a single reader.

Soon the Five Spot, located directly across Manhattan from the Half Note, on the Lower East Side (where all the painters and writers had fled from high rents), was featuring Rexroth, now touring and booked solid for months. He was backed by a group of local jazzmen, now working but wondering about next week's gig.

The appearance of Langston Hughes as a poet-reader with a jazz group at the Village Vanguard pointed to an irony and suggested a partial solution—although, to be sure, Hughes is not a very good reader and has a shaky sense of musical structure.

There is one kind of jazz that has never been a dance or atmosphere music but has been listened to for the poetry that it is. It is the vocal blues. And during the late twenties and early thirties, the blues accompanists had managed, without overriding the singer, to increase the complexity of their roles.

The most sublime and balanced alliance between poetry and music that anyone has so far achieved have been the Provençale songs of the early Renaissance and German lieder. The blues singers and players never developed their art to any such peak, of course, but they made a fine start, and what they did is full of latent possibilities.

Since the twenties, Langston Hughes has taken the poetry of the blues and gospel hymn as the tradition from which to develop his own verses. Now, he may or may not be a first-rate poet. But if Hughes's readings-with-jazz are not a natural development, they at least formed a legitimate alliance.

JAZZ AND THE MOVIES

Movie scores exist in an artistic limbo. But if they are written in a jazz style, they have a unique assertiveness, and their usual blandness disappears. If the heroine flees from her pursuers to quasi-Stravinsky, we may hardly hear it; if to quasi-jazz, we can hardly miss hearing it.

Some very capable men have been involved in movie scoring, of course. Pete Rugolo has worked for MGM films and many a TV thriller (not to mention stripper Lili St. Cyr), and even so illustrious a jazzman as Benny Carter has worked for *M Squad*.

Recently, however, there has been more freedom allowed in jazz movie scoring. It seems to have begun in France. John Lewis wrote excellent music to accompany a trashy little French sex-pot movie (*without* Brigitte Bardot) *Sait-on-Jamais*, called *No Sun in Venice* in American, and the Modern Jazz Quartet performed on the soundtrack.

The *Sait-on-Jamais* score was a success, but what one heard in the film were only snippets of regular MJQ performances edited to fit the action by a sound engineer.

Lewis' music for the Harry Belafonte movie *Odds Against Tomorrow* was another matter. It was scored for orchestra and pretimed in the conventional manner, exactly to the picture's continuity. It is a superior film score, excellently unified, better perhaps than Johnny Mandel's comparable job on *I Want to Live*. And a couple of its parts make sense heard by themselves.

One unique approach to using jazz in a feature film is that in *Frantic!*, made in France as *Elevator to the Gallows* and now being shown here. Miles Davis and a group improvised the score from prearranged patterns and timing, responding to the action as the film unfolded on a screen before them. The LP recording of the results has some really arresting moments. Such things should definitely be tried again and often.

As originally produced, John Cassavetes' *Shadows* had a background score by Charlie Mingus. However, the version of that film now being shown commercially was partly reshot, and very little of Mingus' music remains. The reason seems to be that the music was so poorly recorded at first that it simply couldn't be used; the reflection is not on Mingus but on the engineering.

Duke Ellington has done both movie and television scoring. Certain of his own statements seem to indicate that he thought his writing for *Anatomy of a Murder* was not successful, and many others would agree with him.

Ellington also has been involved with the MGM television series called *Asphalt Jungle*. He contributed the theme music and for some episodes handled the whole score. His music for the episode called "The Lady and the Lawyer" was first-rate Ellington, and one of the best jazz backgrounds yet, a set of excellently conceived and performed variations on his theme melodies, made flexible enough to fit any mood or event in the narrative, and kept musical enough (perhaps too musical) to be constantly absorbing.

The movie *Jazz on a Summer's Day* is a different matter; it is ostensibly a documentary of a Newport Jazz Festival. It has been called a highly successful movie. It has also been said that the film captures the pleasures of jazz superbly.

The opposite opinion holds that in the film, jazz was merely being used for a kind of chi-chi indulgence of cinematic techniques that left the music in the lurch, and that rather than making jazz seem fun, the film makes jazz seem trivial and childish. A *"Vogue's* eye view" of jazz, one man has called it.

In either case, it seems to me that movies are one kind of experience, jazz another. Some kind of alliance is excellent, but why should one medium try to interpret the other? Few things could be more sanctimoniously arty than the efforts of a few years ago to get the movie camera to "interpret" great paintings by ponderously wandering around over their surfaces. And asking us to watch waves and a yacht race while Thelonious Monk plays the piano, as *Jazz on a Summer's Day* did, seems incongruous.

However, the real problem when the music is only background scoring and incidental, particularly in the movies, is that it can be the most thoroughly functional kind of music there is.

Religious music, for example, is supposed to make one feel reverence or, in some cultures, inspire dancing. But at its lowest level, movie music is only supposed to keep an audience from becoming distracted. If it can do some mood setting or actually contribute to the feeling of a scene, so much the better. But the moment movie music starts to draw attention to itself, it is going too far. Therefore, most of it cannot stand on its own. William Walton's score for the Laurence Olivier production of Shakespeare's *Henry V* or Max Steiner's music for *King Kong* sound superb while one is watching those films. But these scores will not bear repeated hearings on records or in concert halls.

There is however, *some* movie music that is effective and unobstrusive in its original context, yet can also be listened to for its own sake. Prokofieff's *Alexander Nevsky* is such a score. So is Aaron Copland's music for *Of Mice and Men*.

It is a high tribute to jazz and its musicians that at least some of the scoring for movies and TV already seems to survive the temptations involved—temptations for it to be mere mood setting and self-effacing craftsmanship.

Meanwhile, if you want to hear jazz movie scores the way they used to be done before anybody got self-conscious at it, catch some of those hilarious early Mae West films the next time around on TV, particularly one called *I'm No Angel.*

JAZZ AND THE THEATER

Bobby Scott (*A Taste of Honey*) and Don Elliott (*A Thurber Carnival*) have both written "incidental" music for Broadway shows. And so did John Mehegan, before them, for Tennessee Williams' *Streetcar Named Desire.* But the one really integrated *dramatic* use of jazz as part of a serious play is in Jack Gelber's *The Connection.*

The Connection has been the subject of some rather moralistic tongue-clucking in the jazz press, and I think its whole intention has been rather misunderstood. Gelber has presented jazz music because some jazz musicians are among the characters in his play, and they are in a situation where they they might naturally play. However the plot of Gelber's play has very little to do with its meaning. Its meaning comes from an interplay of cultural attitudes and characters. Suffice it to say here that—on the surface at least—a group of narcotics addicts are waiting in a loft for their connection to arrive with drugs, while a movie director, dedicated to realism, attempts to photograph them in action. When the drug-bearer does arrive, they all take injections of the narcotic. One addict who passes out from an overdose is selfishly abandoned by most of the group.

The Connection is not a "realistic" play (as it has been called), but a try at an antirealist play. It is as if Gelber were saying that the final parody of realism is to present complacently self-indulgent and self-degrading addicts and, to top it all, make them real addicts on the stage, not actors pretending to be junkies.

But there, precisely, is the flaw, some say, for they are not real addicts but unavoidably *are* actors on the stage. Everyone knows it, and everyone knows that Gelber actually plots their action and speeches on paper like any playwright in order to make them seem to be handling themselves spontaneously on the stage.

Gelber has shown skill in manipulating all the facets of his shocking play, but he has not shown the surpassing kind of skill that Pirandello did in bringing off the same sort of thing. My feeling is that Gelber's artistic focus is not really that of the antirealists, from whom he has obviously learned, but of a sentimentalist. He has portrayed the addict's world, not with the hard, quasi-detachment of a Brecht or a Becket or a Pirandello, but with the fuzziness of a William Saroyan. He has produced an almost popularized modern theater. In tone, he has made a kind of junkies' *The Time of Your Life.* Even his much-protesting line spoken from the audience, "That's the way it really is!" seems to echo Saroyan's reiterated, "All up and down the line, no foundations."

But one must admit that the particular kind of "hard" playing that pianist Freddie Redd and altoist Jackie McLean provide on stage was appropriate to the evening. And the musicians are obviously not required to be anybody's "background."

JAZZ AND THE BALLET

It is possible that a jazzman will produce a dance score as good as *Petrouchka.* But in most of the alliances of jazz with other arts, one artistic experience must dominate. After all, an opera librettist knows that he had better remain a respectable verifier and not a poet, because the primary effect of opera must be musical, and he mustn't swamp it. And (to reiterate another basic point) even the ballet composer, whose role is less secondary than the film composer's and who more often produces music that can pass in the concert hall on its own, knows he still must keep his place.

Several "modern" dancers (of more or less the persuasion of Martha Graham, Merce Cunningham, or Charles Weidman) had been intrigued by jazz for some time. But a few years ago, instead of getting musicians into their recital halls, some of these performers were showing up in the jazz haunts and posturing on the bandstand. Lee Becker could be seen, crowded in with several instrumentalists, at New York's Café Bohemia, or demonstrating to recordings before a gathering of musicians and critics at the Music Inn in Lenox, Mass. Then Eartha Kitt appeared with dancers at the 1957 Newport meeting.

There was also Anneliese Widman's appearance in the short-lived Mort Sahl review *The Next President,* dancing to music by a Jimmy Giuffre group. And there was John Lewis' recent *Original Sin* score done for Lewis Christensen's San Francisco ballet, which was not very well received and which is not really impressive in its recorded version.

Inevitably, some earnestly speak of "new art." Others sagely remembered the wiggling on view at the old Cotton Club in the thirties as Duke Ellington's musicians played behind the papier-maché palm trees. Or they reflected on the many times they had heard everything from Ellington's "Black and Tan Fantasy" to Dizzy Gillespie's "Groovin' High" used by the pit bands at Minsky's while a young woman removed her clothes.

One very good example of such ballets, however, is Jerome Robbins' *Pied Piper.* It is built around a clarinet concerto, written for Benny Goodman by Aaron Copland. Robbins used ballet, "modern," and a few jazz steps to make a wonderful comic dance. However, when something more comprehensive and serious has been attempted, even by Robbins, the results have been considerably less good, and real jazz steps are usually abandoned. The results were certainly less good in George Balanchine's classical *Jazz Variants,* to music by Gunther Schuller for the Modern Jazz Quartet and orchestra, which played at the New York City Center last winter.

There have been other jazz ballets by Sidney Bechet, Charlie Mingus, Dave Brubeck, Rex Stewart—but I am beginning to make a list, and there is no point in that.

In the 1930s, when jazz was a "ballroom" dance music, there was a wonderful, creative interplay between musicians and dancers. A trumpet player's improvised solo might inspire a new step, and a new step might inspire a tenor saxophonist to an extra chorus or two. Two of the great jazz dancers at the Savoy Ballroom in those days were Al Minns and Leon James. Today, these men run a dance studio in New York and tour annually in delightful concert demonstrations of jazz dances from the cakewalk through the lindy. A sympathetic choreographer might do wonders with the lessons they have to teach.

In 1961 in New York, at a club called the Showplace, Baby Lawrence, an almost legendary tap dancer, appeared with the Charlie Mingus group. He got superlative reviews, and he deserved them.

He is an improvising dancer whose art has grown with the music. He has absorbed the rhythmic patterns of modern jazz and dances it as surely as Max Roach plays it. Seeing him gives much meaning to Charlie Parker's words that Baby Lawrence "can cut you with his feet."

Lawrence rattles off the names of a score of other modern dancers whom he admires. Most of them are almost totally unknown to the jazz public, and it is surely a great loss that they are.

THE THIRD STREAM

The alliance between jazz and classical music has recently begun to be fruitful—fruitful in at least one instance, anyway. This is the so-called Third Stream, and the idea is to combine written classical forms with improvised jazz. The pieces are more or less like concertos, with the classical musicians as the orchestra discussing, arguing, agreeing with the improvising jazzmen down front.

Actually the term Third Stream has been so thoroughly misused and abused that it may even have to be abandoned.

It has to do only with the kind of music just described. It is, of course, not a question of an occasional jazz-y effect in a classical piece. It also has nothing to do with jazz musicians' efforts to borrow classical devices and forms—after all this is what jazzmen have been doing, with more or less deliberateness, for more than sixty years. The Third Stream also is not the music of Ornette Coleman, the George Russell group, Eric Dolphy, Jaki Byard, Don Ellis, the new Jimmy Guiffre group, Cecil Taylor, *et al.* Third Stream is not "the new thing" that these players are working on, although some Third Stream pieces have been written around some of these men.

There is, therefore, no such thing as "Third Stream jazz," no matter what liner-note copy says. There can't be; it would be like a male hemaphrodite or a pure-bred mule.

There have been many failures in the Third Stream—some naive, some pretentious, some honest, some not so honest.

The best composition perhaps in the idiom so far on records is Gunther Schuller's "Conversations," written for a string quartet and the Modern Jazz Quartet, and parts of Bill Russo's "An Image," written for Lee Konitz and a string group.

One of Schuller's subsequent pieces, "Variants on a Theme of John Lewis," used jazz material as his point of departure, although his treatment is partly classical and decidedly Third Stream. Another Schuller piece, "Variants on a Theme of Thelonious Monk," is a piece of jazz recomposition and arrangement—and an excellent one.

On the other hand, Schuller's "Concertino" for the Modern Jazz Quartet and orchestra seems to be one of the failures. It sets perhaps pointlessly difficult tasks for the jazzmen in unfamiliar rhythms and structures, and its last movement sounds dangerously like a Gershwin pastiche. However, the "Concertino" is an honorable failure, it is not the "light music" with which Rolf Leiberman and Howard Brubeck have polluted the Third Stream.

The reasons for the success of "Conversations" are important and worth a few remarks.

"Conversations" begins in the contemporary classical manner as the strings gradually move to a peak of tension; at this point, the jazzmen enter, swinging. This piece is a success because Schuller lets the two idioms argue, fight, and agree to disagree. He doesn't try to get the classicist to swing or the jazzmen not to. He trusts the jazz musicians to be themselves and make up their own melodies, and he lets each musical idiom go its own way by its own standards.

By sympathetically understanding jazz and putting his confidence in its players, he has achieved something commendable, which will bring prestige to all concerned. Other composers—also TV producers and choreographers—please harken to the message.

Music 1962—Down Beat Yearbook, 1961

Bill Evans, Introspect

Sunday at the Village Vanguard was recorded before an audience on a Sunday afternoon and evening at the Village Vanguard in New York, by the Bill Evans trio (Scott LaFaro, bass; Paul Motian, drums), just ten days before Scott LaFaro's death. It has qualities preserved on no other recordings by this trio. On the whole, I do not think it is quite so good as their first one, *Portrait in Jazz* (Riverside 315), but in several of its details this Vanguard set surpasses the earlier recitals.

"Gloria's Step" is by LaFaro; it is a good, if not thoroughly original line and on it the young bassist shows the most singularly valuable quality that he had at his death—he selects his notes from unexpected places, and he uses them in an unexpected order that turns out to have its own embryonic logic. It takes sophisticated musical knowledge and a sophisticated ear to do this, of course. But it also takes a developing imagination. On "All of You" the same qualities are even more evident, but there is also a flaw in that there is some rhythmic sameness in his phrasing.

On "My Man's Gone Now" and especially on "Solar" the trio goes a long way toward becoming what it wanted to be—three men simultaneously improvising around given material, each playing musical phrases, no one an "accompanist" or mere timekeeper, and the result an interweaving of three equal parts.

I have spoken almost as if this were a bass player's record (which it isn't), and as if this were really a trio's record (which, happily, sometimes it very nearly is). But it is first of all Bill Evans' record. I think it would be commendably his if only for the way that he handles the improvised impressionism of "Jade Visions"—I still have my doubts about such moods as jazz but I have no doubts about how well Evans can do them. And it is commendably Evans' record even for so simple a matter as the compelling yet gentle momentum with which he handles the theme statements themselves on "My Man's Gone Now," "Solar," and "Alice in Wonderland."

There is hardly a selection here—hardly a chorus here—on which Evans is not musically interesting. And yet, I realize that to hear that he was interesting, I had to give almost constant and careful musical and technical attention. I think Evans has a problem with audiences and with the emotional communication of his music; I think he has, with so fine yet so fragilely introverted a talent, a very special problem in reaching people.

Oscar Peterson's flash and Dave Brubeck's geniality, for examples, are obvious and natural qualities, ready for an audience to grasp immediately. It happens that I doubt if these qualities go very deep in those men but my point is that neither man has had very much trouble getting to an audience emotionally with what he has to offer.

Evans' is a potentially more complex, and therefore potentially greater talent. And so he has to face problems that some men don't have to face and has work to do that not all men need to do. But such problems can be faced honorably and with musical integrity, for during the late thirties and early forties Teddy Wilson was able to play out his melodically inventive, gentle introversion and reach people with it. And I expect it has cost John Lewis a great deal to learn to project his essentially introspective talent so strongly as he does now. A musician can make great emotional demands on an audience—Monk does—but one cannot ask an audience to do a musician's part of the job.

No man could possibly tell another how to go about solving such problems of communication, or what their solution might be for him individually—and certainly it would be an effrontery for a record reviewer even to try. Communication is a much abused word, especially in the public arts, but it is not necessarily a small consideration, especially not for a potentially complex talent. No one could doubt that both Teddy Wilson and John Lewis became better and more expressive players for facing their problems of communication squarely and honestly. The rewards can be as great as the task difficult. And the work to be done, if the problem is there, cannot be run away from no matter how difficult or discouraging.

I think that in having such a task, Evans also has a commanding opportunity not given to all men.

Down Beat, 1962

Giuffre Date

At 4 P.M. on a quiet Friday afternoon a group gathered at the Olmstead Recording Studio to record Jimmy Giuffre's new trio. Besides the leader and his clarinet, there was pianist Paul Bley, a decidedly inner-directed man whose heavy sandals clacked noisily on the steel ladder connecting the studio and the control booth. ("Olmsted, get *that* sound on the record!" a visitor suggested.) And there was bassist Steve Swallow, barely dry behind the ears professionally—but it is said those young ears are already among the fastest in jazz.

Fast ears are what a player needs in Giuffre's music, for it is often almost totally improvised, except for a memorized statement of the theme. The players ad lib their melodies, sometimes without reference to chorus lengths, chord patterns, or any other preset structures. The soloist is free to shift his tempo or his key as he wishes, and the others must follow him. They do immediately. In fact, they seem to anticipate each other even in the most unexpected turns.

The Giuffre trio had just ended a week at Trudi Heller's Downtown Versailles club in New York. Giuffre felt that after such nightly experience at improvising they were ready to record, and he asked Verve's artist and repertory man Creed Taylor to set up a session.

"It's like an instrument, this room," said Giuffre, warming up his clarinet. He had chosen Olmstead's studio himself; Verve, like several other companies, does not maintain its own recording facilities but leases them for individual sessions. Giuffre had asked Taylor for this particular one, which tops a ten-story building on 40th Street in midtown Manhattan. A high-ceilinged room painted in pale blue, it displays several irrelevantly ornate ionic columns on one wall. "It's half of the old penthouse living room," says proprietor Dick Olmstead. "It belonged to William Randolph Hearst."

Olmstead's is also probably the world's only split-level recording studio; the glass-enclosed control booth is set about twenty feet above the studio floor, at one end of the room. It houses the engineer's panel, and will accommodate several visitors.

Olmstead wandered around the studio arranging his microphones. Giuffre cocked his ears for an echo after one of his clarinet phrases. "Yes, this room *is* an instrument. Listen." Swallow plucked a note on his bass and attended the reverberations.

Olmstead climbed up to the booth and slid over behind his complex board. Creed Taylor was at his elbow. Below, on the studio floor, Olmstead had placed one mike close in on Bley's piano, while Giuffre and Swallow were sharing another.

Taylor was there to represent the record company and help Giuffre. He was discreetly quiet, knowing it was best to let Giuffre run the date himself. Unofficially present were Giuffre's wife of only a few weeks, Juanita; young Perry Robinson, a former clarinet pupil of Giuffre's; a photographer, who at first respectfully declined to enter the studio while the tape was rolling; and three friends of the Giuffres who dropped in.

"The name of this piece is "Whirr," said Giuffre. "Spell that," Olmstead said over the speaker, as he bent over his log.

Giuffre pretended to be puzzled. "Well, I will." He looked at the ceiling. In the booth his wife began to laugh. "W-h-i-r-r-r-r-r . . . ," he trailed off.

"Blues in B flat," cracked Swallow, naming the most basic jazz form.

They began fast. Giuffre was playing high and fingering rapidly. "He'll show those critics!" someone whispered to Mrs. Giuffre. (Because in his early days Giuffre seldom played high notes, a French writer had quipped that Giuffre's pupils needed a second instructor for the upper register.) At one point Bley hit the bass strings inside the piano with the heel of his hand to get an abrupt sound. And Giuffre got a brief effect like rushing wind by blowing across one of the stops of his clarinet.

"I think that's it," said Giuffre at the end of the piece.

Giuffre's music has obviously come a long way in the past few years. Most people who know him probably first heard of him when he wrote the highly successful piece "Four Brothers," for the 1949 Woody Herman band. This was the "cool" Herman Herd, and the brothers were a shifting foursome of saxophonists: combinations of Stan Getz, Herbie Stewart, Zoot Sims, Al Cohn, Serge Chaloff, and Giuffre. A second wave of fame came in 1957, when he formed the original Giuffre "3" of "The

Train and the River," "Swamp People," and similar impressionistic pieces. Although his music was then gaining him considerable prestige and respect (he had begun winning fan-magazine polls on clarinet), Giuffre gradually became dissatisfied with the restrictions his style placed on the players.

"I like the pastoral—the country," he has said of these times. "I like peaceful moods." But about then he began listening to Thelonious Monk. "I heard an element in his music—a way of stating things with conviction that was clear and sure. And he played without any restraint—he played it immediately, right in front of you. I also noticed it in Sonny Rollins' music, this same kind of statement. I got interested in this and started to work on it . . . I discovered a lot of things. . . . I was holding back a lot of things. . . . I was afraid of hitting certain notes. . . . I worked—and finally got up enough nerve to throw the rock off the cliff and just play anything I wanted to play when I wanted to play it. It was a revelation."

In all, Giuffre spent more than a year pursuing the idioms of Thelonious Monk and Sonny Rollins. The ultimate result was the new Giuffre style that his current trio plays, but to anyone who has followed his career it also seemed like a revelation. This music incorporates the impressionistic moodiness, the textures, and the compositional refinements of the earlier Giuffre "3." But it also has a new freedom and immediacy. Now, Giuffre the studied composer and Giuffre the player who wants to make strong, spontaneous and uncompromising statements are closer together than ever.

Down in the studio, the trio was ready for the next take. "This is called 'Afternoon.' It feels like a lazy afternoon," Giuffre explained, half to suggest a mood to the players. "I'll spell it for you," he said, smiling up toward Olmstead and Taylor, "A-f-t . . ."

"All right!" Olmstead smiled.

They began with no setting of tempo. Bley was soon answering Giuffre's improvised phrases in a spontaneous, far-out counterpoint. Swallow looked as if he might drop his bass, he was so acutely involved in the music.

After the number, the trio climbed up to the recording booth for the playback of "Afternoon." Giuffre squinted as he listened.

"Let's try that one again," said Giuffre, as Olmstead shut off the tape. "For me—you guys were fine."

Bley protested, "I thought you sounded good." Giuffre quickly affected a comic pompousness: "I always sound *good,* but I can do better."

They clambered down to the studio again. Bley clacked down the steel stairs as Giuffre, behind him, suggested, "Let's leave the chord progression out of this one on the solos. I like the piece but I get tired of that progression. Let's just play."

But Giuffre was persuaded that he had played well, and they decided to return to "Afternoon" later if they felt like it.

They were now about to record "Flight." And again they began without a tempo signal; Giuffre merely quietly said, "Okay, downbeat," as the tape began to roll.

There was a goof in the brief written introduction. "How much after you do I come in?" Bley asked.

"Two and a half beats," said Giuffre. They tried again, twice. Bley interrupted himself on the second. "If I count it, I seem to come in earlier."

"Oh, I forgot. You come in a beat and a half *before* me."

Above, Mrs. Giuffre looked at her husband and laughed quietly; she was around when the pieces were first written.

They started to play. Bley suddenly went into a medium tempo, an easy, rocking jazz groove, and Swallow, too, was on it immediately. Toward the end, Bley surreptitiously reached inside the piano again. The finish of the piece was a long note which Giuffre held softly over the piano's sustained reverberations.

During the playback, Giuffre asked Olmstead, "Dick, can we hear that piece again, on monaural?"

"I don't know why you want it in stereo at all," someone remarked. "I mean with the unity you guys have."

"It still sounds better in stereo to me," said Bley.

"Sure, *you* have a whole mike to yourself," said a visiting musician friend.

The second playback began. Swallow softly clapped his hands to the music and looked at Bley, smiling. At the end of the take, Giuffre's voice was heard, "I'll spell it for you, W-h-i-r-r-r . . ."

Some of the pieces seemed to have little of the quality of jazz in the conventional sense. The trio's work does suggest contemporary chamber music, but only able jazz musicians deeply committed to spontaneity could improvise this way. And only musicians committed to an individual exploration of their instruments and of the personal sounds they can make with them could play this way. No classicists would qualify.

"Everything seems to be going so well," Swallow was telling Juanita, "I can't believe it. It must really be going badly. I feel like when I was in school, if I finished a test and handed it in before anybody else."

Over in a corner Giuffre was earnestly chatting with a new arrival, "At first I didn't know whether we could get along with piano in place of guitar, but Paul is fine."

"Are you kidding? You got this Swallow playing guitar parts on his bass!"

"Hey Paul," said Giuffre, turning to the door, "did you hear a string that's out of tune on the piano there toward the end?"

"On *that* piece?" Bley laughed. "Who could know? No, it was muted. I had my hand on it."

"Well," said Giuffre, as they went downstairs to the studio, "the next thing I'd like to do is record with this group and an orchestra." Bley nodded enthusiastically.

Swallow's voice was picked up from below on the open mikes. "So few notes on that last one. Sometimes with this group I sound like something from the twenties." They ran through the theme of a piece called "Ictus," written by Bley's wife, Carla. The trio had tried to include it on a previous LP but gave up after eighteen unsuccessful attempts to get a good version on tape.

"This time it's going on in one take," someone whispered to Creed Taylor. He was right.

Swallow watched intently as Giuffre invented his coda, so he would know when to come back in for a last bass phrase. Giuffre unexpectedly pulled his last note out of the air at the end of an abruptly asymmetrical phrase, and Swallow was right on it. Bley concluded with something of his own. No sooner had Olmstead shut off the tape than everybody broke into laughter at the humorous appropriateness of it.

The playback got immediate approval. "Now I think this next one should be very loose," Giuffre said, throwing his arms in all directions. "You know—very nondirectional. This is called "The Gamut," he announced to Olmstead.

During his solo, Bley began to hum his melody as he ad-libbed. Neither Olmstead nor Taylor objected. They both agree with Giuffre that it's part of the music as the trio makes it.

Again, Giuffre listened to the playback with his eyes half shut. This time Swallow's eyes were on him, as they had been while they were playing. Suddenly everyone realized that all three of them at one point had spontaneously fallen into playing a little traditional jazz phrase.

"Yeah, that's a good figure there," said Bley quietly. Later he turned to Swallow. "You see, when we set him up, that Giuffre really plays a good solo." They laughed and then listened carefully to the way Bley had finished the piece with an unusual sound from the piano.

"We ought to end with that," said Giuffre.

Creed: "You mean end the *record*?"

"Yes," said Giuffre and Swallow in unison.

Giuffre looked at his watch. "Hey, we've still got the studio for half an hour, haven't we, Dick? Let's hear it all back again. We're all finished. We'll call this album *Thesis*."

"Finished *now*?"

"Sure. After all, we only did one piece twice; there isn't much choice to make, and there's no editing. I'll spell it for you. F-i-n-i-s-h-e-d."

FM/Stereo Guide, January, 1962

Classic Prez

If masterpieces exceed excellence, then there is not a high enough rating for the Lester Young on Commodore 30014, *Lester Young and the Kansas City Five*.

A 1938 session produced the masterpieces: his delicate contrapuntal clarinet improvising behind Buck Clayton and his tenor solo on "Way Down Yonder in New Orleans," his delicately original clarinet invention on "I Want A Little Girl," and his lovely variant of a traditional blues line on "Pagin' the Devil." These are masterpieces.

Excellence comes with his clarinet solo in the faster "Countless Blues," his interplay and tenor invention on, "Them There Eyes."

Surely no horn man between Louis Armstrong at his 1933 peak and Charlie Parker beginning in 1945 produced more original or more beautiful work than the best of Lester Young, and these solos are among the best. And as surely as the best jazz does survive its time and period, these do.

Astonishing: He was a great tenor player, yet for the way he handled the clarinet's sound alone, he would be an exceptional clarinetist, and of the handful of clarinet records he made almost all are gorgeous creations.

The other four titles, "I Got Rhythm," "Three Little Words," "Four O'Clock Drag," "Jo-Jo," with Bill Coleman and Dickie Wells, come from 1944. They are very good on the part of all participants; for Young they are even better than good. But what a different sensibility Young carried after his Army experience!

There are other things to notice on the 1938 sides; Clayton is fine, for instance, on "I Know That You Know" and "Laughing at Life," which do not have Prez—almost as fine as current Buck Clayton, which is fine indeed. Eddie Durham, the leader and a good arranger, has such a very different and older sense of time on guitar from the other men. And notice the group: horns and rhythm with no piano—the idea has been tried since and less casually than this but not really more successfully.

But then, masterpieces never are surpassed. The only thing to do with masterpieces is hear them and treasure them and—if they are jazz—be thankful they got recorded.

Down Beat, May 10, 1962

Concert: Rollins and Lewis

An evening divided between Sonny Rollins and John Lewis held a double promise. Rollins and his quartet (Jim Hall, Bob Cranshaw, Ben Riley) were to play for the first half of the program at the YM-YWHA. Lewis was to premiere his score for a new Italian film, *The Milano Story.* And there would also be a performance of Jim Hall's "Piece for Guitar and Strings."

For Rollins, the promise was fulfilled brilliantly. From his opening choruses on "Three Little Words," it was apparent that he was going to play with commanding authority and invention, and with a penetrating humor which included a healthy self-parody.

His masterwork of the evening was a cadenza on "Love Letters," several out-of-tempo choruses of easy virtuosity in imagination and execution, and a kind of truly artistic bravura that jazz has not known since Louis Armstrong of the early 1930s.

The performance included some wild interpolations, several of which Rollins managed to fit in by a last-minute, witty unexpected alteration of a note or two. To my ear, he did not once lose his way, although a couple of times he did lose Hall—and that is nearly impossible to do, for the guitarist has one of the quickest harmonic ears there is.

Rollins' final piece was a kind of extemporaneous orchestration on, "If Ever I Should Lose You," in which he became brass, reed, and rhythm section, tenor soloist, and Latin samba percussionist all at once and with constant musical logic.

Hall's piece was carefully rehearsed and better played than on its recorded version. It is a work of skillful lyricism, but I wonder still if it has the depth of, say Hall's lovely improvisation on "I Can't Get Started" earlier in the evening.

Lewis' five-part piece was a disappointment. It seemed naive in its scoring, in development of its ideas, and in abrupt transitions from jazz to quasi-Italian schmaltz and back again.

If the film is a farce comedy, the score may have a deliberately guileless quality in context. But a concert performance is another matter. In the past, Lewis' detractors have accused him of a kind of academicism. There was nothing very academic about this score. And much hasty commercialism has shown better craftsmanship. It is hard to believe that the man who wrote and scored *Odds Against Tomorrow* wrote this. It is almost impossible to believe that the same man also wrote "Three Little Feelings." And it is no pleasure to say so.

Delta Blues of Robert Johnson

The sixteen titles on Robert Johnson's *King of the Delta Blues Singers* (Columbia 1654)—some of them previously unissued and some of them alternate takes—were done at several sessions in 1936–37, the only recording dates of self-accompanying Mississippi Delta blues singer Robert Johnson.

Johnson died not long after the last date and before he was twenty-one. Since then his reputation has been almost legendary. I think this commendable LP proves that it was deserved. He was a haunting singer, and he was a poet. I might also say that his work is a stark lesson to anyone who thinks that jazz and its progenitors are "fun" music or a kind of people's vaudeville. But one could say that about any good blues singer or any really good jazzman.

Johnson's work apparently is the direct and uncluttered product of the Mississippi Delta blues tradition, and it is also a revelation to those who believe that the authentic "country" blues is limited in emotion and tempo to the slow moodiness of, say, Bill Broonzy's later days. For there is a variety of tempo and rhythm and attitude here that is a credit to the tradition, and in the hoarse directness of Johnson's voice there is an immediacy that cuts directly through the twenty-five years since these tracks were made.

The best blues deal in their own way with basic human experience, with things that all men in all times and conditions try to come to terms with. If I did not believe that, I would not call them poetry.

Me and the devil was walking side by side/I'm going to beat my woman until I get satisfied.

I got stones in my pathway, and my road is dark as night.

I got to keep moving, I got to keep moving./Blues falling down like hail, blues falling down like hail./I can't keep no money, hellhound on my trail/hellhound on my trail, hellhound on my trail.

Those words are strong on paper, but when one hears Johnson sing them they are stronger still, and beautiful. His kind of emotional honesty takes bravery. And if jazz did not have such bravery in its background, it would surely not have survived.

Honor Robert Johnson.

Down Beat, May 24, 1962

When the Big Bands Played Swing

In the fall of 1939 a fist fight broke out between two boys in the corridor of a New Jersey high school. The fracas soon spread to half the student body, and took all available faculty members to quiet. The bone of contention was not baseball or girl friends. It seems that Benny Goodman and Artie Shaw were both appearing in Newark during the same week and one young man had declared Goodman the best. The other young man wasn't having any of that. As hostilities spread, the belligerents formed themselves into firm battalions: one group shouted that neither Shaw nor Goodman but Tommy Dorsey was "the greatest"; another (smaller but no less vocal) declared for Bob Crosby; still another group (highly excitable, mostly composed of freshmen and therefore indicating adulation to come) shouted for Glenn Miller. And so events marched.

It was all part of what jazz writers call (somewhat pompously perhaps) "the swing era," the period of greatest mass popularity that any jazz style has ever had.

The accounts usually say that everything started in March, 1937, when the Benny Goodman band played an engagement at the Paramount Theatre in New York. From the moment the musicians came on stage, there was shouting from the seats, dancing in the aisles, panic followed by resignation from the ushers and the management—and 11,500 paid admissions the first day.

Of course, a few rumbling voices declared at the time that this "swing music" was not really anything new, that it was just "another name for jazz"; and, as if to prove their contention, the hit group of 1917, Nick La Rocca's Original Dixieland Jazz Band, was revived at the New York World's Fair. These dissidents notwithstanding, the fact was that between 1917 and 1937 jazz had been through a major revolution affecting not only the size of the jazz orchestra but the jazzman's basic ideas of rhythm and melody. Among the early contributors was one man whose name is indeed well known—Louis Armstrong—and two whose names are not so well known—pianist-leader and arranger Fletcher Henderson and alto saxophonist and arranger Don Redman.

Actually, the teen-age swing fans described above were fighting a battle about very little. There was not really very much difference between the Goodman and Shaw styles. Goodman had a disciplined brass section and the scores leaned heavily on it; Shaw's band was, in contemporary parlance, "cooler," and depended on its highly disciplined sax section. Both were simply popularizing a kind of music that had begun in the early twenties and had already reached its maturity by 1933. Tommy Dorsey and Bob Crosby, as we shall see, were also derivative, if from different sources. And as for Glenn Miller, however good his music was as dance music, it is rather hard to take it seriously as jazz. For one thing, Miller never had any really good soloists except Bobby Hackett, and Hackett spent most of his time striking guitar chords in the rhythm section. Second, the Miller band's ideas of rhythm frequently reflected the archaic phrasing of commercial "hillbilly" music. On the other hand, two of the great creative big bands of the late thirties, Duke Ellington's and Count Basie's, didn't even raise a voice among our high-school devotees.

But we are getting ahead of our story. As I have already indicated, the roots of big-band swing style go back to the twenties. Three major forces that shaped it came together in 1924, when Louis Armstrong, a shy young man wearing red underwear and big-toed work shoes, joined Fletcher Henderson's orchestra in New York. Don Redman, Henderson's chief arranger, has said, "Louis, his style and his feeling, changed our whole idea about the band musically." To the layman, Armstrong's rhythm and melody—in short the *swing*—that was to dominate the contribution is perhaps at once the most nebulous and the easiest to recognize. It was he who first dramatized the phrasing, the ideas of music, and the mode of improvising that was to influence every jazz player no matter what his instrument.

But before Armstrong arrived, Redman and Henderson had already given this music a basic framework and style in their orchestrations. Before the improvising soloist gets to it, swing music belongs to the composers and arrangers, and the first successful arranger for big bands was Redman, working for Henderson's orchestra.

Like most "second-generation" jazzmen, Don Redman came from a middle-class background. He was born in 1900 in Piedmont, West Virginia, and it is said that he played trumpet at three. His father was a member of a brass band and young Redman learned every instrument, as well as elementary harmony and theory, before settling for alto saxophone. Later he attended conservatories in both Boston and Detroit. When he came to New York after making a reputation as a player and arranger in Pittsburgh, he went to work in recording studios, accompanying singers, generally finding himself in the company of a young pianist from Georgia named Fletcher Henderson. Gradually, a kind of semipermanent "house band" began to gather around Henderson and Redman for these sessions, and it usually included tenor saxophonist Coleman Hawkins and drummer Kaiser Marshall. On one occasion, these men—still leaderless at this point—were asked to record some instrumentals, one of them called "Dicty Blues." Later that same day they auditioned for the Club Alabam', using the same piece, and got the job. Then they decided to make Henderson the leader because he was nice-looking and a college graduate (in chemistry and mathematics).

Redman as arranger first shaped the style of the Henderson orchestra. Apparently he saw that the future of jazz lay with more control over the group yet more freedom for the individual soloist. The "collective" improvising of New Orleans jazz seemed to have gone as far as it could—at any rate, more and more often such groups were using soloists with rhythm backing. What Redman did was to abandon the New Orleans approach almost entirely. He took a conventional American dance band of the time—with its separate sections of saxophones (doubling on clarinets), trumpets, trombones, and rhythm—and managed to convert it into a new kind of jazz band. He even made some use of the dance band's basic style, but the rhythms had to be jazz rhythms, the solo passages had to be jazz improvisations, and the written variations had to be in the jazz style. One more thing became characteristic: Redman borrowed the "call and response" patterns heard in Negro church services.

When the familiar biting brass of a swing band plays a brief musical phrase and the saxophones answer with another short phrase and an exciting back-and-forth of these phrases follows, the music echoes the preacher's prodding question, "Do you want to be saved?" and the congregation's, "Yes, Lord!" Some of the early arrangements by the Henderson band seem crude today, and some few imitate the style of King Oliver's New Orleans band or the New York Dixielanders of the time. But in the best of them can be heard the style that was to become a national and world craze in the late thirties.

By 1927, Armstrong had left the Henderson band, and Redman and Henderson were also going their separate ways. Redman first led the famous McKenney's Cotton Pickers around Detroit. Later, he returned to New York to lead his own band in competition with Henderson's orchestra. Basically, both groups played the style their leaders had earlier worked out together.

Henderson, however, continued to get the soloists. At various times in the twenties and thirties, in addition to Redman, Henderson had Hawkins, Armstrong, and Kaiser Marshall; pianists and arrangers Fats Waller and brother Horace Henderson; trumpeters Joe Smith, Rex Stewart, Tommy Ladnier, Henry "Red" Allen, and Roy Eldridge; clarinetist Buster Bailey; saxophonists Russell Procope, Benny Carter (who also arranged), Hilton Jefferson, Ben Webster, and Chu Berry; trombonists J. C. Higginbotham, Benny Morton, and Dickie Wells; drummer Sidney Catlett—to name only the best known.

In the early thirties, Henderson had just about formed his band's style: the arrangements and soloists worked together beautifully, the fire and the phrasing Armstrong had inspired were in both the individuals and the group, and many of the famous arrangements that Goodman was to use were already in the books. By 1935, Henderson had recorded "Sugarfoot Stomp," "King Porter Stomp," "Henderson Stomp," "Somebody Stole My Gal," "Honeysuckle Rose," "Down South Camp Meeting," "Big John Special," "Wrappin' It Up," and "Rug Cutter's Swing" in virtually the same scorings that Goodman played later. Even the Henderson soloists sometimes directly inspired Goodman's—compare Red Allen's "Wrappin' It Up" improvisation to Harry James's with Goodman for example. Later Henderson organizations, between 1936–38, recorded "Christopher Columbus," "Sing, Sing, Sing" (which the Goodman band ad-libbed into a marathon grandstander), "Blue Lou," and "Stealin' Apples"—music still well worth listening to.

At the very time—in 1932–33—when the style was finally perfected, however, work began to get very scarce (Columbia's recent four-disc documentation of Henderson's recorded career, C4L19, is aptly titled *A Study in Frustration*), and through producer John Hammond, Henderson was introduced to Benny Goodman. Goodman's new orchestra needed arrangements, and Hammond thought Henderson the man to provide them. Goodman agreed and Henderson became chief Goodman arranger, although for some years he also tried to keep together a band of his own.

Perhaps the best single introduction to the Redman-Henderson style is the celebrated Henderson arrangement for Goodman of "Sometimes I'm Happy." It begins with muted brass instruments carrying the familiar melody; they play it fairly straight but with phrasing that makes it swing. Every time the brass pause, however, the saxophones interject a phrase that is now part of the tune; clearly that musical phrase is saying "Yes, indeed!" After one chorus, the jazz soloists enter—first a trumpet, then a tenor saxophone with the brass answering his phrases quietly behind him. Next, the saxophones play a written variation on the theme which sounds as natural and fluent as a good improvised jazz solo. Then the trumpets join the variation. Finally, the record ends with a two-part conversation for the brass and the clarinet improvising against them.

There are many highly talented big-band arrangers during the swing period, of course, but they all owed a basic conception and many of the details of the music to the work of Redman and Henderson. Some arrangers put the ideas to a very personal use, to be sure, and one such particularly worth mentioning here is Sy Oliver. Oliver was chief arranger for the later Tommy Dorsey band, after having worked for several years for Jimmy Lunceford. Today one can also hear the influence of Redman and Henderson in the work of such diverse talents as Gil Evans, Quincy Jones, and such current arrangers for Count Basie as Ernie Wilkins and Neal Hefti.

Redman and Henderson made a big swing band out of a conventional dance band, but there were other approaches employed in the thirties. One of these was the idea of a big "Dixieland" band. Both Goodman and Tommy Dorsey had toyed with this notion in their earliest days, using the help of a talented arranger named Deane Kincaide. The early Woody Herman band was also such a big "Dixieland" group. But the most successful was the Bob Crosby orchestra. Crosby himself was the front man—he stood there and smiled and waved a stick and his real function was an occasional song. The Crosby book was provided by the band's director, Gil Rodin, and the arrangers, including clarinetist Matty Matlock and Deane Kincaide.

The earliest band to achieve any national identity using an expanded Dixieland format was New Orleans trumpeter King Oliver's 1926 group, and at about the same time Jelly Roll Morton was flirting with the same idea. Oliver did what Redman did not do: he tried to build on the jazz band and style that already existed. He expanded his two-trumpet New Orleans group by substituting a reed section using written parts instead of the single improvising clarinet of his earlier music. The sound of the older style could be retained by having the sax players frequently double on clarinets and take clarinet solos. Oliver profited by Redman's example (and he used an arranger named Billy Paige, for whom Redman had worked in Pittsburgh) but only as a guide to expanding what he already had. To hear the most interesting evidence of the evolution of this style compare Oliver's 1923 "Riverside Blues" with the 1936 Crosby band's "Dixieland Shuffle," obviously inspired by "Riverside."

Duke Ellington learned from Redman and Henderson, too (indeed some of his early recordings are virtually imitations), but he abandoned the dance band idea and started all over again for himself—and his conception proved to be the most brilliant and durable of all.

Ellington has been a major jazzman for over thirty years, and his achievements are large enough to cut across any considerations of period or style. But it was precisely at the height of the swing craze that he was doing some of his greatest work and his was one of the few groups of this period that had a really original approach to big-band jazz.

In 1927, Ellington's orchestra was hired by the Cotton Club to provide music for elaborately staged and lurid floor shows. Acts by talented singers and dancers would be separated by wildly absurd production numbers in which sheiks abducted innocent American heiresses, or "white goddesses" ruled native African tribes with bullwhips. Here Ellington's talent was released, and he soon found himself with a new sort of band. In effect, he converted a pit or show orchestra into a jazz group. The emphasis fell on refinement in orchestration, on the integration of solo and group, and on creating varied sounds and textures.

Ellington led the band, but everyone contributed. As he later commented: "The music's mostly written down, because it saves time. It's written down if it's only a basis for a change. There's no set system.

Most time I write it and arrange it. Sometimes I write it and the band and I collaborate on the arrangement. Sometimes Billy Strayhorn, my staff arranger, does the arrangement. When we're all working together, a guy may have an idea and he plays it on his horn. Another guy may add to it and make something out of it."

Ellington's whole career is full of excellences, but between 1938–41 he produced one exceptional record after another. "Rumpus in Richmond," "Ko Ko," "Harlem Air Shaft," "Sepia Panorama," "Bojangles," "Concerto for Cootie," "Across-the-Track Blues," "In a Mellotone," "Blue Serge"—these are surely the jazz masterpieces of their time, and in them the composer, the solo improviser, and the group form an emotional and musical whole which surpasses the sum of its parts. Ellington has influenced everyone (including such acknowledged followers as Charlie Barnet, to whom he once even loaned his library of arrangements), but he has had very few successful imitators.

One other band that was inspiring musicians in 1939 was Count Basie's, and it gave the Goodman orchestra such pieces as "One O'Clock Jump," "Sent for You Yesterday," and "Jumpin' at The Woodside." But in Basie's orchestra—with its special kind of light swing and the nearly revolutionary ideas of some of its soloists—particularly the brilliant tenor saxophonist Lester Young—we hear the beginning of a new kind of music which a few years later was to become "modern jazz."

The innovations in the Basie band were the handwriting on the wall for the big swing bands, it seems to me. Their demise has often been attributed to economics, but I think the real reason is that the work of all but the very best big bands was done. By the late thirties, the swing style had made a musical summary and synthesis of fifteen years of jazz. Great numbers of bands had spread the news and popularized the music. Artistically, it was time for something new, and that something new eventually came from individual improvisers working in small groups. Only the most truly creative bands of the forties could endure both the artistic impact of "modern" jazz and the spiraling expense of keeping so many men together.

Today, Henderson is dead, but Goodman periodically gets out the old book and forms a new band to play it again. Don Redman's chief occupation is writing arrangements for Pearl Bailey. And Ellington? Well, of course he still leads the best big band in jazz.

The Return of Sonny Rollins

The Bridge (RCA Victor LPM/LSP-2527) was the first new recording by tenor saxophonist Sonny Rollins after a self-enforced retirement in late 1959, when he withdrew from all concert and night-club appearances.

By then, Rollins had already proved himself an authoritative soloist, and he had shown the rare capacity to combine a grandstanding bravura with artistry, the like of which jazz had not seen since the Louis Armstrong of the mid-thirties. His style was his own, to be sure, but it echoed both the forceful tone and assertive manner of Coleman Hawkins and the deep love of melody of Lester Young. Rollins also had a dexterous but disciplined rhythmic authority obviously learned from Charlie Parker. Almost single-handedly Rollins has made a synthesis of over fifteen years of modern jazz, and his best solos combine the spontaneity of improvisation with the thoughtful sense of design of good orchestration. Thus there was "Blue 7" (Prestige 7079), in which Rollins based tantalizing chorus after chorus on his major theme, distilling, abstracting, and elaborating, in both witty parody and serious respect. Or there was "Blues for Philly Joe" (Blue Note 4001), which turned out to be a kind of free, extemporaneous rondo, alternating choruses of theme-statement, thematic variation, and outright invention—in the form A, A, A1, A2, A3, B, C, A4, D, D1, E, A5, A, to be academically exact.

When he returned to active playing last fall, Sonny Rollins was the same, only much more so. On his best nights his work was as imaginative as ever, and sometimes even more comprehensive. I remember one concert which he finished by suddenly transforming himself into a Latin band, alternately becoming its reed, brass, and percussion sections, while simultaneously retaining his role as jazz tenor soloist—always with a musical taste and easy logic that was far beyond crowd-pleasing stunt-work. On the same occasion he played an astonishingly challenging cadenza of several out-of-tempo choruses in which he did nearly everything conceivable to trip himself up—and did lose his accompanists a couple of times—but did not lose his own way once.

All of which make *The Bridge* doubly disappointing. To be sure, there is plenty to admire: there is the marvelous momentum which Rollins' phrasing and swing give to popular songs like "You Do Something to Me" and "Where Are You?" and Rollins' original "John S." develops from a striking idea. There are, in fact, ideas aplenty, but Rollins and his quartet seem to be playing down. It is as if he were trying to popularize himself. It happens that the very best Rollins is the most popular Rollins already, which means that he is in a very happy position for a popular artist, and surely one he should take advantage of.

To anyone who knows tenor saxophonist Sonny Rollins largely from his records, the music on *What's New?* (RCA Victor LPM/LSP 2572) will seem some of the best Rollins there is. But to anyone who heard Rollins in person after his retirement, it will be—once more—something of a disappointment. The set is built around the gimmick of various "Latin" meters, has a couple of pop tunes ("If Ever I Would Leave You," "The Night Has a Thousand Eyes") taken as bossa novas, includes some conga and bongo drumming, and (goodness!) even a chorus chanting "Brownskin Girl." Rollins' response to these rhythms is, as usual, personal and sound. That is, they propel him, but, beyond an adjustment in his phrasing, they propel him in doing the same sort of thing he already does.

He seems on "Brownskin Girl," for example, to need no help at all, overriding both chorus and drums to become, with a sustaining humor, a whole calypso band unto himself—including the percussion. "Bluesongo" has hints of how Rollins can tease and coax a theme-melody, but they seem comparatively mild ones. The most successful track is the twelve-minute "If Ever I Would Leave You," which almost catches the sustained power and daring of Rollins at his best. It shows his compelling love of melody, his deep humor, and especially in some climactic exchanges with the percussion, his authoritative power. Finally, "Jungoso" is a tour de force, a hoarse and almost ceremonial incantation led by Rollins with string bass and conga drum. The saxophonist uses his horn in starkly passionate declamations, and once or twice even inflects two tones simultaneously. Not so incidentally, guitarist Jim Hall has a touchingly melodic solo on "The Night Has a Thousand Eyes."

Saturday Review, June 16, and December 15, 1962

Gillespie in Concert

By the mid-twenties jazz music was being recorded more or less regularly, and if those who heard the legendary figures of the past insist that the records by King Oliver or Bix Beiderbecke or Fletcher Henderson are a shadow of the reality, at least the records are there and in some quantity. A more recent legendary event, the appearance of Charlie Parker-Dizzy Gillespie quintets in the early forties, is now as much a part of the established jazz tradition as Oliver's Creole Band, but their music hardly got recorded at all.

In 1945, a small company, hastily formed as Petrillo lifted a ban on record-making by AFM musicians, was willing to do six instrumentals of the then new music. Only five of these are now available (on Savoy 12020), and three of the five have an overloaded and inappropriate rhythm accompaniment. Still, one can hear the sometimes intricate unison lines, beautifully executed by Gillespie's trumpet and Parker's alto, breathing musically as one. And the solos are still excitingly personal after all the years of honorable assimilation by Parker-Gillespie followers, and not-so-honorable imitation by others.

Otherwise, to hear Parker-Gillespie on records, we have to depend on later re-creations. There is that searing 1947 concert, preserved on half of Roost LP 2234, with hazily recorded rhythmic backing, but with Parker in dazzling performance, playing as if he were out to get Gillespie, and the trumpeter responding as if he were just not going to be got. There is also a 1950 studio date on Verve MGV 8006. Parker, particularly, was in excellent form and produced some of his best-recorded work; Thelonious Monk was on piano; and the strange choice of drummer Buddy Rich cluttered things up from time to time.

Then, finally, a 1953 concert in Toronto did get recorded and now reappears on Fantasy 6003, *Jazz At Massey Hall*. If a reunion of Parker (pseudonymously "Charlie Chan") and Gillespie is not enough, also present are Bud Powell and Max Roach, *the* pianist and drummer of the idiom—a truly illustrious gathering not otherwise represented on records.

True, the music is from a concert, just as it happened and without benefit of studio retakes or corrections. But that also gives it a directness and immediacy that studio recordings don't have. The occasion caught Parker only about a year before a musical deterioration overtook him, and it caught Gillespie as his style was going through an effective retrenchment and simplification.

There is evidence on some numbers of a backstage bickering which carried over into the music, but nevertheless, the players make it musical —and they sometimes make it humorous as well, as when Parker and Gillespie banter with the unison parts on "Salt Peanuts." Or when Parker, in the first solo on "All the Things You Are," an otherwise graceful virtuoso exploration, jokingly runs off one of Gillespie's favorite interpolations before the trumpeter even gets his turn at the piece. Later on "Peanuts," by the way, Roach has a nearly melodious drum solo. On "Wee," Gillespie fluffs a few notes (if it matters) and the breakneck tempo nearly gets the better of Powell, who had not played publicly for several months before this appearance.

Then there is "Hot House." The piece always inspired Parker to interesting things, and here he builds an intriguing structure, alternating a shimmering complexity of phrase with a subtle simplicity. And finally, "A Night in Tunisia," with everyone in very good form—a succinct demonstration of the integrated trinity of imagination that these men possessed in rhythm, melody, and harmony.

Also largely taken from the same concert is *The Bud Powell Trio* (Fantasy 6006). There are good Powell records available (Blue Note 1503, 1504 and Roost 2224); and there are poor ones, made at a time when Powell's rhythmic coordination was decidedly off. This LP is one of the good ones, and the best of it offers some of the best Powell we have. Several of the ballads on the LP are largely excursions in voicing and harmony, but pieces like "Cherokee," "Embraceable You," and "Jubilee" (actually "Hallelujah") show Powell's fleet, agile melodic invention, and they also show (should there be any doubters left by now) his soundly personal assimilation of his elders, particularly Teddy Wilson. Accompanist Max Roach has a marvelous contribution on "Cherokee." And bassist Charlie Mingus contributes so much that it is little wonder the rumor persists that he later rerecorded his part on these pieces, whether it is true or not.

The aforementioned "A Night in Tunisia" is the basis of *Tunisian*

Fantasy, a part of another concert recording done at Carnegie Hall last year by Dizzy Gillespie, who led a large orchestra of brass and percussion assembled for the occasion (Verve V/V6-8423). The *Fantasy* (which, incidentally, might have been better rehearsed in a couple of spots) is a set of variants on Gillespie's piece, one of them based on the main theme, one built around the interlude that introduces the soloists, etc.

It is the highest compliment to Gillespie's pianist Lalo Schiffrin, who wrote the *Fantasy*, to say that the work is as generally unpretentious as many comparable jazz pieces are pretentious, that it is almost constantly interesting, and that it fulfills one of its main functions beautifully—it inspires the trumpeter to play with joyful variety and with the compelling graceful bravura that is Gillespie at his best. Schiffrin is Brazilian and he can authentically handle the kind of Latin percussion that the trumpeter has always found propelling.

The other selections on the LP are a mixed bag: a new version of Gillespie's "Manteca," this time done largely as a bounding exercise for the percussionists and with a tongue-in-cheek that its title (meaning *lard*) might call for; "Kush," featuring Schiffrin's episodic Latin piano; "This Is the Way," with Gillespie's altoist Leo Wright; and "Ool Ya Koo," with amiably theatrical scat singing by Gillespie and Joe Carroll —but never mind all that.

Saturday Review, August 25, 1962
Copyright © 1962 Saturday Review, Inc.

Jazz Clubs, Jazz Business, Jazz Styles in New York: A Brief History and a Cultural Lag

During the summer a large New York jazz club, the Jazz Gallery. which had a touch-and-go career for a couple of years, finally closed its doors, this time apparently for good. Business at all other jazz clubs is reportedly poor, and there are constant mutterings from the owners about "putting in some strippers."

Actually, the strippers might not help, for current business at all other night clubs in New York City is evidently bad.

It does not always go this way, however. Sometimes when the jazz clubs are packing them in, the uptown comics are playing to half-empty houses. And other times, even the most popular jazzmen can't make the overhead for a clubowner, while the latest French chanteuse or a comic plus ballroom dancers and a dog act can pack the house.

What does all this mean? Shall we give the usual answer and say that in the night club business there is just no telling how things will go? Perhaps. But for the jazz clubs there may be a better answer. The history of such places—especially in New York but also in other big cities—has been directly tied to the evolution of the music. And most jazz clubs come and go as styles rise, become popular, and decline in their following.

For example, there is convincing evidence that the surest sign that there would be some business decline in clubs featuring modern jazz came about two years ago. By that time, an only slightly watered-down version of the modern idiom was becoming commonplace in the bars along 125th Street in New York City and in cocktail lounges and hotel watering-spots throughout the country. If something that sounds like modern jazz is being heard nearly everywhere, the music will probably soon begin to lose its special attractiveness for a segment of its following. This is not a matter of how things should be, of course, but of how they are.

There was a great deal of jazz in New York before there were any jazz clubs. And there continues to be good jazz of all styles played in many a bar and dance hall that has no reputation for specializing in the music.

Public awareness of night clubs specifically devoted to jazz music came with the repeal of prohibition, and the first jazz clubs in New York City were converted speakeasies, along 52nd Street, between Fifth and Sixth Avenues, and in Greenwich Village.

The village spot was Nick's. The music was not advanced, but in those days it was generally very good, and it found a small audience. Eddie Condon's club is a current off-shoot of Nick's, and if the music in both places is not always as lively and interesting as it once was, it is more popular. Indeed, one or another sort of Dixieland has become a kind of solace music for the tired businessman who may well have attended Nick's during the thirties. Such a cultural lag, plus the nearly constant revivals that the Dixieland style experiences, keeps Nick's open, keeps

Condon's open, and, until the wrecking crews moved in, kept Jimmy Ryan's open.

Other, now nearly legendary, 52nd Street clubs have long since gone. When they began, the Onyx, Famous Door, Kelly's Stable, and the rest had a real cultural, perhaps artistic, purpose. They presented small-group swing after it had developed among players who were refugees from the early big bands and before it had become popular. Some of the most advanced jazz of the mid-thirties was first heard along this street. And as the style became more accepted, these clubs flourished—with Coleman Hawkins, Roy Eldridge, Billie Holiday, Charlie Shavers, Pete Brown, Art Tatum, and so on.

Then, when modern jazz began to develop in the early forties, it was soon heard along 52nd Street. But in presenting it the clubs were at first simply following their policy of booking the most interesting and talked-about younger players, players they could afford to hire.

Meanwhile, as swing became the established jazz style, a group of slightly more pretentious and more expensive clubs sprang up, popularizing it further and bringing it to a slightly more affluent audience. After its downtown start with such music, the Café Society was even able to move uptown with Teddy Wilson, Albert Ammons, Pete Johnson, *et al.* And with such popularization, there inevitably came borderline artists like Hazel Scott, as today there is Nina Simone.

Soon, just about every patron who was going to discover swing music had done so. And elsewhere the surface devices of the style became commonplace. The first clubs to go under were the expensive ones like Café Society Uptown.

Then 52nd Street saw that modern jazz was not just a certain group of young players but a whole new school of music, and the clubs tried to make the transition in full. One narrow basement spot even jammed Dizzy Gillespie's 1947 big band onto the small bandstand.

It was too late perhaps; the street's work was done, and the music was new. The clubs tried strippers, and a few tired locations were still holding out with the unclad women and the blue lights when the hard-hat crews arrived a few years ago to tear down the area and make way for office buildings.

Gradually, modern jazz found refuge in a new group of clubs, just as swing had done before it. They were the Royal Roost, Bop City, and Birdland. Only the latter has endured, probably because it has consistently booked the popularizers of the style and its early successes—

George Shearing, for one—and even people like Perez Prado and Big Jay McNeely as they became popular.

For several years, Birdland was the only modern-jazz club in New York City. One of the first signs that, at long last, modern jazz was about to receive a wider public popularity and acceptability was the mid-fifties' appearance, first, of the original Basin Street and then of several new downtown jazz clubs—the Café Bohemia, then the Five Spot on the east side, followed by the Half Note on the west. And most recently, a switch from folk to jazz at the Village Gate.

The Bohemia had a short career with jazz but, for a while, a highly successful one. Its success announced a larger audience for modern jazz.

But as leaders like Art Blakey and Miles Davis began to get their new audience, their prices inevitably rose. At first, the Bohemia tried to keep up by raising its own prices. But finally the club dropped jazz. Meanwhile, there were the Five Spot and the Half Note, which, to establish themselves, booked good but less expensive players.

With the close of the Bohemia, there was the Village Vanguard to take up some of the slack with name groups like Davis' and the Modern Jazz Quartet.

The Vanguard has had one of the most interesting histories of all New York City night clubs. In the late thirties, it provided a haven for the then-established swing idiom, fulfilling something of the same function as the two Café Society clubs. In 1940 Roy Eldridge was there, demonstrating that by that time, even an advanced swing player such as he was finding a larger following, and it was possible to make him the top of the bill at the Vanguard.

By the time modern jazz was developing, however, the Vanguard was presenting cabaret acts—some of the best cabaret acts. For examples, Judy Holliday and Betty Comden and Adolph Green did some of their first work at the Vanguard.

It was probably inevitable that once modern jazz had become more acceptable, Vanguard manager Max Gordon, who likes jazz and wants to present it, could book it in as the main attraction, and he did, beginning a few years ago.

There are other cultural-lag clubs besides Condon's and Nick's, of course. There are clubs like the Embers (slightly more expensive, slightly more ornate), and a more rowdy version of the same approach, the Metropole. The general fare, however, is a somewhat watered-down swing, most often featuring trumpeters.

The lag has begun to catch up, by the way. Our tired businessman no longer gets a shock from Charlie Shavers, or even from Jonah Jones in one of his more advanced, Eldridgelike forays. Apparently, it all sounds pretty much the same to him now; 1938 has become just as acceptable as Dixieland. Such clubs probably will go on and on, and in ten years or so, they probably will be offering some diluted Gillespie—or perhaps even the real thing.

By and large, then, clubs rise and fall as jazz evolves, in direct relationship to changes in the music, the gradual spread of taste for those changes, and the clubs' adaptability to those changes. Some exist to harbor new styles, some to present those styles as they become more popular, others to offer jazz as middlebrow nostalgia. If a club is flexible enough, it can find new purposes for itself, or modify its old ones, and endure.

In the short run, such a view may not be very encouraging or helpful to a young musician worrying about next week's gig, or to a clubowner worrying about last month's bills. In the long run, it may be helpful to a musician planning a career, or to an alert clubowner looking to his future.

The implication here is that the work of some existing jazz clubs in New York City may be almost done now and that this is the reason business is not good. If there is some advice that might profitably and properly be given to the owner of a smaller and less expensive club, it might be: don't put in the strippers and don't hire the safe, bland conservative groups unless you absolutely have to. Try to hang on. In the long run, you may be better off if you identify yourself at least partly with the most advanced playing around. Put in a good group, playing an established style that really *plays*, and complement it with a newer group. You may soon find yourself with the next young jazz audience in attendance. And to stay in business, that is the audience you will have to get. You may be sure that whoever gets that audience will be running the next successful jazz club in New York.

Down Beat, November 8, 1962

Stitt in the Studio

Alto saxophonist Sonny Stitt was one of the first jazzmen to grasp Charlie Parker's style, and he had apparently recognized an aesthetic kinship with Parker long before most followers of jazz had heard of either man. His absorption of Parker's ideas is so complete that, as one commentator has put it, Stitt is the kind of player who refutes every concept we have about originality, even personal expression, in jazz. Yet Stitt plays with spontaneity, involvement, and conviction. If he lacks Parker's brilliance and his daring quickness of imagination in rhythm, harmony, and melody, Stitt nevertheless is not playing an imitation, and his work is far from pastiche or popularization. He simply finds his own voice in Parker's musical language. He may construct a solo almost entirely out of Parker's ideas, but he will play them so as to convince you that he discovered each of them for himself. As if to give a final contradiction, Stitt also plays tenor, usually in different, somewhat simpler style, but with no less effectiveness. By almost all we profess to believe about jazz, it cannot be. But it is.

Stitt has recorded in several settings, but most often with himself, piano, bass, and drums. He has most often appeared that way too, sometimes touring alone and picking up local rhythm sections from place to place. He recently undertook to record for Atlantic, a new company for him, and everyone agreed that it was time to try Sonny Stitt in a new setting. Thereby the date obviously held promise. It also involved some compromises. Stitt was to be provided with a large group consisting of ample brass and rhythm sections, and with scores by Jimmy Mundy, who was doing powerhouse arrangements in the early thirties, and by Tadd Dameron, one of the first and best to do big-band modern jazz arrangements. But some weeks before the date, Stitt had made some appearances with the modishly successful sax and electric organ setup. So the rhythm section was to include organ instead of piano. Also,

Mundy's scores proved to be capable but rather safe reworkings of commonplace blues phrases.

As the musicians gathered at Atlantic's studios, it was obvious that the chairs assigned to the three trumpets, one French horn, three trombones, bass, drums, and organ would be filled by some well-known players. Not the least of them was Philly Joe Jones, currently one of the most celebrated drummers in jazz.

Sonny Stitt entered the studio, a tall and almost unbelievably thin presence, graying slightly at the temples now but otherwise looking still like a man in his early thirties. He spied veteran trumpeter Dick Vance first and, more given to gestures than talk, immediately fell on Vance's neck.

Soon the altoist was warming up, not up, not with scales or exercises but with some of his own favorite phrases, and Mundy took his position in the center of a semicircle of horns. Nearly thirty years of jazz music were represented and ready to go.

Mundy did not seem to be carrying himself exactly with the assurance of a veteran among these mostly younger men, but he was obviously impatient to get to work. "Let's go. Let's try 'Boom Boom,' he said, calling for one of the scores which had been placed on music racks before the players. And turning to Sonny, "Play me a D minor chord?" Stitt obliged with an arpeggio. "Okay, everybody ready?" Mundy asked, raising both arms wide apart, and to about three-quarter mast. "I'll give you four bars for nothing," he said, beginning to count off, and the players came in for a very ragged start. When they began it again, the piece proved to be assertive and based on a simple blues bass figure.

"Now let's try it just a trifle brighter," said Mundy, meaning in jazz language that he wanted it a little faster.

Stitt briefly crossed to the corner of the studio to bum a cigarette from a visiting friend, remarking with the hint of a smile, "He's got some screaming brass there, hasn't he?"

Mundy was addressing Atlantic recording engineer Phil Iehle, "Can we get the French horn in closer, please? It's isolated over there away from the other brass."

As Iehle moved the horn chair, Stitt, now back in position, made his request, "I don't dig this sitting down playing."

"Oh, you want to stand up?" Iehle raised Stitt's microphone.

The reshuffling had an obvious and immediate effect on the next run-through of "Boom Boom"; the written parts went down with a spirited crispness and Stitt was really beginning to play the blues. Mundy looked up. "Want to take one?"

"Yeah," Sonny agreed, "let's take one."

And Phil Iehle began to roll his tapes and receive the first try at "Boom Boom."

At jazz record dates, the end of the first take is often an unofficial signal for a brief break. And this break was marked by the arrival of Ahmet Ertegun of Atlantic, who was to supervise the session. Ertegun is the son of a Turkish diplomat and, along with his brother Nesuhi Ertegun, he has been involved with jazz most of his life. He entered, announcing to the assemblage with a smile that, of course, it is musicians who are supposed to be late for record dates, never A & R men. He shook hands with Mundy and Stitt and joked briefly with Jones. Then he crossed the room to greet Tadd Dameron who was sitting with a couple of friends, waiting his turn after Mundy's.

Ertegun heard the first playback in the engineering booth, instructing Iehle, "Phil, this is basically Sonny Stitt, rhythm and organ. Let the brass be more like punctuation and bring up the organ especially." In the studio, on the other side of the glass panel that separated the players from Iehle's tape machines and control board, Mundy stood with his ear glued to a loudspeaker. The rest of the room, including Stitt, strolled around and chatted, apparently unconcerned with what the playback was revealing. But they were hearing it, nevertheless.

When the speakers were silent again, Ertegun, Iehle, Mundy, and Stitt had heard how things were going, and the date was in earnest.

Another take. The organist, a capable young girl named Peri Lee, who knows all the hip phrases, was playing harder now, but the brass was so pungent as to balance out. And from time to time Stitt even improvised on top of some of the high brass screams, gracefully unintimidated.

At the end, Iehle and Ertegun wanted to test the microphone balance of drums and bass, and Philly Joe and bassist Joe Benjamin began to play alone as Iehle moved his mikes and adjusted his settings. But almost immediately Stitt got interested and was playing the blues along with them.

Minutes later, they had done an almost perfect take, and Ertegun said quickly over the studio speakers, "Can you do another one right away?" They did. Stitt stood up for his solo, played with his knees slightly bent, rose to his toes again as he reached for his ending.

Ertegun: "Okay, I think we got it."

Mundy's final blues had efforts as fashionably hip as its title, "Soul-ville." "Ashmet," he said into a studio mike, "can we keep the organ up? And can you fade out the ending in there on the board?" They did a run-through and a take, Mundy exuberantly conducting with both arms. Mutually, Mundy and Ertegun suggested the piece could carry more improvising by Stitt and a solo by trumpeter Blue Mitchell as well. As the tapes were rolling again, Mundy hurriedly expanded his arrangement, making signals to the men to return to section "B" by holding up several fingers on both hands to describe an awkward "B," or to repeat "C" by inscribing a "C" in the air with his right fore-finger.

At the end, Ertegun from the booth made a long announcement over his microphone to the effect that it sounded like the rhythm was slowing down at certain points, although it might not actually be, etc. Philly Joe Jones, apparently having heard all he intended to listen to, started talking loudly to the speaker on his right, "Okay, okay, okay, baby! Okay, Amhet! Okay Ahmet [this time pronouncing it *Ak-med*]! When we stop the shuffle beat and go into the four it sounds like the rhythm drops, see? But it doesn't. See? Okay, okay."

In the next take Stitt was playing strong blues, and he was carried away enough to improvise an extra chorus. Mitchell followed him and everyone else made necessary adjustments, with Mundy's arms flagging the assemblage on, 1-2-3-4, 1-2-3-4. And Jones fixed things so one didn't notice the change of rhythm, although he still made it.

At the end Ertegun entered the studio. "All right," Stitt said, crossing over to him, "you like that one?"

"Yeah!" They shook hands.

"That's it, then," and Stitt returned to his position in the semicircle of musicians, pausing en route long enough to give Mundy a polite embrace of thanks.

Meanwhile, Tadd Dameron, a keen, sharp-eyed man, had been distributing his own music around the room. His first piece had been given the hasty, last-minute title of "The 490" after Dameron's street address. It was, by Ertegun's request, an eight-bar blues. But the musicians' first run-through revealed that Dameron had written an ingeniously ballad-like theme within the traditional but often neglected blues form, and had scored it quite interestingly. Once he had signaled the tempo and got the musicians started, Dameron sat quietly facing them, listening to the results with sober face and piercing look. Only once did he raise his hands, to quiet the brass behind Stitt's first entrance. And the room had taken on a new life.

At the end, Dameron was immediately exhorting the trumpeters to "Sing it! Sing it! Everybody!" He started them again, this time knowing what to listen for and conducting them modestly with one hand. "Hold it! Hold it!" he stopped them, turning to the trumpeters. "Play it this way, boo-ob-de-*wahhh.*"

"Hold it, Sonny," Dameron smiled an interruption toward the end of another run-through. "That's the intro."

"Oh," said Stitt. He had momentarily been improvising with his eyes shut; as the music had become more challenging, he had become more serious. "I was back at the second ending?"

"You were wailing though, man," said Dameron, signaling a general laughter.

They tried "The 490" onto tape. Dameron smiled at Philly Joe's exciting and propelling delayed entrance. Gradually, the composer had begun to do more active conducting. But he was not keeping time for them so much as he was signaling dynamics and encouraging feeling, and he frequently sang along silently with the brass as Stitt effectively juxtaposed passionate slow blues improvising against the more sedate ballad-blues writing. In a peak in the coda, Sonny lifted his left foot abruptly behind him, and Dameron held his finger to his lips for the last big chord from the brass.

"Well!" announced Philly Joe at the end of the playback, "that ain't no easy tempo to keep going."

Dameron began to work with the players on the next piece, "On a Misty Night." Again he was calm and strictly business, and again the musicians were quietly enthusiastic. "More legato. Make it slurred more right there. Good. Good. Thank you," he said, interrupting them and singing the passage for them twice.

Dameron increased the tempo each time they ran the piece through, and a huge, but decidedly lyric brass sound gradually emerged. For one crescendo he raised himself to his full height, moved forward and conducted the semicircle with both arms. Stitt had begun to sit down during these rehearsals, but he was playing like Sonny Stitt standing up nevertheless.

"Trumpets, it's supposed to go do-*wah.* You're playing do-*dah.* Dig?" Stitt's coda was of a length dictated by his own inspiration, and Dameron had to bring the brass in under him for the ending when he intuited that Stitt was ready.

"How long is that tag?"

"Till you get tired," Dameron answered quietly, laying aside one of his several white handkerchiefs.

"What's my chord?"

"B flat 7."

Each time Stitt made a different ending and each time Dameron knew when to signal the group to reenter. But, when the take was under way, Stitt made a mistake at the end. The rest of the performance had been so good they decided to do just the ending again and splice it on.

"That's it," Ertegun announced through the speakers. "But Sonny, Blue, and the rhythm section, can you stick around a second?" The idea was to do one informal quintet number.

Two minutes later, Stitt had taught Mitchell a little thirty-two bar theme he had apparently made up on the spot by expanding a little traditional jazz phrase, and the rhythm section had fallen in with them. Six minutes after that, the quintet had played it and improvised on it expertly, and Iehle had the results on tape. Then they tried it a second time, but it didn't come off. So, by unspoken agreement, they decided to accept the first version as much the better.

Everyone knew then that the date was over. The musicians joked a little as they packed up their instruments, and Iehle silently disconnected his microphones. Then everybody left.

Evergreen Review 27. January–February, 1962

Mulligan and Desmond at Work

Studio A at RCA Victor Records is a large rectangular room, and recording engineers will tell you they get a very special sound there. If the group of musicians is a lot smaller than the room they install baffle boards and place their mikes carefully, and the sound they get is still special. The four-man group that Victor engineer Mickey Crofford was to record in Studio A on a warm summer evening was small in size, but not small in fame or talent—saxophonists Paul Desmond (who, of course, does most of his playing with Dave Brubeck) and

Gerry Mulligan, plus bass and drums. And they were to improvise freely around arrangements written by Mulligan, which he had kept modest and flexible, with plenty of room for solo invention.

Like most jazz recording dates, this one combined constant pressure, banter, and even levity with utter seriousness, hard work, and musical accomplishment.

Desmond was early, and by 7 P.M. he was seated in the engineer's booth just off Studio A. The booth is also a rectangular room, smaller than Studio A, with elaborate tape recorders and control boards at one end, and a comfortable visitors' area with chairs, couches, and a table at the other. From this booth there is a clear view of the rest of Studio A through the wide glass panel which runs along one end.

Desmond was going over some of Mulligan's scores with A & R man George Avakian, who had arranged for the date, and Avakian's associate, composer Bob Prince. As usual, the alto saxophonist was dressed in a neat brown Ivy League suit, white shirt, tie, and fashionably heavy-soled shoes. Also as usual, his suit was slightly in need of a press, his shirt a bit rumpled, and his shoes not recently shined.

Avakian seemed vaguely worried—for no good reason, but Avakian usually seems worried at the start of a recording date. Desmond seemed serious; Prince, confident. And Crofford was busy in the studio and in the booth with his switches and dials.

Suddenly, all heads bobbed up as a knock on the glass and a broad grin revealed that Mulligan had arrived in Studio A. In contrast to Desmond, he was dressed in a pair of khaki slacks, a sports shirt, and a thick cardigan sweater. He was obviously ready to go to work: ready to exchange his black shoes for the white sneakers he was carrying, and to take his baritone sax out of its canvas sack and start playing.

Desmond had selected the Modern Jazz Quartet's Connie Kay as his drummer, and Kay entered almost on Mulligan's heels, waving his greetings and going immediately to work setting up his drums. Bassist John Beale, who had arrived soon after Desmond, was quietly running over his part to Kay's right. Kay had just returned from San Francisco with the Quartet. "Glad I finally got to you, Connie," said Desmond, crossing from the booth to the studio. "I was about to send up a sky-writer—Connie Kay call Paul Desmond."

Crofford had placed music stands and high stools for the two horns facing the rhythm, with Desmond's alto on one stereo microphone and Mulligan's baritone on the other. Avakian—busy enough to be just now grabbing his supper, an oversized and somewhat over-drippy sandwich

—was seated with pencils, note paper, and a stop watch beside Crofford's complex array of knobs, switches, and dials.

There had to be at least one run-through to test balance and mike placement. "We'll try one, okay?" said Avakian into his microphone, as Mulligan turned to Desmond with a mock serious frown to remark, "And please try not to play your best chorus now."

"Yeah, I'll save it," he answered, perhaps implying that he really had no control over the matter.

The piece was "Easy Living," with Mulligan carrying the melody, Desmond inventing a countermelody behind him and taking the first solo. The performance was promisingly good, but Prince and Crofford decided there was too much mike on Kay's cymbal, and went in to the studio to move things around a bit.

After another partial run-through, Avakian asked, "Want to tape one to see how it sounds?" But Paul and Gerry had their heads together over the music sheets.

"Try that last ensemble bridge again," Mulligan was saying. "You have the melody. It's the part down there at the bottom of the page." He pointed. "It could be a little more legato sounding." Desmond looked it over.

"I just wrote those notes in so you could see the pattern," Mulligan reminded Beale. "You don't have to play anything."

"Suppose I blow what you're playing along with you?" They tried it, and everyone commented that it sounded good.

"Want to tape one?" asked Desmond, affirming Avakian's suggestion. "We can figure out from the playback what's wrong."

In a few minutes there was a preliminary take of "Easy Living" on tape, and after the last note of the playback had echoed through the studio, it was obvious that this was going to be a relaxed and productive record date. Even Avakian seemed convinced of it. Mulligan had played with buoyancy, Desmond with fluent melodic ideas, and the improvised counterpoint had had fine emotional and musical rapport. As one visitor said, "Yeah, tonight they're going to *play!*"

As saxophonist of the Brubeck Quartet, Desmond is in a rather odd position, for his talents are more respected by musicians and critics than those of his pianist-leader. There is, in fact, constant wonder in the trade as to why Paul doesn't leave Dave and go off on his own. At the same time, Desmond is of a cooler and more lyric persuasion than some of the hard-blowing funk merchants who sell well on records nowadays, which puts him out of fashion in certain circles. Mulligan is something of an elder statesman as things go in jazz: his popularity dates from the early fifties and the days of the Mulligan Quartet. Since then he has held a large following, while leading both large and small groups. Recently there has been as much talk of Mulligan the movie actor (*The Subterraneans, Bells Are Ringing*) and of Mulligan the Broadway composer (a promised musical version of *Happy Birthday* for Judy Holiday, who will also contribute the lyrics) as about Mulligan the jazzman.

Several visitors and friends were in the booth by now. And each time the door to Studio A was opened, the grinding monotony of a rock and roll date being held next door in Studio B assaulted the ears. It soon developed that some rather illustrious jazzmen were involved in that music next door, and their aesthetic escape proved to be frequent brief visits over to the Desmond-Mulligan session to hear what was going on.

After a good version of "Easy Living" had been put on tape, there was some banter in the studio about, "Okay, that's it. Everbody come back the same time tomorrow." And there was some serious unwinding over cokes, while Connie Kay pulled out one of several hamburgers he had brought with him. But discussion of the music didn't stop, and Mulligan was soon demonstrating a point, seated at the piano that stood in the far end of the studio.

Desmond said he wasn't sure he had quite done his best by "Easy Living," and requested they try a slightly faster tempo—that they "make it a little brighter," as he put it—and all agreed to try the piece again. Just then Avakian threw his switch inside the booth and announced over the studio loudspeakers, "Gentlemen, I hate to say this, but I suggest you tune up a little."

"What? How could you even imply such a thing?" protested Mulligan with affected seriousness. And he carried his heavy horn over to the piano again to correct the matter.

When the tapes were rolling, Mulligan felt free enough to do some improvising even in his written parts.

At the end of the new take, before anyone had spoken, there was silent acknowledgment that it was the best yet. "Fine," said Avakian into his mike. "Want to hear it back?"

Mulligan again affected his cantankerous tone. "It's bad enough making these things without having to listen to them." He turned to Desmond, bobbing his eyebrows à la Groucho Marx, "Right? That a good attitude?" And a moment later, "Well, Paul, what other tunes do you know?"

"I know 'Melancholy Baby.' "

Mulligan crossed to the piano again and played some deliberately pompous neoclassical runs, stopping abruptly to announce, "Well, I guess I'm fired, huh?"

Soon they were into "The Way You Look Tonight," somewhat faster, with Paul playing slightly crouched over his small horn, and Gerry standing with his feet apart, swaying from side to side as he listened to Desmond, or swaying back and forth as he made his unwieldy horn wieldy in solo. Connie Kay was playing with his eyes closed—a good sign. Inside the booth, Crofford waved his arms as if conducting, smiling, "Ah. I like these four mike dates. This morning I had to keep track of nearly twenty mikes on a big band behind a vocalist."

On a second take Desmond played a solo that was, for him, almost gutty, and Mulligan danced the phrases off his horn in a very different rhythmic manner. As the musicians entered the booth to hear the playback, a visitor remarked, "My, that was . . . well, that was *jolly!*"

"I would be inclined to accept that take," said Avakian looking directly at Desmond.

"If only to get out of here, *right?*" he cracked back.

They did "The Way You Look Tonight" again. Maybe it was a bit less "jolly" this time, but everyone looked more satisfied at the end. Desmond's lyric presence was still firm and Mulligan had corrected something that was apparently bothering him before. No one seemed to need a playback, and Avakian called through the speakers, "Well, what's the next tune?"

Desmond: "Did you bring in that blues?" It was a way of announcing that the time had come, as it does at least once in most jazz record dates, to play a twelve-bar blues. If a blues is recorded at exactly the right moment, it can lift everybody's spirits, and it usually goes on tape satisfactorily in one or two tries.

They ran through Mulligan's written theme, and before they had decided on the order of the solos Desmond asked, "Want to play some counterpoint on this, too?"

Crofford, in the studio to untangle a wire, remarked casually to Beale, "One thing I never worry about is the bass."

"It's the only thing I do worry about," Beale smiled.

In a few minutes they were ready. Avakian announced onto the rolling tape, " 'Walking Blues,' take one," and signaled the musicians to start.

"It's called 'Whistling Blues,' George," called Mulligan. "I just changed it."

"Who are you? Tex Beneke?" Desmond whispered quickly.

As Desmond improvised his solo, Mulligan again did his side-to-side strut. Then, with the tape still rolling and Desmond still soloing, Mulligan signaled to the rest of the group for a round of four-bar phrases from player to player, before he and Desmond went into the counterpoint choruses that finish the piece. An arrangement changed even while it was being recorded. They played the "fours," and as the saxophones were restating the theme at the end, Mulligan began to improvise and merely suggest the melody with a few key notes, as Desmond was playing it in full. It was an effective idea. This was really becoming a cooperative two-man date.

At the end of the take, Mulligan registered approval by turning his heavy horn horizontal and laying it across a raised knee. Paul entered the booth and asked almost shyly, "Where'd that coffee come from? Is it a local concern?"

They heard the playback of the blues with satisfaction and a few minutes later in the studio they were running through the arranged parts of "All the Things You Are." As they finished the conservative Bach-like ending Paul asked, "Isn't that a little daring?"

"Maybe," Mulligan countered. "It'll go okay in the Middle West."

As all this talk filtered through the open studio microphones into the visitors' booth someone muttered, "Maybe those two are trying to work up some kind of act. The bantering, and this Alphonse and Gaston about who's got the first solos and who has the melody and who the harmony. Maybe they could take it on tour."

"Connie," Desmond was saying, "do you remember the tempo of the last take you did?" Kay started to brush his snare drum with perfect memory, and unbelievable lightness.

On another "All the Things You Are" at a faster tempo, Paul seemed to be more comfortable. Gerry had been better at the slower one. Their only musical disagreement so far.

In a final take of "All the Things You Are," Mulligan was smiling broadly as Desmond went into his opening "break" over suspended rhythm, and then invented a lyric solo as the beat resumed. He was still playing hunched over his horn, but this time he was allowing himself a slight motion of the legs in time to his improvising.

At the end, everyone seemed pleased with the performance. But the playback revealed a once-in-a-thousand accident: one of the microphones had briefly cut off during the counterpoint, and some bass notes didn't get on the tape. Desmond was especially disappointed, and for a moment looked as if he didn't want to play any more.

With their heads together, Avakian and Prince decided they could rerecord the bass part later and blend in the few missing notes, saving the performance.

"Otherwise, Bob," said Avakian, as everyone's relief settled in, "did you ever see a more relaxed and easy date?" Mulligan had again sat at the piano and was somehow running through a Mexican waltz, alternating it with some raucous low-down blues.

The ending Mulligan had designed for "Stardust" was rather complicated but Connie Kay had it after one explanation, and with no music sheet to refer to.

Mulligan said after a run-through: "Did you play a B flat there instead of a B natural?"

Desmond: "Um huh."

Mulligan: "Goodness gracious!"

As the take started, there was a fluent opening exposition by Mulligan, and it was evident from his first phrase that "Stardust" has a special meaning for him; he became so involved in his playing that at first he didn't hear Avakian calling out that there was not enough tape on the machines to finish the piece, that they had to put on another reel before making a full take.

On the next try, more new ideas rolled out of Mulligan's horn, and then Avakian waxed philosophical. "Very good! But it always seems to me if you get a very good one you should try another. A very good one may be a sign that an excellent one is on the way."

"Well, I don't hear anything *dramatic* about it," said Desmond quietly, "but otherwise it was very good."

They did "Stardust" again, and Mulligan's involvement was unabated. At one particularly delicate turn of phrase, a visitor in the booth yelled out audibly. And in the studio Paul indicated his pleasure by smiling and pretending to conduct Kay and Beale, waggling his right forefinger in the student conductor's double-triangle 1-2-3-4, 1-2-3-4.

At the end, as they heard it played back, Mulligan smiled and laughed aloud at one of Desmond's phrases, and he danced a bit during the ensemble.

When the speakers were silent again, Desmond said quietly, "I think it's about time to amble on home, for me, anyway."

Mulligan started to play his theme song. And Kay had his cymbals almost packed away.

Evergreen Review 28, January-February, 1963

Charlie Parker Made Easy

Sonny Stitt is not simply a popularizer of Parker's ideas, but he has served something of that function, not only by perpetuating the style, but by carrying it to the audiences who were not ready to receive it as first expounded by Parker himself. Lou Donaldson, however, *is* a popularizer; he uses only some of Parker's ideas and manner of phrasing (but, oddly, Donaldson still attacks individual notes in a rather academic manner), and he now plays them in a kind of up-dated version of the urban rhythm and blues music that audiences accept casually as a part of big-city, and largely Negro, barroom and nightclub life.

The name of Donaldson's new LP, *The Natural Soul* (Blue Note 4108); the use of down-home titles like "Funky Mama," "Nice 'n' Greasy," and "Sow Belly Blues"; the fact that the recital includes the requisite electric organ, guitar, plus a slightly watered-down modern jazz trumpet—these tell the story. It is inevitable that Parker's ideas should sift to this level, but one cannot honestly say that it is as "unassuming" or "unpretentious" as other such blues playing. There is something calculated about its earthiness and its grinding reliance on a handful of devices. But Donaldson can make unaffected music, consult his "Blues Walk," for instance, on Blue Note 1593.

Cannonball Adderley is something of a popularizer too, but a popularizer of a different sort from Donaldson. Adderley does not make the neighborhood bars, he makes the jazz clubs. Further, his style is both more personal and more varied in its inception (besides predominant Parker, one hears early Benny Carter, a bit of late John Coltrane, and recently a wholly unexpected snippet of Ornette Coleman), and he has a virtuosity that on occasion tosses out notes like handfuls of unicolored confetti. *Jazz Workshop Revisited* (Riverside 444) returns Adderley to "live recording" at a San Francisco club where a few years ago he did "This Here," a rather posturingly executed gospel-style blues that became a hit. Adderley's current group is a sextet, still with his brother Nat (Miles Davis with extra notes) on cornet, and with Yusef Lateef (a sort of forcefully sophisticated but becalmed Illinois Jacquet) on tenor saxophone and flute.

At present the sophisticated blues-band approach is more varied and is often laced with big band effects. "Jive Samba" reflects the current fad for bossa nova for a relentless eleven minutes. Cannonball takes a well-shaped solo on "Marney," seems to mean what he plays on "Mellow Buno," and makes a few knowingly engaging announcements to the audience between some of the numbers.

However, I should not leave Adderley without recommending his disciplined improvisations on "Autumn Leaves," available on Blue Note 1595 with a group that includes the real Miles Davis, for they are very good, and the record is probably Cannonball's best.

Saturday Review, May 11, 1963
Copyright © 1963 Saturday Review, Inc.

Whose Bossa?*

A little over a month ago a national magazine reported that there were some forty bossa nova, or "jazz samba," LPs on the market. By now, there may well be twice that many, ranging in price from 97 cents to $4.98. There are also certain international recriminations in the air. The Brazilians are saying that the Americans get the rhythm all wrong, or that they are playing the old "heavy" samba beat, or that they just

* From the *Saturday Review,* February, 1963 As a postscript to the above, the following from a *Down Beat* column, later in the year:

I have been wondering, since this bossa nova jockeying started, just what it is about Brazilian musicians that has set reputable U.S. jazzmen to raving. Having heard Bola Sete's Fantasy LP (3349). I now know. His is a rare combination of innate musicality and mastery of one's instrument.

don't have the right touch, anyway. Further, they add, the one undisputed hit, the Stan Getz-Charlie Byrd version of Antonio Carlos Jobim's "Desafinado," is played incorrectly, with wrong harmonies and without the proper bridge.

The Americans might retaliate that if they get the samba wrong in the jazz samba, the Brazilians are weak on the jazz. It does not seem altogether inappropriate that one of the most blandly derivatively American jazzmen has been told by Rio musicians (at least according to his publicity) that he plays bossa "like a native." At any rate the Brazilian improvisers heard on *Do the Bossa Nova with Herbie Mann* (Atlantic 1397), recorded in Rio, seem rather derivative, if not exactly bland, but guitarist Baden Powell is lovely in his own idiom on "Consolacao." (Incidentally, since bossa nova is, in Brazil at any rate, a music and not a dance, one wonders how one is to "do" it, with or without Herbie Mann.)

The best, or I would say the most authentically sympathetic, American bossa nova performances that I have heard are on a Dizzy Gillespie LP, titled (inappropriately enough) *Dizzy on the French Riviera* (Phillips 200-048). Besides a dubbed-in moment of some French children noisily enjoying themselves in the breaking surf, there is a quite authentic reading of "Desafinado," plus a ten-minute exploration of Jobim's romantic "No More Blues." There are more Latin rhythms in Lalo Schiffrin's "Pau de Arara," and "Long Long Summer," and Gillespie's "For the Gypsies," plus a decidedly North American blues called "Here 'Tis, You Hear?" and a ballad, "I Waited for You." Gillespie's well-established affinity for almost any and all "Afro-American" rhythms is, of course, tellingly evident. The best American bossa novas, yes. But it is surely not the best Gillespie LP I have heard, and that is perhaps some kind of comment on the nature of bossa nova.

Further comment on its nature is contained on an LP which is something of a sleeper. It is the film score to *Black Orpheus* (Epic LN 3672) and it was one of the earliest examples of this contemporary Brazilian popular music to be issued in the United States. In its original context, some years ago, this music generally fulfilled a romantically lush, mood-setting function very well. A moody, slightly nostalgic romanticism is apparently essential to bossa nova; at least it is essential to the songs of João Gilberto, who is one of the most celebrated performers in the idiom. He can be heard on Capitol T 10280, and on the recently released Atlantic 8070, called (I'm sorry to say) *Boss of the Bossa Nova*. My impression is that Gilberto is a very engaging popular singer. He does not offer the self-conscious emotionalisms of the continental cabaret singer, but in his lightly lovelorn or quasi-philosophical airs he shows neither the emotional power nor the spontaneous musicianship of a good jazz singer; indeed, I doubt that one's interest in him is really musical. However, he does not have much rhythmic poise, especially in the way he handles the bossa nova syncopations. And his work divertingly illustrates one consistent device in this music: the tension between a comparatively simple melody, with romantically unexpected intervals and twists, and an accompaniment in a contrastingly busy but flexible samba rhythm, lightly played.

Saturday Review, February 23, 1963
Copyright © 1963 Saturday Review, Inc.

Martial Solal

One of the best jazz pianists in the world plays in France and, as far as I know, to this writing has not been in the United States. He is Martial Solal. He was born in Algiers and began playing jazz in 1940. After the Second World War, he inevitably gravitated to Paris. As I imply, it is enough to say that Solal is exceptional for a European jazzman: it could be that Solal will develop an importance which, like Django Reinhardt's, is greater than considerations of geography or even of instrument.

Not that I would particularly like to demonstrate any of this by those of his recordings which have so far been released over here. One LP presented him when his style was still largely unformed, and the most recent offers a Solal doing an incongruous Errol Garner pastiche (but there is discreetly assimilated Garner in his best playing) and also performing some more or less experimental, unaccompanied pieces— pieces of a sort which do not seem to suit his fundamentally conservative approach. However, we have also had released here his delightful variations on "Bemsha Swing" in a scoring of the piece by André Hodeir. And we have heard his wonderfully sympathetic joint recordings with Sidney Bechet. These included a couple of rare moments by Solal, particularly in the way he humorously abstracted the melodic line of "All the Things You Are" and rephrased and almost constantly reharmonized the single-note motif on "It Don't Mean a Thing."

Solal's best playing invites one to deal with basics, and deal with them in a rather awed way: what a completely *natural* musician this man is! To pay him the highest compliment, he seems as natural a musician as was Bechet. The foreign jazzman's usual problem seems not even to occur to him; not only can Solal swing, he swings with a vitality that is personal, and a sureness which allows him rhythmic variety and variation of a sort that many American jazzmen of his generation have not tempted. He has fine pianistic technique, but it reveals itself so soundly and so musically that one may be almost unaware of his proficiencies. He puts nearly every idea to a directly musical use, and time and again one notices Solal quietly employing effects which might easily be turned into blatant grandstanding by a less discreet and dedicated player.

Above all, Solal answers the basic criterion: he invents interesting, fresh, and personal music.

Solal apparently feels that a serious jazz player should provide most of his own repertory, one appropriate to the larger considerations of his style. I wonder if many of his pieces (at least the few that I have heard) would be more than "interesting" in the hands of another player, or, let us say, in the abstract. But they become increasingly suited to Solal's own work. Most important, they allow him performances which seek to be a continuum; that is, in which a theme-statement at the beginning and its reiteration at the end do not seem so isolated as they have for so long in jazz. In this I think Solal (like Charlie Mingus and, on occasion, Cecil Taylor) has faced one of the most pressing problems of form. For it no longer seems sensible in modern jazz for the exposition of a theme merely to set a tempo and a chord structure for improvising, and then disappear completely.

Perhaps this sort of thing is easiest to see in the way that Solal handles familiar thematic material of another man. As he performs Duke Jordan's "Jordu," his opening exposition is rather free, allowing for rhythmic variation, melodic paraphrases, interesting changes of register, and fleeting embellishments. As the performance unfolds, one realizes that these alterations are rather specific hints of the personal way that Solal will later improvise on the material. Further, many of his variations are thematic or at least make use of fragments of the theme-melody. And about halfway through the performance, he reiterates the theme rather directly as if to reestablish the order of things. Solal uses these organizing thematic signposts with the same naturalness that Thelonious Monk does. They also allow him striking forays into the implication of a piece without inviting disorder. Most fascinating of all is a kind of improvising in which Solal alludes to the structure of the theme almost phrase by phrase and rest by rest. But he echoes this structure, not with paraphrases of the theme but with *new* melodies which fit its patterns of phrasing.

The performance of "Jordu" that I have been discussing is on an LP called *Jazz à Gaveau* which was recorded at a pubic concert by Solal's trio (Guy Pedersen, bass; Daniel Humair, drums) and which I shall briefly review. The masterpiece of the occasion was "Aigu-Marine," a contemplative but never precious improvisation, beautifully rendered, and with a striking technical discipline. It is probably the best example of the continuous flow of theme-into-variations in the recital, although "Dermaplastic" also seems very good in this respect. Both "Gavotte à Gaveau" and "Nos Smoking" (yes, a bilingual pun) alternate two separate tempos with complete naturalness (again, one thinks of Mingus) and on the fast portions of the latter, Solal performs with a really delicate ease. On the former, staccato fragments that at first seem isolated soon reveal themselves as part of a careful, yet still spontaneous, structure (here one thinks of Charlie Parker and Ornette Coleman as well as Monk).

I seem to be indulging in a panegyric. I do not mean that. I will take one exception—perhaps it is subjective—that Solal's wit is perhaps too prevalent. Thus, a piece like "Averty, C'est Moi" is in blues form but that seems merely a convenience or convention—he is obviously neither a blues man in the traditional sense, nor does he discover the contemplative mood that players like Benny Carter or Earl Hines have found in the idiom. But perhaps it is more of—what shall we call it?—understated, puckish Solalian lyricism.

Third Stream Problems

In his *Rhapsody in Blue* George Gershwin, according to the phrase of the twenties, "made an honest woman out of jazz." Perhaps he lay down with her and produced a bastard? Or perhaps, since she was an honest woman to begin with, Gershwin only borrowed a few of her jewels?

The *Rhapsody* and Gershwin's other "serious" works, are basically European concert music, and a rhythm here, a slur or blue note there—even a twelve-bar blues form—can't really make them jazz. Gershwin was not the first man to indulge in such borrowings, he was merely the first from the other side of the fence. There is reason to believe that European composers were exposed to jazz and its progenitors as long ago as Brahms. There is a Brahms caprice that might have been influenced by American minstrel music (but then there is an eighteenth-century Scarlatti sonata that sounds rather like Meade "Lux" Lewis).

Gershwin's relationship to jazz—or jazz's to Gershwin—is an intriguing proposition. It is not quite enough to say that his concert works are not really jazz, or to say that his popular songs gave jazzmen some favorite vehicles for their own interpretations and improvisation. "I Got Rhythm" has been deeply inspiring, not only in its harmonic sequence but in its implied rhythmic patterns, to nearly every important jazz musician from Sidney Bechet through Ornette Coleman, and it has become the most durable pattern in the repertory after the twelve-bar blues. Further, anyone who has heard Gershwin the pianist on a piece like his "I Got Rhythm Variations" knows that there was more jazz in him than we generally suppose. His contributions would seem far from superficial, but they are rather subtle for a critic or historian to deal with.

It is easy enough to make a list of composers who heard ragtime and jazz early and tried to make some use of it in their work—Debussy,

Milhaud, Stravinsky, Ravel, etc. And names like Ives and Copland only begin an American list. Some of the pieces that resulted have been successful, some have not. But in very few cases does the success or lack of it depend on either the authenticity or the extent to which the composer has employed the jazz idiom. One exception might be Ravel's sonata for violin and piano, which attempts to go deeper into jazz than most, and whose middle movement turns out to be a disturbing and unintentional parody of the blues. The most successful early work is probably in Milhaud's "La Création du Monde." In form, it is pure European classicism; in melody and rhythmic effects it is made up of the jazzy clichés of the twenties, but nevertheless one gets the feeling that, of all these composers, Milhaud might have developed the most authentic grasp of the jazz idiom had he been interested in pursuing it with discipline. But he was not. Stravinsky begins with engaging "light" pieces like the "Piano Rag Music" or sections of *L'Histoire du Soldat*, but when he writes a more serious work around a jazz orchestra, he produces the *Ebony Concerto*, which hardly gives jazz a telling glance.

Today, almost any American or Western European composer will at least be aware of this vital musical idiom in our midst. Many are also showing an increasing understanding of its real qualities and its heritage, and inevitably some of these men reflect that growing understanding in their own work. It has become apparent that a casual or superficial reflection of jazz is not enough. Gradually, certain composers have sought to use the jazz idiom with more commitment—to use its way of handling sound, its way of phrasing, to use its musical forms, and most recently even to use jazz improvisation itself. At the same time, certain jazz composers have looked in the other direction, not merely to borrow this or that device or practice from Western concert music and assimilate it into jazz (that is a continuing process, anyway) but to form musical alliances comparable to those the classicists have undertaken.

Composer Gunther Schuller was the first to speak of such activities as a "third stream" of music. But his phrase has since been subject to so much journalistic abuse that it may well have to be abandoned. There even appeared an LP called *Third Stream Jazz*—rather like an orange tangelo, I suppose. The first stream was, of course, the Western or European concert tradition, as it continues in Europe and as it was long ago transplanted here. The second stream is the continuing evolution of jazz. And the third stream seeks to combine the two, using written forms for classical players, and improvisation by jazzmen, to make *concerto grosso*-like works.

It seems to me natural to ask if some Third Stream composers are attracted to jazz, perhaps unconsciously, because of its ready audience as well as its natural vitality. And it is good to ask if some jazzmen are not attracted to concert music because of false notions of prestige. Some are, in each case, to be sure. But a blanket accusation of opportunism hurled at all the classicists, or of self-defeating delusion hurled at all the jazzmen, is much too facile. For one thing, it misunderstands a commonplace response of many an artist to his environment. Better to accuse contemporary classicists of hopeless effeteness if some of them did not respond, and respond deeply, to jazz. And after all, any opportunism involved will reveal itself in an opportunistic and shallow music that results. To sniff suspiciously around *all* Third Stream efforts on principle is perhaps to find an easy way to avoid real appreciation or evaluation of the results.

The problems in Third Stream music are complex, even if some of them are fairly obvious. One work, evidently inspired by obvious analogies of early jazz to Bach and Handel, pits à more or less "Dixieland" style *concerti* of players against an *orchestra*. But in performance, the Dixieland men are simply drawn from the symphonic ranks, and their phrasing is frequently stiff and occasionally ludicrous. Also, the ability of such men to indulge in a real improvisation may turn out to be almost nil. Only experienced jazzmen can play jazz. And nowadays few classical players can improvise well in any idiom.

A somewhat more intriguing work, which received a great deal of attention a few years ago, is Swiss composer Rolf Liebermann's *Concerto for Jazz Band and Orchestra*, which juxtaposes a big jazz band and a symphony orchestra, again in *grosso* style. Liebermann did not ask for improvising; still that would not really prevent the jazz involved from being jazz. But Liebermann's concept of jazz was almost a hold-over from the twenties: the term seemed to mean almost any North American (or even South American) popular music. Further, his knowledge of these idioms seemed to have its gaps to say the least: a section marked "boogie woogie," for instance, has little or nothing to do with boogie woogie. Also, it was rather painfully obvious that Stan Kenton is very much to Liebermann's taste. But Liebermann's final section, marked "mambo," is undeniably a crowd-rouser, and a diverting one.

A piece by Gunther Schuller called "Transformation" shows much more awareness of the problems involved in Third Stream music— problems not only of phrasing but, at last, of using real improvisation. Schuller is well equipped to deal with them. He is primarily a classical player and composer whose knowledge of jazz is not only sympathetic but historically authentic and penetrating—"knowledge" is not the right word; let's call it love.

"Transformation" begins with a small classical orchestra in Schuller's contemporary compositional idiom. A jazz group makes itself known, at first complementing the classical lines. But gradually the jazzmen begin to coax the classicists over to their way of phrasing. Soon the piece is completely transformed as the jazzmen begin to improvise on the blues. After a bit, the classical players return, reverse things into their style again, and it is largely they who finish off the performance. (Incidentally, the recorded version of this work is especially graced by the improvising of pianist Bill Evans.) There may be something a bit too polite, too self-effacing, in using such a mutual deference of each idiom for the other. But "Transformation" was a firm step.

Subsequently, there were some other steps that seemed backward, or at least sideways. Leonard Bernstein and the New York Philharmonic premiered a rather pretentious and aridly "experimental" piece by Teo Macero for jazz group and orchestra. Under the same auspices, there was performed Howard Brubeck's *Dialogues for Jazz Combo and Orchestra*—an example of bad conservative classical writing, with sometimes genially *ersatz* jazz from Howard's brother Dave.*

Firm steps forward were again taken at a 1959 Town Hall concert, jointly performed by the Modern Jazz Quartet and the 1959 Beaux Arts String Quartet. Each group offered pieces from its own repertory, and the two groups joined for John Lewis' "Sketch" and Gunther Schuller's "Conversation."

Lewis' brief piece is perhaps even less than a sketch. In a sense, it is a curious little Haydn pastiche, built around a single descending phrase which is handled with some ingenuity by each group of players in its own idom. But at the same time, the piece meets the Third Stream composer's major problem directly. For Lewis made no effort to get the classical players to use jazz phrasing, an especially difficult proposition with string players. Nor did he ask the members of the MJQ (as he has done in some of his jazz pieces!) to deport themselves like classicists.

Gunther Schuller's "Conversation" used the same principle, but it went further. And instead of trying to ally the idioms gradually as in "Transformation," Schuller let each assert itself fully. In outline (and with some simplification), the string quartet begins "Conversation" in

---

* I am inclined to except Bernstein's later performance of Larry Austin's piece "Improvisations for Jazz Soloists and Orchestra" from such censure, however.

Schuller's contemporary atonal idiom, but with some percussive and harmonic complements from members of the jazz group. (How could one add anything effective to so delicately balanced a medium as the string quartet? Schuller did.) When the strings have built a deadlock of tension, the jazz players arrive almost abruptly, relieving it with easy improvisation. As the jazzmen build their own kind of tension, the strings reenter beneath them. And a debate ensues. The piece concludes on a somewhat John Lewis-like resolution—a respectful agreement to disagree.

It has been said that it is incongruous to hear a jazz bass player suddenly begin walking quarter-notes after some twentieth-century atonality. But that is precisely the point of this piece, precisely its structural premise. The tension between these two idioms, with each allowed to express itself fully, even competitively, is what makes "Conversation" successful. And such a structure is in almost complete contrast to the kind of deferences between the groups of players that Schuller used in "Transformation."

Schuller has done one other Third Stream piece that was initially conceived for the Modern Jazz Quartet, this time with a full orchestra, a strangely Gershwinesque *Concertino for Jazz Quartet and Orchestra*. The score does raise the problem of getting at least a few of the symphony men to swing and use jazz phrasing. But it throws far more difficult tasks at the jazzman: meters they are not used to, unfamiliar forms (a thirteen-bar blues—why?), and the task of deliberately accelerating their tempo. Under the circumstances, it would seem almost impossible to get a comfortable and relaxed performance of the *Concertino*.

In "Abstraction" Schuller took still another approach. The piece is a brief serial composition, in mirror form (the second part is an exact reversal of the first), for augmented string quartet. It was originally conceived for Ornette Coleman, who improvised against its first and second parts and invented a cadenza between them. The idiom is predominantly classical, but Coleman is asked to play his responses to it in his own way. In the recorded version he darts in and out, sometimes playing with the strings, sometimes against them, but the performance is an emotional whole.

Schuller has also written two sets of "variants" on established jazz compositions, one on John Lewis' "Django," the other on Thelonious Monk's "Criss Cross." The former is perhaps not quite so successful in conception, or in execution on the recorded version. There are some rather surging and turbulent moments, both written and improvised, that will seem out of place to some people in a lyric work like "Django." But it seems to me that the implications are there in Lewis' piece, for there is more to "Django," in any performance, than lyricism. One problem in the "Django" variants is the viola solo that introduces the second part: I have heard it several times and it always comes out as Viennese schmaltz—quite a contrast to the lovely way Jim Hall's guitar opens the first section on some of the same thematic material.

The "Variants on a Theme of Thelonious Monk," on Monk's "Criss Cross," are on an already major Monk piece, indeed one of the major compositions in the jazz repertory. And except perhaps for one slow interlude (the second variant), Schuller has actually produced a brilliant jazz arrangement, which owes little or nothing to classicism except for forms and skills that Schuller has assimilated in his own experience as a composer. The improvising in the first section is especially intriguing, being done in a kind of relay form with each soloist momentarily overlapping the previous player in sometimes simultaneous invention. On the recording, the juxtaposition of Ornette Coleman and Eric Dolphy, and the differences in the way they phrase, is tellingly dramatic, as is the Monkish understanding Coleman uses in rephrasing the theme itself, early in his solo.

In a sense we have come full circle here, with the Monk "Variants" as a jazz arrangement, on a major jazz piece, done by a classical and Third Stream composer. Beside this, the current efforts of classicist Lukas Foss to get his players to improvise in their own idiom is perhaps only the other side of the coin.

Two recordings, one written by an important jazz player and writer, the other by a well known composer-arranger, attracted a great deal of attention when they were first issued. Both are more or less in the Third Stream idiom. The first is J. J. Johnson's "Perceptions," written for Dizzy Gillespie. The piece shows increasing orchestral subtlety and skill on the part of the composer and it must have delighted the musicians who played it. To others, it may seem only a succession of perhaps commendable effects. In either case, it seems to me that one problem is that it was not really written *for* Gillespie, or perhaps anyone like him, for it asks him to execute written parts of a sort that are hardly his wont. And in only a couple of places does "Perceptions" call on him to do what he does best—open up and play!—and those moments are a joy. The other work is Eddie Sauter's "Focus," a skillful but occasionally derivative string work, against which Stan Getz improvised. "Focus" is a rolling tour de force for Getz, but Sauter offered a sort of advanced

David Rose writing with some of the schmaltz drained off. At any rate, the juxtaposition of Getz and the orchestra never seems to cut very deep. An LP recital called *An Image* was written by Bill Russo around Lee Konitz. Konitz improvised with a string group augmented by a few jazz players, and some of the pieces are in a classical idiom. Russo has also on occasion arrived at a provocative use of strings in jazz by having them play with minimum vibrato and supplementing them with a guitar.

Two other recent pieces dramatize the current problems of the Third Stream. "Around the Blues" by André Hodeir is perhaps not really a Third Stream work, but it surrounds several choruses of Milt Jackson's blues playing with orchestral sections, with plaintive flutes predominating. The piece leans heavily on Jackson. In the end we may feel that basically we have what we had already: Milt and the blues. (Perhaps if Hodeir the composer of the *Jazz Cantata* could work with a major jazz improviser?) German composer Werner Heider's appropriately titled "Divertimento" (it is a diversion at best, I would say) alternates statements by the orchestra and statements by the Modern Jazz Quartet effectively, each in its own idiom, but Heider's writing seems less commendable. But it is a joy to hear the Quartet executing its sudden entrances with such immediate swing.

I have heard Mercer Ellington and a group of highly spirited (although otherwise not particularly notable) jazz players encourage the later members of the Beaux Arts Quartet into a momentary swing (the group reorganized in about 1960). But in a sense the problem rests where it is left by "Conversation," "Abstraction," and the "Monk Variants": one can still find only a few classical players who can phrase in the jazz idiom, and one can find only a few technically skilled jazz players with an interest in undertaking more complex written classical parts.

Are we deadlocked for the moment at the point where Third Stream pieces *must* let the two idioms argue and even battle? At the point where few classicists will truly understand the jazz idiom and few jazzmen the classical? But where at least one or two jazzmen can improvise well, even within classical structures? Perhaps. And perhaps that is all we should wish for or expect. It is conceivable that the Third Stream is not a stream but actually an eddy, but I do not think it likely.

As I say, we have had some few successful pieces—*works* quite beyond the status of "efforts" or "experiments." But there are several signs that the future will be different. A recent concert piece by a young composer, David Reck, contains a part for tenor saxophone—a rare event in itself, but the part is marked to be played with a tone like Ornette Coleman's, and the writing shows considerable knowledge of Coleman's work. Further, the piece contains a few brief spaces in which the players—whoever they are and whatever their background—are asked to improvise. And the beautifully shimmering ending can be extended ad lib, the players being cued according to the conductor's discretion and feeling for the moment. Yes, the future will be different.

Evergreen Review, May-June, 1963

A Conversation with Martial Solal

Pianist Martial Solal arrived in the United States this summer from Paris for his first visit, an extended stay at the Hickory House in New York, and an appearance at the Newport Jazz Festival. The reputation that preceded him was that of a dazzling player, one of the best jazz pianists in the world, and perhaps the best and most original European jazz musician since guitarist Django Reinhardt.

Solal was born in 1927 in Algiers, where he first began to play jazz piano, and moved to Paris after his army service. For several years he was in effect the house pianist at the Left Bank Club St. Germain, work-ing with expatriates like Lucky Thompson, Don Byas, and Kenny Clarke, with the best French jazzmen, and with visiting Americans.

American musicians have for years returned from Paris with high praise for Solal, but until now others have heard him only on a sporadic series of records, not always ideally selected from those he has done in France. (I might mention that some of the best Solal I have heard is on *Jazz à Gaveau*, recorded at a concert by Pathé.)

I decided it might be fruitful to set up a three-way conversation with Solal and an established American pianist, Dick Katz, whose experience has included work as accompanist to singer Carmen McRae, pianist with Kenny Dorham, with the J. J. Johnson-Kai Winding Quintet, etc., as well as his recording work with many others, including his own groups.

We met at Katz's 11th Street apartment and our talk was tape-recorded. (I should add that I have done a bit of brushing up on the transcript; M. Solal's English is very good, but not quite as good as it appears below.)

WILLIAMS: Martial, you can imagine that Dick and I are very curious about the background and experience of so accomplished a jazz musician who does not come from our country. I should ask you first when you began to play piano.

SOLAL: I was exactly seven years and two months. You are the first men I have said that to—I always say seven.

WILLIAMS: Was your family musical?

SOLAL: Yes. My mother studied piano for a long time, and she used to sing classical. She learned at the Conservatoire in Algiers. She was not professional, but she was very much a musician.

WILLIAMS: When did you first hear jazz?

SOLAL: Oh, the first time was when I was about thirteen or fourteen.

WILLIAMS: Do you remember what it was?

SOLAL: A man in Algiers, a pianist. His professional name was Lucky Starway. He was playing a popular song, but not the way exactly that it was written. He changed some notes in a sort of improvisation. I thought it was wonderful, very exciting.

KATZ: This man was an Algerian? He wasn't an American?

SOLAL: No, he was French, but he lived in Algiers. Then I went to him and he taught me jazz. He was the only teacher in all Africa and Europe who could. He played several instruments, piano, trumpet, saxophone, accordion. . . .

WILLIAMS: What was your family's reaction to your wanting to play jazz?

SOLAL: Oh, they were very happy for they loved music.

WILLIAMS: Good. Not all American parents who love classical music would approve of jazz.

SOLAL: Well, mine were less happy when I said I was going to leave school when I was fifteen or sixteen. I wanted to be a musician and I couldn't go ahead at school and work too, so I left school.

WILLIAMS: Well, by that time were you listening to a lot of jazz?

SOLAL: Yes, many records. Fats Waller and Benny Goodman with Teddy Wilson—that kind of record. This was about 1942.

KATZ: Did you hear the big bands—Basie, Ellington?

SOLAL: Then I knew mostly small groups. Later, of course, I learned of the great orchestras.

WILLIAMS: When did you hear more modern musicians?

SOLAL: I first heard Errol Garner when I was in the Army. This was in 1948. I heard him on the radio. I still don't own many records, by the way.

WILLIAMS: You must have liked Garner immediately. And that fascinates me, because anyone who hears Errol Garner, I think, knows right away that he is a self-taught musician. He still cannot read, you know. You are trained—one hears in your work that you have studied the classics. Your style is your own now, of course, yet immediately one hears the early influence of Garner.

SOLAL: Maybe that's still true in my playing. I know it was true.

KATZ: I recall when I was in Paris in 1951, the first time I heard you play—and I really enjoyed it, but you reminded me somewhat of Oscar Peterson.

SOLAL: Probably.

WILLIAMS: Did you admire Art Tatum?

SOLAL: Oh, always!

WILLIAMS: I notice that several of the people you admired make a happy or optimistic music—Fats Waller, Errol Garner, Art Tatum. How did you actually feel about Fats Waller, for example?

SOLAL: I was fascinated by the sound first. It was so clear, so clear a piano, like the sun. And his left hand was like two men playing together. I also heard Lionel Hampton about this time. It was very funny. You know the way he played the piano—he played with his two index fingers, using them like the mallets of his vibraharp, while there was another pianist playing the bass? Well, I believed he was playing alone, all by himself. And the first time I heard it, I said this is too much. I can't believe it! I tried to imitate it. Oh, I tried. But it is impossible.

WILLIAMS: When did you decide to leave Algiers and go to France?

SOLAL: In 1950, just after my military service. There was no work at all in Algiers. I was just teaching some little boys, six years old, and working in night clubs, playing tangos, and things like that. It was not very enjoyable. In Paris, it was very bad for me. I knew nobody. I had to wait about three months without speaking to anyone. I did not know where the streets were. I knew nothing about Paris. I just knew some musicians, two or three. Soon I had a chance to work with a popular band. Also about that time, I decided that I had not enough technique, so I decided to work more. I want to be able to play everything I hear in my mind. I still can't do that.

KATZ: How did you go about that? Did you practice things that you had learned earlier? Exercises and things?

SOLAL: Yes, exactly. But in different ways.

KATZ: Did you play any of the classical repertoire for practice— Chopin études and things like that?

SOLAL: Yes, exactly, Chopin études.

KATZ: Bach?

SOLAL: Not so much. You see, I forgot the book of Bach pieces in Algiers, but I had Chopin with me.

KATZ: Well, I've always thought that a lot of the technical problems in Chopin are applicable to jazz.

WILLIAMS: I might ask you at this point about Bud Powell, since he is a very famous American pianist who's been living in France for several years now.

SOLAL: I used to love Bud Powell, and I think I still have many things from him. Maybe more than from anyone else except Tatum. He was very exciting to me, especially when he plays chords. Not his single-note lines in his right hand, because that is so much like Charlie Parker. But he plays some chords ten notes or eight notes together, you know. He has a very unusual way to play these chords. It sounds——-

KATZ: You mean the voicing of the chords or the way he attacks the instrument?

SOLAL: Both—the voicing and maybe more the way he played it.

KATZ: Because whenever I've discussed Bud Powell with other pianists, they've agreed that the most elusive part of his playing is his rhythmic attack, which no one has ever really been able to get—that certain kind of swing he has.

WILLIAMS: Well, when you were practicing, did you ever try, say, imitating Powell?

SOLAL: No, not practicing. Never.

WILLIAMS: You once made a very interesting record with Sidney Bechet and Kenny Clarke on drums. How did that come about?

SOLAL: I wanted to prove that any style of jazz could be played with any other. It was very exciting to make this album. The session went so fast and easy for us, one tune after the other. In two hours we made about eight numbers. I think it became a big success in Europe, my best selling record.

WILLIAMS: When you accompanied Bechet did you play more conservatively?

SOLAL: Oh, perhaps I tried, but I can't even when I try.

WILLIAMS: Well, Bechet sounded entirely comfortable.

SOLAL: I don't know this record, actually. I have not heard it since. I just remember the session was very enjoyable.

KATZ: Well, you have a wonderful surprise in store.

WILLIAMS: In France, now, you have your own trio.

SOLAL: Yes, Daniel Humair, from Geneva, on drums, and Guy Petersen, who is French, on bass.

WILLIAMS: Do you work in night clubs?

SOLAL: Not since three years. Once a week, when we are in Paris, we work on Thursday nights at the Club St. Germain. Two years ago we used to work every night.

WILLIAMS: But now you can earn your living just playing concerts?

SOLAL: Yes. But because I also write music. I write film scores. But if I just had to wait for a concert in France! There are not that many and they don't pay very much. We play in other countries. But this year in France we had a big tour for the Jeunesse Musicale de France, almost seventy cities in four months. That organization sponsors classical music, ballet, and theater in small communities all over France for young people. We were only their third jazz group.

WILLIAMS: In general, you would prefer not to play in clubs at home, but you came here to play in a night club.

SOLAL: Yes, I was so happy to come here I would have accepted to play almost anywhere, even for dancing maybe. Well, no, not dancing.

WILLIAMS: You know, some American musicians will expect your playing to change while you are here. They remember that some European musicians have felt that if they came over here, in the original environment of jazz, their style will change.

SOLAL: That would be true if I had never had a chance to play with American musicians, but I have been doing this already for years in Paris.

WILLIAMS: The trio that you're working with over here, with Paul Motian on drums and Ted Kotick on bass—did you know their work from records?

SOLAL: I had heard one record where they played together with Bill Evans.

KATZ: When Paul Motian and the late Scott LaFaro, the very talented bassist, worked together with Bill Evans, the three of them evolved a style, a departure from the traditional concept of the bass and the drums accompanying the pianist. They had more of an equal participation by all three men, a lot of counterpoint, both rhythmic and melodic, on the part of the bass. And Paul played musical phrases on his drums.

SOLAL: I heard those records only after I had come over here. And then I asked Paul to play as he plays with Bill. He's playing for himself, as a soloist, you know. But bass and drums have to play together.

KATZ: Well, since you've started playing at the Hickory House, have you noticed a change in the way Teddy and Paul play with you?

SOLAL: Yes, I think it is much better now that we are used to playing together. I suppose that Bill Evans and Paul had much experience before playing this way. In France, I try to get the trio to play with each one as a soloist. May I put it that way? But not always, because naturally it clashes sometimes.

KATZ: Other than the famous pianists like Fats Waller, Art Tatum, and Teddy Wilson—those you told us you liked very much when you were young—were there other instrumentalists?

SOLAL: Yes, I can mention many of them. Maybe it will seem very funny to you, but, Benny Goodman, Django Reinhardt. And later Stan Getz. Some of his harmonic things I still use. Charlie Parker.

KATZ: Doesn't sound funny at all.

SOLAL: It's so far away from the piano.

WILLIAMS: Incidentally, you made some recordings with Django Reinhardt.

SOLAL: Just one. I played very bad on it. It was my first record and it was his last.

KATZ: What about Thelonious Monk?

WILLIAMS: Yes, especially in view of Monk's sense of form—and yours.

SOLAL: He plays so many unusual figures. I am sure that I received much influence from him, but not as a pianist. Still, I think he has influenced every modern pianist in harmony.

KATZ: What do you like best about his music—his playing?

SOLAL: Essentially, what I like best is his writing. I love his writing. But I think when he is playing, he is still composing, no? That's maybe why he doesn't play so much—not such big piano. He is still composing.

KATZ: One other question: I hear in your playing things that I've heard in modern classical music, particularly harmonically and in some rhythms. I was wondering if this is just a coincidence or that you are influenced by some of the contemporary classical music that you have listened to. Prokofiev's piano music, for instance.

SOLAL: No, this is really a coincidence. I'm sorry to say that, but I don't know classical music after Debussy. Really, it's a shame. I've never read any of Prokofiev's music. I intend to read it, sometime.

Saturday Review, July 13, 1963
Copyright © 1963 Saturday Review, Inc.

Mulligan Rediscovered

We know that a jazz soloist is most often improvising, and this knowledge makes us listen with a special receptivity. But a good jazz solo is a good melody. Certainly it should be well played, and a player should assume a meaningful musical relationship (chiefly rhythmic) to his accompaniment. Still, a good jazz solo is a good melody almost in the abstract; if we wrote it out note for note, a good solo would seem good even on paper. Indeed, it is one of the glories of this American music that its best improvisers invent superior melodies, usually superior to other popular melodies, and often so superior that they create standards of their own.

All of which is preliminary to saying that on an LP by Gerry Mulligan called, after his nickname, *Jeru* (Columbia CL 1932/CS 8732; now Odyssey 36-16-0290), the baritone saxophonist has a solo on "Get Out of Town" that is very good indeed, and beautifully recorded. It is also, for me, somewhat unexpected.

Mulligan's early reputation in jazz was as a highly promising young composer-arranger who also played good baritone saxophone. That reputation reached a peak in 1949 and 1950 through his work with a nine-piece ensemble led by Miles Davis, with scores by Davis, Gil Evans, John Lewis, Johnny Carisi, and Mulligan. Eleven performances by this ensemble are collected on Capitol T 762, in an album titled, after the style it more or less founded, *The Birth of the Cool*. Mulligan's arranging included "Godchild" and "Jeru" (the nickname again), both of which took a rigid thirty-two-bar "popular song" form as a point of departure, and each of which burst through its all-too-familiar structures in highly provocative ways. Mulligan also contributed melodically appropriate baritone solos on several of the titles.

The Davis group may have provided a jazz style, but by the time that cool music had become something of a fad a few years later, the group had long since broken up and its members scattered. Mulligan was in California in the early fifties, and there he did some recordings as leader of a pianoless quartet that brought him and trumpeter Chet Baker almost instant popularity. (Examples are preserved on Pacific Jazz 1207 and Fantasy 3220.) This group made a genuine attempt at an ensemble style and occasionally at collective improvising. But I expect that its basic rhythmic simplicity, its general air of jaded yet boyish sophistication, and a repertory of fairly familiar ditties had more to do with its popularity than the quartet's intrinsic musical merit.

Mulligan himself had obviously become a more proficient baritone saxophone player, but a less effective jazz soloist. For one thing, his patterns of phrasing often had a decided rhythmic sameness, not to say monotony. For another, there was a kind of edgy compulsiveness in his work, as if he were unable to let the music flow or happen but had to coerce it. And he seemed always busy—trying out this idea, that motif, the other run, but without larger melodic design. In short, he was playing at playing solos rather than playing them.

I have high praise for a collaboration between Mulligan and Paul Desmond (*Two of a Mind*, RCA Victor LPM/LSP 2624) and particularly for Mulligan's improvising on "Stardust." The LP also seems to me a sign that, for the first time in over ten years, Mulligan had again begun to play solos of selective cohesiveness.

The *Jeru* LP confirms my feeling. Mulligan's first improvisation on "Get Out of Town" is, as I imply, an excellently developed jazz solo— it may even be a great one. But by singling it out I do not mean to neglect the tellingly varied patterns he uses on "Here I'll Stay," the fine momentum of his choruses on "Blue Boy" (a light but not trivial blues), or the delicacy with which he reads "Lonely Town." On that latter Mulligan gets an almost impeccable accompaniment from pianist Tommy Flanagan, and Flanagan's fine combination of lyric delicacy and rhythmic range is nowhere really overshadowed by Mulligan. The ensemble has the added percussion of a congo drum but its use is integrated and happily ungimmicked.

Spring is Sprung (Philips PHM/PHS 200-007), on the other hand, finds Mulligan returning to his quartet with Bob Brookmeyer's valve trombone, a thing of bemused tartness, as the other horn. The occasion is not entirely pianoless, for both Mulligan and Brookmeyer undertake the instrument for one number each—something the notes call "bench warming," with (one assumes) unintended innuendo. The players let us know they were having a good time. But, except for Bill Crow's bass solo on the "Four for Three" waltz, this seems lightweight stuff, with a lot of regressive *doodle-de-do-ing* from the leader.

Besides such periodic returns to popular quartet format, and his general freelancing in the record studios, Mulligan has led a large ensemble, the Concert Jazz Band, off and on during the past few years. The recording activities of this group have included such commendable projects as the introduction of scores by young Gary McFarland and the reorchestration of George Russell's fascinating "All About Rosie" (on Verve 8415), but the performances have been, to me, somewhat bland—as if we were listening to a first-rate studio group running down good material.

However, on *The Concert Jazz Band on Tour* (Verve 8438), recorded variously in California and Europe, the ensemble showed a spirited personality of its own. And on the new *Concert Jazz Band '63* (Verve V/V6 8515), the brass digs in with rapid accuracy on "Little Rock Getaway," for example, and the easy ensemble swing of "Big City Blues" is almost worthy of Basie. McFarland contributes again with three Ellingtonesque pieces that culminate in "Bridgehampton Street" and prove that you can learn from the master without copying him. And Mulligan on "Little Rock" and his own "Ballad" is once again a first-rate improvising melodist.

Saturday Review, June 15, 1963
Copyright © 1963 Saturday Review, Inc.

Record Date—
Art Farmer & Jim Hall

Trumpeter—and nowadays more frequently fluegelhornist—Art Farmer has formed a quartet featuring guitarist Jim Hall, and the alliance promises to be fruitful. Both players are lyricists. Farmer, as a direct heir to the innovators of the late 1940s, has his virtuosity, while

Hall, his own roots more obviously stretching back to the late thirties, is a somewhat gentler player. Therefore, there is likely to be musical empathy, plus good contrast and little that is stylistically redundant in an alliance of Farmer and Hall.

Farmer, in style and temperament a modernist, is also something of the complete popular artist. That is, he can undertake almost any musical task—reflect any passing fancy from cool through soul and almost any Tin Pan Alley ditty—with honesty and integrity, without artistic compromise or calculation.

Another musician might tone down his style to the point of inhibition on this or that number. But Farmer simply does his straightaway best on whatever material he undertakes. It is a rare quality. And it should go without saying that Farmer's best is something special and personal

Soon after its inception, the Farmer quartet was signed by Atlantic records, and its first LP was undertaken in late summer.

Farmer's determination that the record should show the quartet at its best, plus the use of some still-unfamiliar material on the LP—not to mention Atlantic's usual care in recording—led to a series of three recording dates. And before it was over, the third of them proved singularly fruitful. Following is a description of the session.

It is an evening session, scheduled to begin at 8 p.m., in the Atlantic studios. By 7:45, drummer Walter Perkins and bassist Steve Swallow are on hand. Perkins has his set assembled, and Swallow already has been "miked"—a microphone, wrapped with foam-rubber padding, has been tucked into the bridge of his instrument by Atlantic's engineer, Tommy Dowd.

Hall is outside the studio door chatting with a friend when Farmer steps off the elevator, shakes hands all around, and turns to the studio door with the apology that he needs to warm up.

Inside, Farmer's warming up soon proves to include not only exercising fluegelhorn and lip (with some George Russell scales, by the way), but also his learning a new piece by running it over attentively on the studio piano. It is a gently appealing waltz called "Some Sweet Day," which sounds as though it might be Jim Hall's. However, Hall explains it was written by a friend, a composer-singer from Argentina, Sergio Mihanovic, whose family comes from Yugoslavia.

Bassist Swallow complains that he can't seem to get an unwanted buzz out of his E string, as Hall, his guitar and amplifier set up and properly microphoned by Dowd, consults with Farmer.

Perkins has begun energetically demonstrating a tambourine he has hopes of using on a piece by Tom McIntosh called "Great Day." Farmer's "I don't like the sound of that—play it on the drums" is met by an almost crestfallen look from Perkins.

"Aw, I practiced all week getting my technique down," he says.

Swallow is rehearsing the first piece (not by running over a bass part of chord changes but by playing the melody itself), and it now appears that composer Arif Mardin, assistant to Nesuhi Ertegun, jazz A & R man for Atlantic, and Ertegun himself, have arrived.

Ertegun delivers his greetings as Swallow and Farmer are running down the skeletal arrangement of McIntosh's piece. About the ending, "Make a cymbal bash on that big note," Farmer instructs Perkins, who sits at his set, surrounded by three microphones and an appalling tangle of wires. Perkins gives a sample of his best bash. Then Farmer continues talking to Swallow and Hall in his usual firm understatements: "Yeah. And y'all play the big fat chord."

So the ending is set. They go back to the first chorus, but that in turn leads to further changes. ("We're going to have to change that tag." "Let's simplify and play more unison.")

Soon they are running through "Great Day" from the top. Farmer plays a lovely solo, an example of his special unruffled sprightliness. He is undoubtedly only half trying—just running through the arrangement —and he plays as he walks across the studio to resume his place at his own microphone after a consultation with Hall. But it sounds lovely.

McIntosh arrives, entering the studio with an apology that he knows his piece needs some changes, but Farmer, smiling, immediately reassures him that they had been working on it and he thinks Tom will like what they had done.

"Great Day," it turns out, evokes a happy spiritual, and thankfully proves to be without the affectations and clichés of "soul music."

Farmer takes a final run-through. There are a few brush-up corrections ("Walt, do something harder on that last note") before Ertegun suggests from the engineer's booth, through the loudspeaker, "Let's try it, Art."

"Okay."

"Stand by. Here we go. Seven one three four, 'Great Day,' Take 1."

The performance unfolds.

Hall, without being derivative about it, suggests a contemporary Charlie Christian.

At the end there are two further changes in the arrangement, and a two-bar break goes back in, and Ertegun voices approval of the sound and balance Dowd is getting after they hear the playback.

"Jim, you have to get out your rock-and-roll guitar to play that last note," Farmer chides. And then through his microphone he addresses Ertegun and Dowd: "Ready to try another one?"

"Any time," Ertegun responds. And as Dowd nods, he formally announces for the benefit of the tape, " 'Great Day,' Take 2."

As they play, Swallow is curved around the side of his instrument, standing on tiptoe as if he were about to climb up its side. Hall looks as unruffled as always and plays calmly but feelingly. And Farmer has taken off his loafers.

At the end of the take, Ertegun encourages over the studio loudspeaker, "Very good except for the ending. A beautiful take otherwise."

But Farmer doesn't quite agree and says:

"Let's try another one on it. It's still a little tight."

After a pause he adds, "Hey, Nesuhi, could you play us back a little bit of the first chorus."

Soon they've heard the playback, commented on the arrangement, and are about set for another take.

As he leaves the studio to reenter the engineer's booth, McIntosh pauses and says, "Let Walt have two bars after the solo." And as Farmer thinks this over, he adds, "You got two good takes already though."

"Good," says Art—and as a sly afterthought, "they can use them in the memorial album."

During the last take of "Great Day," Swallow adds some further toeing and dancing to his bass climbing . . . and as the last notes die, Ertegun asks for an extra ending, to make up for the one that didn't do so well. That done, the studio fills with casual conversing and a bit of laughter.

Gradually the business at hand begins to re-emerge as Hall recalled the previous two sessions with a question to Farmer, "Did we ever get a good take on 'My Little Suede Shoes'?"

"Yes, we finally did last time."

"Art"—it's Jim Hall again—"do you want to do the ballad?"

"Why don't I join in?" asks Swallow, glancing at a copy of "Some Sweet Day" on Hall's stand. "I can read off of Jim's part."

They begin slowly and quietly. Behind the glass of the booth, Dowd is readjusting his levels to fit the new dynamics. He operates his control board almost as though he were playing a piano, using several fingers of each hand simultaneously on the various colored buttons, adjusting them to raise this microphone level or lower that one.

"That buzz in the E string on the bass is still giving us trouble," he remarks to Mardin.

At the end, Hall says, "That sounded much too serious. It shouldn't be a driving waltz."

Another try. Perkins uses his brushes to much better effect.

Dowd, meanwhile, is responding to some kidding about having three mikes on the drum set. He says that, usually, little of the true quality of jazz drumming comes through on records. "All you have to do on some dates is go in the studio and hear what's really being played, then listen to how little of it the tape is picking up."

At which point Ertegun reminds him, "Tommy, we *have* to get that middle cymbal."

When the take is over, Ertegun says into his mike, "It could be a little faster, Art."

Farmer nods.

Another try at "Some Sweet Day," and from the opening bars, it is obviously going to be a good one. Swallow sways widely in time to his own solo, causing Dowd to remark, "It's a good thing we've got the mike strapped inside the bass, otherwise we might not be getting but half of this."

McIntosh looks pleased at the whole performance.

In a few minutes, Farmer is in a huddle with Perkins across the studio as Ertegun calls over the loudspeaker, "Art, I think you should hear this played back!"

At the end all agree it was a beautiful take, and Farmer affirms that he is now relaxed about the way the piece is going by casually telling an anecdote about Dizzy Gillespie's fluffing a note during a performance of the "Star-Spangled Banner" at the Monterey Jazz Festival.

However, in a few moments, Ertegun suggests, "Just for safety let's do another one—and maybe we'll use the first one at that."

Hall solos with his eyes shut, embracing his instrument. And in his solo Farmer shows that on fluegelhorn he gets the intimacy of a Harmon- or felt-muted trumpet with the warm sound of an open horn.

A few minutes after the final take of "Some Sweet Day," Farmer and Perkins have begun to kid around in duo with the theme of a light and brash Richard Rodgers ditty called "Loads of Love." The kiddings comes off so well that someone is soon suggesting they record the piece as a couple of duets—first Farmer and Perkins and then Hall and Swallow.

They run it down that way a couple of times, but it seems to be falling into two separate halves. Farmer and Ertegun suggest that Perkins continue his sock cymbal under a solo by Swallow and then under Swallow and Hall in duo.

"Want to try it a little faster?" Hall asks, looking up at Farmer.

"Well, if I have to start worrying about the tempo and the changes, too . . ."

Meanwhile, Dowd has made it a real evening session: he has turned out the studio lights except for a couple of pinlights on Perkins' drums and for the much softer glow through the glass of the engineer's booth. It is as if he were deliberately preparing for something.

A couple more takes of "Loads of Love" and Farmer is asking Perkins, "Can you keep the feeling of 'two' but play around it a little more? I think of it as a solo almost." After several false starts, they get a couple of good takes on the piece, and Ertegun suggests, "I think that's it. Okay?"

Farmer agrees: "Yeah. Let's do a take on 'Embraceable You'—all right?"

Almost immediately, the tape is rolling, and they are into the piece. It is beautiful from the first notes: Farmer's opening solo, the sensitive interplay with which Hall supports him, Hall's own passages, Swallow as sensitive as Hall under Farmer's later chorus.

At the end there is a moment of silence as the studio reverberations whisp off. Someone says quietly, "Wow!" Then Ertegun's voice comes simply over the speaker, "A masterpiece."

The rest is anticlimax: Hall is unplugging his amplifier, Perkins is packing his cymbals, and Swallow is slipping the cover over his bass.

As all this is being done, Ertegun says, "Art, listen to the last take of 'Loads of Love' again."

But Dowd, before getting to a playback of "Loads of Love," reruns the tape of "Embraceable You." Nobody minds. And one has the feeling that the reputation of these players and their group might stand by that one performance alone.

Rehearsal Diary

The Tuesday afternoon gathering is at Carroll Instrument Studios on West 49th Street. The occasion is the first of three rehearsals for the final concert in the Carnegie Recital Hall series "Twentieth Century Innovations" directed by Gunther Schuller. The series began with Stravinsky, Schonberg, and Webern; it moved in later concerts through the American premiere of several concert works (including one by Barraqué); and it is to end with "Recent Developments in Jazz." Originally, some Third Stream pieces were to be presented, but these were combined with the "Early Experiments in Jazz" of Stravinsky *et al.*, at the previous concert.

Schuller stands in the brightly lit room, intently facing the players, his scores spread on a music stand before him. Some well-known jazzmen are present. Nick Travis and Don Ellis are on trumpets, Britt Woodman and Jimmy Knepper on trombones. Among the reeds are Phil Woods and Benny Golson. Drums and percussion are Charlie Persip and Sticks Evans. There are two basses, Richard Davis and Barre Phillips. Jim Hall is on guitar.

"Let's go," Schuller is saying. "Get out the Lalo Schiffrin piece," calling for the toughest work they are to do, a twelve-tone serial composition, "The Ritual of Sound," involving jazz motives and phrasing. They discover there are no markings of sections or subdivisions on the score. "You'd think a big copying house would question a thing like that," Schuller observes.

"Well," (it is a voice among the brass) "there are so many metronome markings—why don't we just use those." The shifting rhythmic complexities of the piece call for indications scattered throughout the score.

"At the first two-four, let's call that A. B eleven bars later. C at the first tempo change . . ." The players mark their scores as Schuller continues. "Wait a minute. I'm calling this off, but not marking it myself." "Where was B, Gunther?"

"Lalo's here! He just walked in." He is a quiet, sober presence of medium height, dark, and currently slightly stout around the middle.

The piece, like most serial works, has notes and melodic fragments scattered from instrument to instrument in waves that carry us across the orchestra and back. But much jazz phrasing is called for, and not only in the few obvious growls and shakes from the brass.

"Right there before D, it's *do-wat, do-wat*. You know, like the Ellington thing," Schuller instructs. Then to Lalo, "This is pretty fast." (To the left of the room, a good-looking female enters quietly.) "Is the trumpet open there, Don?" he says, stopping Ellis.

"Oh, you're right. Still cup-muted," says Ellis as Schiffrin peers over his shoulder at his part. Down in front, among the reeds, Benny Golson looks at his part, bemused but interested. Over on the right, Richard Davis is smiling—but then Richard Davis is frequently smiling.

"Now listen, all of this section is jazz, remember. Play it *do-la-DAH!* But basses, you're rushing. Try that again, just the basses. No, watch the markings. It's very slow here."

Then, a voice from the center of the group, "Gunther could we go back to G?"

"No, I don't want to rehearse it now. I just want to read it."

They are at about the middle. The tempo changes radically, yet the musical momentum seems continuous. "Hold it! That's too slow, but Richard you got there too early."

And a few moments later comes a topper: "Everybody, at L it gets complicated. But Lalo, aren't there some wrong notes in here?"

Schriffrin comes forward and stands beside Gunther, addressing them in his slightly Spanish-accented speech. "You see, any one of these phrases would be an *ostinato* riff in jazz or in any African-influenced music. But I have gone from one to the next instead of repeating, and given each one its own rhythm, separately."

They are into it again. The reading is still rough, but in the places it should, it is beginning to swing a bit.

"Hold it, hold it. Come on, you can read better than that. You'll just have to count."

And finally, when the last notes have hesitantly scampered by: "We'll have to spend a lot of time on that tomorrow. Now, get out George Russell's 'Lydian M-1.' "

There is some shifting around: Persip moves into the drums; the reeds move over to include Phil Woods; Schiffrin takes his place at the piano; Travis is out; etc. They begin. The intro is Persip setting a quick tempo. Then Russell's theme, a curiously compelling rapid succession of notes tightly knit, and giving the impression of a narrow range melodically, but a wide one rhythmically. It must be tough enough to read them, tougher still to get the phrasing and accents. "Hold it! You can't read this fast?"

"No. Gunther, you'd better get Barry."

"No, look, Barry isn't going to be here. Can't you——"

"Okay, I'll work on it tonight and have it tomorrow."

"So far, so bad," mutters Nick Travis on the sideline.

Soon Gunther is saying, "Let's just take a break and then we'll do the Hodier pieces. I want to read through everything today." Only about two-thirds of the players leave for the coke machine in the next room. The rest are running through tough passages they have already played, or running through the opening section of André Hodier's "Jazz Cantata."

Out by the hall phone booths someone is saying, "You know, the trouble is that if you sent down to the corner music store for the worst pop song in the house, handed it to Thelonious Monk or Sonny Rollins and said, 'Want to try this?' in ten minutes he might come up with something that would knock you out." (He has a point, and a big one, but one that every good jazz composer is aware of.)

Inside, Gunther gathers the players, calling out for the "Cantata." "And remember the phrasing—most of this is just plain old jazz." The good-looking woman takes her place beside him. She is of medium height, with almost black hair and fair, almost white, skin. She takes an authoritative stance as she holds up a vocal score at eye level.

The first section is very fast. She lets go with a darting, wordless, scat melodic line, very high for jazz singing. Behind her Phil Woods has a rapid alto part to play in the style of an improvised solo. The singer is dashing off her notes with a combination of ease and drive.

At the end of the first section, she protests, "I didn't get all the notes." She is saying it over a spontaneous scattered applause from the musicians.

"You stayed with it all the way through!" Gunther counters. "Gentlemen, this is Susan Belink. She has never sung jazz before. She's in opera."

They are into the second part of Hodier's "Cantata." The performance moves along well enough, but at one break Jimmy Knepper says, in a near-whisper, "That note is awfully low." Several of Hodier's parts skip rapidly from high to low and back again.

Gunther asks, "Have you got one of those long fiber mutes? Use that." Britt Woodman, to Knepper's left, silently provides one.

Soon they begin Duke Ellington's "Reminiscing in Tempo," one of his early long works, first done in 1935. At one brief interruption, Schuller ejects, "Hey, this sounds good!" And at the end, "Good. I think we can get that one. But somewhere along the line we're going to have to add some more rehearsal time."

"How about starting at one o'clock Thursday afternoon instead of two?" someone suggests, to general agreement.

"Right now as much as we can of the other Hodier pieces, 'Paradox I' and 'Tension-Détente.' From now on I'll just call that 'Tension,'" he says, pronouncing it in English. "Anyone who doesn't have a part in these can leave."

"Trouble is," one of the players is remarking to a friend as he heaves on his overcoat, "that in jazz the players always come first. No matter how well we do that Ellington piece, it was still written with Harry Carney's baritone sound in mind. And Johnny Hodges' sound, and Cootie Williams' sound, and Rex Stewart's sound. Don and Nick are doing especially well with those trumpet parts, but no matter how well any of us do, we can only produce an imitation."

"Well," says the friend as they push through the door, "what about George Russell's piece? He didn't necessarily write that for specific men. True, it was commissioned for that Teddy Charles record, and he more or less knew who would be playing it. But he still wrote it sort of in the abstract. Any group of good jazz players ought to be able to play it as well as any other group."

"Yeah—theoretically. . . ." They are both smiling as they reach the street.

Wednesday, 9 A.M. Second rehearsal. At Carnegie Recital Hall itself. The small auditorium seems hazily lighted at this unaccustomed morning hour, but the stage is harshly bright. Almost everyone is prompt and assembled, instruments unpacked, on stage by five minutes to nine. And at five minutes past, Gunther is saying, "Oh, Jim, there you are. Fast as you can."

They begin Schiffrin's piece again. Gunther conducts with both arms, but somehow always with his right more than his left. He bobs up and down, bending his knees a bit, almost awkwardly, and moving slightly from side to side. "Remember, all of this has more jazz phrasing than we gave it last time." Hall is crawling around the stage as they play, searching for an electrical outlet for his guitar amplifier and trying to trail his wires so that no one will trip over them.

Schuller stops everyone, looks down at his score, lays down his baton. "Start that again, but just the trumpets."

"Okay. Now one trumpet at a time. You first, Nick."

"Now just the trumpets and the trombones."

"Okay, good. Now the whole six-four section, all the brass." Breaking it down had worked.

Travis signals a private joke to Phil Woods who is sitting in the auditorium and they both laugh broadly but silently.

At the end of a wildly contrapuntal texture, there are pleased looks all around. Schiffrin, who had been standing in back of the house, makes only one quiet comment to Schuller, so quietly that I don't catch it.

"Now, just the guitar and vibes on the eleven-four." Sticks Evans is having trouble with this part, but even so he almost makes it swing. Too infectiously perhaps, because by the end of one section Schuller is saying, "Now fellas, here don't play swinging eighth notes. These are all legit eighth notes."

Out in the auditorium there is some reasonably good-natured joking to the effect that, "Maybe Lalo sniffs airplane glue or something before he writes something like this."

10 A.M. They are still on Schiffrin's piece. "Did I tell you to shorten those notes yesterday? Well today I'm not so sure."

"Britt, those triplet accents . . ." Gunther sings the phrases and Travis spontaneously begins to play them on his trumpet.

Jim Hall, asked for a particular dotted effect, says, "It's been so long since I played a mandolin."

By 11:05 the final notes rise in an orderly pattern and hover over the stage, the composer applauds them from the back of the house.

"Okay, in five minutes we'll do the Ellington." He says it to the men in the auditorium as well as those on stage, and some of the former begin to take their places with the group.

Phil Woods warms up by playing "Donna Lee." Gunther is telling Britt Woodman, "I'll rely on you here."

"But I never played this piece with Duke."

"But you know the style."

"Where did you get the score?"

"I asked Ellington for it a few years ago to use at a concert at Brandeis University. He never sent it. Maybe he couldn't find it any more. So I just took it off the record."

They are into "Reminiscing in Tempo," playing it with only a couple of interruptions and corrections. "Soft," says Gunther over the music. "Full!" "Relax." "Up!" It is as if Ellington's gentle but firm melody had a momentum of its own that carried the players along with it. "Hey that sounded great. We'll do this some more tomorrow."

11:20. "Real quick, get out the George Russell. Wait, somebody's missing." He faces the back of the house. "Hey Buff, is Harvey out there?"

After two false starts, they have slowed down Russell's rapid tempo to work on the accents. "Lalo, you'll just have to play louder. I can't hear you."

"Charlie, you're rushing. No, don't look at me in this piece. There's no point in my conducting a piece like this, anyway. Just watch for that one bar in three-four. Otherwise, keep playing all the way through the tempo I give you in the beginning."

At the end someone asks, "Could we add another rehearsal?" He sounds almost plaintive.

Thursday, the afternoon of the concert, 1 P.M.

"Get out the George Russell," Gunther announces loudly and hopefully to the harshly but brightly lighted hall. Not all of the musicians are there, and only half of those that are seem ready. Gunther crosses for a consultation with Jim Hall over the score.

In a few minutes, they're assembled. Schuller signals the tempo. Persip's brushes chip a snare drum. "Wait, wait. Hold it. Charlie, you started faster than I set it." ("Oh? Sorry.") Persip cooks up his brushes again. Everything is falling into place. Hall is laying down his guitar line with confidence. The difficult horn accents are coming more correctly.

"Let's stop there. Charlie, help us out there with some fills. If you play right through, you leave a hole. Now, begin again at M for Monk."

"Very big on those D's. At the end, Lalo and Richard louder to help everybody out. Make a big thing of it!" They do the final part again.

"Okay. Now from the top, just guitar, piano, vibes, bass, and drums. No horns. We've got to get this. First we'll try it very slowly." It sounds good slow.

"Hey! This is a hell of a piece!" says someone suddenly as they finish the first marking.

Schuller, emphatically: "There is not one extraneous note in this whole piece."

Golson, laughing: "Except in the solos!" He had just played one.

Then, George Russell's "Lydian M-1" from the top. It goes down very well, the accents fall right, the players are more relaxed and a group drive has developed. Schuller seems cheerful for the first time today as he calls out for the Ellington piece.

"Play it more evenly, Lalo. And these ensembles have got to be right. It's like playing Mozart—everybody knows the style." Again, a very good reading.

But Gunther is a bit strained as they turn to the tough one, the Schiffrin "Ritual of Sound." "Please concentrate. I have no more time and I've got to do the Hodier pieces. Where's Phil? Benny, is Phil out there?"

"Joe, always strong!" They are about halfway through it now. "Always with energy." Schiffrin himself is in the rear of the house quietly commenting to a friend in Spanish—a good sign presumably.

"Drums, you're late. *Wum-b-um-bum*. We'll work this out later between us." Travis makes a mistake—his first, as I remember.

At a final run-through, it goes the best yet.

"The Hodier. The Hodier now," clapping his hands and beginning to shift a couple of chairs around. As they begin the first section, Susan Belink joins them, singing her part from a seat in the house. Schuller asks her to hold it, he wants to rehearse the players alone first. "Don, watch your dynamics."

Then Miss Belink moves toward the stage. She is dressed quite informally compared to her first appearance. And today her sentences feature a couple of scattered "man's" and "like's."

In the first section she and Woods make the shifts of tempo together in sudden, compelling bursts. Her head tosses back slightly on high notes, and Woods's feet lift and curl up under his chair as he plays. At her last strong note, a sudden burst of "Wow!" goes up from the group, and the whole room is smiling broadly.

It is nearly three o'clock. An engineer has set up a mike which somehow picks up more Woods than Belink, although she is singing directly into it. They move singer and mike to the center of the stage. Gunther suggests to Don Ellis that for his trumpet solo in the fast section, "We have the mike, so use the Miles Davis mute."

"Yes, well, I'll try the Harmon, with the stem, in close to the mike." Somehow it doesn't work; it doesn't get the Miles Davis sound. "At home I have a Miles Davis bucket mute and a Don Goldie mute and a —let's try the cup mute." Gunther goes out into the auditorium to hear the balance again now that the mike is on Ellis.

They begin the first section of the "Cantata" again. As Belink brings out her last phrase Gunther turns to the visitors to ask, "Could you hear that?"

"We couldn't miss it!" "Sure did!" (Visitors now include composer Milton Babbitt and tenor saxophonist Lucky Thompson.) There is a five-minute break, and Golson immediately climbs off the stage and goes over to Thompson, seated in the rear of the house, with a warm welcome. Several players exchange tips on the food at nearby lunch rooms as they hurry out.

In about five minutes the players are reassembled on stage for the "Cantata" again. It goes excitingly and there are smiles and scattered applause at the end.

4:20. "Okay, the other Hodier pieces. Get out 'Tension.' We're really going to be hopping it. And we're not going to rehearse past five. The rest of you, who don't play these last two pieces, be here tonight by 8:15 at the latest. And have a good dinner. It helps. Wait! Before you go, just let me run down the final number. You know, Eric Dolphy and his quartet will be on in the second half of the program, playing their own things. At the end we want to have an improvisation for almost everybody on 'Dona Lee.' Solos by you, Phil, by Don, Benny, Jimmy, Nick. But don't anybody play the theme in the first chorus unless you really know it. When we finish the solos we play the theme again. But don't take it out, because then Eric will play two choruses very high, you know the way he does. Phil, you improvise at the same time, but in the middle. And you guys," gesturing to the other horn men, "play a riff under them. Okay? Now let's go on to 'Tension.' "

In the back of the hall Milton Babbitt whispers, "So *that's* how they arrange an improvisation!"

On the stage, Gunther is instructing, "Joe, remember it is a vibe solo, but he's written it out. Try to play it like you're improvising it."

"Richard, you know that little hole in there, give me a Ray Brown walk. And everybody, you know this little measure I'm always bitching about. Softer. Not *da-da de-du dit-do-WAH*, but *da-ut da-it dit-da-do*. Begin again."

4:40. "Okay. Now, 'Bicinium.' Don't goof now." He is speaking quickly and almost sternly, but suddenly he laughs, turning to me, "Martin, are you getting all this?" It breaks the tension.

Again, Golson and Knepper have to move quickly from high notes to low. Their chops must be aching. Persip claims he's getting blisters on his feet. "Come on," Gunther encourages. "Just imagine you're back with Dizzy. He worked you much harder than this."

4:55. "Let's take a breath and we'll do it again. We have another one to rehearse after this. Good music is always hard."

"You *mean* that?" says Travis genuinely puzzled. "I've played good pieces that were easy."

"When?"

A pause. "Oh, I remember one in about 1948."

"Just these three rehearsals and the cost is $2,500," Schuller muses. "Sometimes I think all regulations are deliberately antiart."

And in a few minutes, "Okay, now 'Paradox I.' Only Charlie, Richard, Jimmy, and Benny. The rest of you can go. By the way, this will be the first number on the program."

Evergreen Review 31, October-November, 1963

Gospel at the Box Office

Whatever it takes to attract the jaded tastes of the more avid midtown Manhattan nightclub patrons—a strangely close-knit amalgam of press agents, actors' managers, and what we shall call (for lack of better terms) "celebrities" and "socialites"—a new club called the Sweet Chariot seems to have it, for the time being at least. For about a year and half a kind of *voyeurism* drew more or less this same crowd to the Peppermint Lounge, where jean-and-black-leather jacket-clad teenagers did the twist. Now the fad has changed to the nearby Sweet Chariot, where gospel song, quasi-secularized as "pop gospel," is the attraction. And the attraction seems to be spreading to other big cities as well.

The contrived atmosphere of the Sweet Chariot Club is bizarre almost beyond belief. There are, for example, "hostesses" clad in choir robes that reach only to the thigh, where they meet opera-length stockings. Yes, and there are small wings attached to the shoulders of their gowns and wire halos topping their coiffures. Customers are offered tambourines for participating in the music. The only thing missing, it would seem, is an assurance from the management that the Chariot is insured against unexpected thunderbolts, well aimed from the blue.

Columbia Records, and its subsidiary Epic, have recorded these frenetic proceedings on a series of three LPs, done at the club, and complete with announcements by an MC named Howard Saunders who occasionally sounds like a crowd-haranguing fugitive from a carnival midway. The music is performed in a manner quite appropriate to such surroundings. On *Introducing the Sweet Chariot* (CS 8861/CL2061, $4.98) we first meet the pat (albeit strident) routines of the Golden Chords, who offer some not very attractive female voices, plus the applause-begging of a screaming and affected frenzy at the end of their four numbers. Following the Chords, we hear an ugly strain of voices and emotions in a four-number parody of gospel by the Nathaniel Lewis Singers. And finally there is a brief appearance by the Sweet Chariot Singers (formerly called the Philadelphia All Stars!).

On *Everybody's Shoutin' Gospel* (Epic LN 24062, $3.98), the Herman Stevens Singers, led by Helen Bryant and Evelyn Archie, offer a program that reaches back to the spiritual ancestor of gospel in "Joshua Fit the Battle of Jericho" and forward to the fine, contemporary antiphonal piece, "Didn't It Rain." Their work is quite skillful in its way, and if it were not so edgy and compulsive, it might have had some of the compelling momentum and swing that gospel singing should have.

Indeed, lurking beneath this recorded display, and particularly in the voice of Nathaniel Lewis, there is often a hint of the power and beauty that can be found in the gospel idiom. That is true also for the young Sweet Chariot Singers themselves who further offer (it says) *Shoutin', Wailin', Hard Drivin' Pop Gospel* on Columbia CS 8862/CL 2062 ($4.98). As a final irony, two of the Chariot Singers, visible in the album's cover photo, are holding tambourines clearly marked "not for sale." *Oh yeah?*

For a better insight into the history and compelling beauty of this remarkable American idiom of gospel music there is Folkways album RBF RF 5, *An Introduction to Gospel Song* ($5.95). The set begins with proprietary efforts to Europeanize the traditional Negro spiritual by Fisk University and Tuskegee Institute Singers, recorded in 1913 and

1917, respectively. It passes through examples from the late twenties, by the Rev. J. M. Gates and F. W. McGee and their respective congregations, of how collective, spirited songs grew more or less spontaneously, from chanted sermons. The set ends with two quite lovely pieces by the moving Spirit-of-Memphis group (chorus, bass drum, tambourine, and delicate solo voices) recorded in 1954.

"Gospel Song" is a selection on a remarkable recital by a young man named Sandy Bull, who plays various stringed instruments on *Fantasias for Guitar and Banjo* (Vanguard VRS 9119, $4.98.). "Gospel" is a set of variations on the traditional sacred piece, "Good News" (which incidentally has also found currency as the rock and roll ditty, "I Got a Woman") by Bull on electric bass and Billy Higgins on drums. Bull approaches a wide variety of musical idioms on this LP, with succinct understanding and with an immediately apparent and innate musical sensibility. By double-tracking, he offers William Byrd's "Non Nobis Domine," with two of its contrapuntal lines on banjo and a third on guitar, and the results are stately. Also on banjo, he abstracts the Southern mountain air, "Little Maggie." The first side of the LP is "Blend" by Higgins, drums and Bull's unamplified guitar. It is an evolving tissue of fantasias, echoing jazz, the modality of Indian and Arabic music, and with hints of various other folk idioms. If I say that these twenty-plus minutes of music are not entirely sustained, I do not mean to imply that the shifting textures are not remarkable and musicianly.

Saturday Review, August 31, 1963
Copyright © 1963 Saturday Review, Inc.

Steve Swallow

"I'd rather play with either Jimmy McPartland or Bud Freeman or with the Jimmy Giuffre Trio than play be-bop."

This provocative statement comes from Steve Swallow, one of the best of a remarkable group of young bass players who have participated in the most recent developments in jazz.

"New thing" music (to use that graceless and even ambiguous but still necessary term) can now boast three or four outstanding reed men and three or four accomplished trumpeters at best. But the good bassists who have been involved in it! . . . Charlie Haden, Jimmy Garrison, the late Scott LaFaro, Ron Carter, Gary Peacock, David Izenzon, Chuck Israels Swallow—not to mention a venerable progenitor like Charlie Mingus or a recent apprentice like Barre Phillips.

Swallow is not alone among younger players in having an articulate sense of jazz history and his own relationship to it. He elaborated:

"Orthodox modern jazz is difficult for me because there are so many things that are given, so many inflexible idiomatic requirements of exactly what each player is supposed to do in the music. And a man can make the music sound wrong if he doesn't meet those requirements.

"The Dixieland players know that they are part of history, and they have less concern with the sanctity of their idiom. The style is refined, but it always sounds stylized, sounds like Dixieland, in a variety of formats and instrumentations. In that sense, it is flexible.

"The basic Dixieland instruments have certain ensemble functions, but beyond that a player is free to find his own way. Drummers don't play the flow of the rhythm, for example, but its demarcation. George Wettling is superb at this. And the ensemble deals with a varied texture. Therefore, I feel free to find a sixth voice.

"Because I play with such a variety of groups, some people assume I play in a variety of styles, but I don't. Actually I'm not sure there was ever an exact place in Dixieland for the bass, and some groups, I think, sound better without one.

"And today the swing-period players can allow the same sort of freedom to a bass player in their style.

"Bud Freeman, whom I love to play with, long ago found a place for his tenor in the Dixieland ensemble. Anyway, the best things in Bud's style are bigger than category, not the things that make him an ensemble player or make him a swing-period soloist.

"By now, be-bop is historical too, but many of the players don't know it yet. And be-boppers still want things done only along well-established lines. Of course, some players thought of as modernists are too mature to need absolute orthodoxy. I never assume with Art Farmer that he wants me to play any way other than the way I play."

Swallow has worked, within the same month, for George Russell and Benny Goodman. And as of this writing, he is simultaneously bassist with the Jimmy Giuffre Three, the new Art Farmer-Jim Hall Quartet, and the Marian McPartland Trio. He also is likely to respond positively

Albert Ayler. *(Courtesy of Impulse Records)*

Jimmy Garrison, Ornette Coleman, Bobby Bradford, and C. M. Moffett in rehearsal. *(Courtesy of Herb Snitzer)*

Thelonius Monk.
(Courtesy of Columbia Records)

Ray Charles.
(Courtesy of ABC-Records)

Miles Davis.
(Courtesy of Columbia Records)

The Modern Jazz Quartet: Percy Heath, Connie Kay, John Lewis, Milt Jackson.

Pharaoh Sanders. *(Courtesy of Impulse Records)*

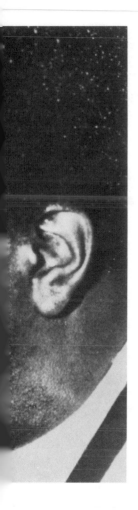

Archie Shepp.
(Courtesy of Impulse Records)

Bill Evans and his Grammy Award.
(Courtesy of Verve Records)

John Coltrane. *(Courtesy of Impulse Records)*

to any calls from Bud Freeman or Al Cohn and Zoot Sims if he can
sandwich in the gig. Obviously such a multiple musical life cannot continue for him, for he simply will not have the time.

Swallow is a native New Yorker, born there in 1940 and raised just
across the river in Fairlawn, N.J. His father is an electrical engineer by
profession, but as a part-time musician he worked his way through college, with an alto saxophone and trombone and later continued his interest in the jazz of his own day.

Steve was a trumpet player when he was a youngster, and he wanted
to play jazz.

"My father played me records by Jelly Roll Morton and Bix Beiderbecke, and I liked them," he said. "Actually, I was a rotten trumpet
player. In junior high school I wanted to jam with some fellows who
were playing jazz, so I got a book called *50 Hot Licks for Trumpet by
Ziggy Elman*. I learned them all right away, in all the keys, and went
off to the session. I could make a solo just by stringing together my
Ziggy Elman licks. The other players tolerated me.

"I can't say I ever actually switched to bass—it was just that there
was always a need for a bass player, and I was a rotten trumpet player.
From the beginning I seemed to get the right notes on bass, but I can't
say that my time was too good then."

Swallow was sent to prep school, and there he met Ian Underwood,
an exceptionally talented flutist and reed player. They had what Swallow calls "real amateurs' zeal" and used to get up early to play together before school breakfast.

The association with Underwood continued at Yale University, where
the bassist became a member of the local Dixieland outfit, the Bullpups.

"They needed a bass player, and I needed the money and enjoyed the
trips we made," he recalled. "That was about all there was to it really.
At that point I wasn't even the zealot I had been in prep school, but I
realize, looking back, what important lessons I was learning.

"The bass player that I admired most on records then was Percy
Heath, but there were excellent swing-period musicians at Yale functions. I got to work with Buddy Tate, Buck Clayton, Rex Stewart, Dickie
Wells. I learned especially from Dickie—he is such a clear and precise
player, you know. I would often follow him and simply play his solos
back note for note. He didn't seem to mind, and it was superb training
for me."

The knowledge that music held more for him than an outlet for amateur's zeal or a college student's part-time job came to Swallow abruptly

and fatalistically. In the fall of 1959, pianist Ran Blake, then himself a student, held his second jazz festival at the small Bard College in New York State. Blake invited one of his favorite pianists, Paul Bley, to participate, and Bley got Paul Cohen, then a good drummer and now a young Pennsylvania lawyer. Cohen recommended Swallow.

"I had no idea how Paul Bley played," Swallow said, "and I hurried around trying to find one of his records. They were out of stock every place I went. The afternoon of the concert, we held one rehearsal. I was deeply impressed with Paul's music but seemed to get nowhere playing it. That evening on the program we followed the gospel singing of Prof. Alex Bradford, which of course the audience loved. When we started to play, my back was against the wall, and I found that I was managing to produce a real affinity with Paul's music. It was a very strong experience, the whole thing. I was physically sick afterward, but I knew then that music was going to be my life.

"I left Yale before midterm exams. I went to New York, and I just called Paul Bley, asking if he needed a bass player."

Bley said that he did. It was rather a lean time for them, but they had a job at Copa City with blues singer Big Miller, and Swallow had the Dixieland and mainstream contacts he had made at Yale, particularly Jimmy McPartland and Freeman.

"Paul set me the most important challenges," Swallow said. "He set all the fast tunes slightly faster than I could play and all the ballads slightly slower. In four months he whipped me into shape. I had gotten through the instrument; I had learned the bass. He felt that the instrument itself simply has to be gotten through. And I played it the same afterward, until Jimmy Giuffre got hold of me."

Swallow had arrived in New York in the winter of 1959, in time for Ornette Coleman's first Five Spot engagement with Don Cherry, Charlie Haden, and Billy Higgins in his quartet. Swallow was quickly introduced to Coleman's music by Bley, in whose group Coleman had played in California. So, besides the workouts with Bley and the Dixieland jobs, there was frequent attendance at the Five Spot.

In the summer of 1960, Swallow went with Ian Underwood on a European trip that included a long stretch in Germany.

"We played nothing but Monk tunes and Ornette tunes," he said. "Learning the Monk repertory is the only meaningful training in composition I have had, by the way, except for some brief study at Yale with Donald Martino, an ex-jazzman who is now a serial composer. That and knowing Carla Bley's music."

Back in New York there were frequent weekend sessions at the Phase 2 coffee house. These often included, besides Paul Bley and his wife Carla, trumpeter Don Ellis and pianist Jaki Byard.

It was at these Phase 2 sessions that the players began to change tempo and key, and leave chord structures altogether, to keep the young, amateur be-boppers out of the jamming. Shades of Gillespie and Monk at Minton's! The effort of the Phase 2 players was not to disparage Gillespie and Parker or the achievements of bop. Rather, they wanted to acknowledge that the musicians of their own generation had to stop walking in Bird and Dizzy's shadows—after nearly twenty years of modern jazz—and find their own way.

Paul Bley had already joined Giuffre by the time Swallow had got back from Europe, and Swallow went with Bud Freeman. But when Giuffre's regular bassist was caught in a traffic jam. Swallow made a rehearsal. He soon found himself having to choose between Bud Freeman and Giuffre, and he says, "It was a hard choice."

"At first the Giuffre book was full of simple song forms," he said, "but gradually Jimmy's ideas began to emerge, and they made sense to me. He has been a big influence, chiefly by making it clear that he would not accept common practice—although, of course, he does not want to avoid it just to be avoiding it.

"We approach a piece phrase by phrase rather than setting a tempo first and keeping it. All of my own playing is related to a tempo, but when the Giuffre trio played that extended job at the Take 3 coffee house last spring, we really managed to break through. Tempo still exists in our music but in a way that permeates—if that's the word. I still play in reference to it, not because the tempo makes the music swing—tempo doesn't—but because a consistent proportioning of the time establishes relationships. To put it another way, each musical phrase takes it own shape, and it may deny the time and the tempo.

"These things have become so fundamental to us that Jimmy didn't realize that on 'Spasmodic' and 'Divided Man' on our *Free Fall* LP, there are stretches in strict tempo. And of course, that's good, because it means he was thinking in terms of musical phrases."

Swallow finds a further challenge in the work of players past and present, not all of them bass players. He will mention Pete LaRoca, Marian McPartland's drummer, as having "the ideal solution for drums." And he found Art Tatum's virtuosity a fundamental personal incentive for a while.

But on his own instrument "if someone says that I remind him of

Charlie Haden, I have to admit that I remind myself of Charlie Haden. I have decided to let my sources rise to the top and be obvious because that is the best way to assimilate sources. Charlie's influence is clear to me, but the others are less clear because they aren't directly related to the bass. But I know that I listen to Django Reinhardt's records for instruction as well as for pleasure. I think you can hear the effect of his sound in my playing, but I am also fascinated by the way he used triads. He used them in part to organize tonality, and I am not interested in that aspect of it, of course."

Swallow says that he used to be able to play faster than he does now, but he is not talking about rapid tempos, as will be seen. The admission brought him to some remarks on fellow bassist Gary Peacock, who, he says, has been a very big influence.

"I tried for the concentration, the density, of his playing, and I just couldn't do it," Swallow remarked. "If I hadn't been exposed as strongly to the style through knowing him and hearing him, I could have spent a long time trying to play that way and got nowhere. I am very thankful there are important differences between me and such an extraordinary player as Gary.

"His concern with velocity is fundamental to what he has to say. With Bill Evans, he will inject, in a single moment—even between Bill's rapid phrases—a finished idea. I need half a chorus to develop an idea most of the time. That's why I say I play more slowly now."

The admiration for Peacock is mutual, and the latter especially credits Swallow with exploring the range of tone and sound beyond that supposed to be legitimately possible on the bass.

A lot is said about the new jazz as a "free" music, but Swallow declared, "The word freedom is really meaningless to me—musically I don't even consider it. I am a member of an ensemble, and most of what I do is in reference to the other music being made on the bandstand."

Down Beat. October 10, 1963

Mostly Mingus

Surely the name Charles Mingus should be writ large in the history of recent jazz. For one thing, he was the first bass player in twenty years to rethink and reinterpret the function of his instrument. Since 1939 and Jimmy Blanton, the bass has had an exact harmonic function. In the modern jazz ensemble, it has also long carried the rhythmic lead. But Mingus at key moments does not so much "accompany" with his strings, one-two-three-four/one-two-three-four, as he manages also to enrich the ensemble texture with a spontaneous, interplaying, countermelodic part.

Mingus has contributed a great deal more than that. As an instrumentalist, he is one of very few bass players with the technique, quick imagination, commanding presence, and energy to be a truly authoritative soloist. (A superb example is a piece called "Cryin' Blues" on Atlantic 1305.) In his small group he has also rediscovered the semi-improvised ensemble style, the thrilling collective spontaneity that has been missing in jazz since Dixieland descended to its current boozy geniality as a substitute businessmen's bounce.

Mingus also has a capacity that only an exceptional composer-player can have: he encourages merely good sidemen to much better than good performances.

But the name Charles Mingus is writ large in recent journalism for quite other reasons. Mingus declares that white men cannot play jazz, and a flock of reporters quote his words. (But he nearly always uses white musicians in his groups.) Mingus announces that he is disgusted with the United States and is leaving shortly for Spain. (But he does not go to Spain, and a handful of insiders nod that of course they doubted that he would.) Mingus is sued for assault by a long-faithful sideman.

But the name Charles Mingus was never writ quite so large as it was the morning after a certain night in December, 1962, when he had held forth at Town Hall.

The occasion was supposed to have been a public recording date, but the producers' announcements and ads somehow came out reading "concert." At one point during the proceedings, Mingus shouted to his audience, advising, "Get your money back!"

The musical results of that evening of turbulence, chaos, and (yes) some achievement, have now been issued on United Artists UAJS 15024 —or that part of the results that the company felt could be salvaged for LP. The cover photograph tells a part of the story: strung out across the Town Hall stage is a great pile-up of musicians, some in shirtsleeves, some still stiffly in tux. In the midst, Mingus is instructing one of his saxophonists, Eric Dolphy. Not visible are the music copyists, who were placed conspicuously at center stage, working on the next piece—or perhaps the conclusion of the piece in progress.

As if to give final embellishment to such pouring chaos, the LP itself is mislabeled. The descriptions in Bill Coss's accompanying program notes are correct, but six titles on the LP label are wildly juggled. Further, what is labeled "My Search," but apparently should have been labeled "Epitaph II," is actually a version of an earlier Mingus work, "Pithecanthropus Erectus" (a performance of almost overwhelming impact in its original version on Atlantic 1237). And what is labeled "Epitaph I," but should have been labeled "Finale," is actually a spirited version of Duke Ellington's "In a Mellotone," which the group simply began to ad-lib at the close of the evening, as the management was sternly attempting to bring down the curtain.

Several soloists do shine on this LP—Mingus, Dolphy, and trumpeter Clark Terry, who is a brick throughout. Yet one cannot say that the music is successful. Paradoxically, it is also fascinating. Even through a sloppily played or draggingly rehearsed ensemble, one is forcefully aware of the abiding musical energy and personality of the bass-playing leader. One also senses what a distinct loss the evening was, for Mingus has recently shown (particularly on two recitals for Columbia, CL 1370 and CL 1440) a continuously developing grasp of large ensemble composing and playing.

The Charlie Mingus Quintet, now released on Fantasy 6009, featuring drummer Max Roach on one track, was actually recorded in a night club a few years back. The set contains versions of "Love Chant," "A Foggy Day," and "Haitian Fight Song" that are not nearly so forceful as the originals (again, these are on the fine Atlantic series, 1237 and 1260). Mingus also offers a total and superior recomposition of the melody of "I'll Remember April." Most of the pieces have relatively uncomplicated solos by tenor saxophonist George Barrow, an improviser gifted with fine natural swing.

Saturday Review, December 14, 1963
Copyright © 1963 Saturday Review, Inc.

Contemporary Blues

Periodically, the basic, so-called country vocal blues tradition is declared dead at the roots. And just as often an authentic, colorfully named, and relatively young bard—a "Muddy Waters" (McKinley Morganfield), a "Bo Diddley" (Elias McDaniel), or a "Howlin' Wolf" (Chester Burnett)—emerges to wail such declarations into nothingness. Similarly, commentators periodically discover that singers generally thought of as wiggling rock 'n' rollers are authentically talented blues men—Chuck Berry and Rufus Thomas, to pull two names out of a hat that contains dozens.

In more sophisticated areas, there were during the thirties and forties several good singers who carried on an authentic blues tradition within the mainstream of developed, instrumental jazz. Chief among them were Jimmy Rushing, with the Count Basie Orchestra, and Joe Turner, whose pianistic associates on recordings included such disparate sensibilities as those of Art Tatum and Pete Johnson.

Modern jazz has had its singers from the beginning, of course, first in the remarkable presence of Sarah Vaughan. But no younger bluesmen were directly associated with a more or less instrumental idiom until the mid-fifties. Then, two such singers appeared: Joe Williams and Ray Charles.

Interestingly, both these men began as ballad singers, and Charles was a particularly subdued stylist in the manner of Nat "King" Cole. Ironically, when they switched to the blues, each of them began using crying, shouting vocal devices that echo the most earthly and archaic country performances.

Joe Williams began singing blues with the re-formed Count Basie Orchestra in 1954. It was collective musicianship that sustained that group, but it was numbers with Joe Williams like "Every Day," and "All Right, Okay, You Win" that gave it hit records.

Half of a recent re-released Verve album, *The Count Basie Band with Joe Williams at Newport* on Verve V/V6-8560 (the reverse is by Dizzy Gillespie), gives examples from 1957 of an enjoyable singer doing four of his specialties. Williams can bend, quaver, and wail a note; he can double, triple, and quadruple it; he can stretch and elaborate one phrase and condense the next. His beat is nearly perfect, well varied, and never monotonous. And the whole performance is delivered in a calculated and stylized rococo. Indeed, if one has ever heard the Joe Williams of the late fifties do the same number twice, he has probably heard every effect, down to the last hoarse grace note, delivered in exactly the same place and the same way. And one is left with the impression of having heard a respectful but mannered imitation of the vocal blues.

More recently, Williams has gone out on his own and has reintroduced balladry, along with a little more spontaneity, into his repertory. It was this Joe Williams who returned to Newport last year, with such company as Clark Terry, Howard McGee, Coleman Hawkins, and Zoot Sims, and whipped the audience into a loudly appreciative (and, some felt, threatening) throng. Victor recorded the event and released it on LPM/LSP-2762. Williams is broadly banal on a broadly banal piece like "Without a Song." The tempo is too fast on "Roll 'em Pete" and the line too cluttered with notes for a vocal version of "Gravy Waltz." But Williams glides along at medium tempo with an unobtrusive, swinging grace on "April in Paris." And (as the audible crowd on the record knew well) he hit his level with what is actually a rock 'n' roll style blues about the current dance steps, "Some of This 'n' Some of That." There is also one slow blues, a beautiful traditional piece by Leroy Carr called "In the Evenin'." Ray Charles has recently recorded the same piece, and the difference between Williams and Charles is the difference between a good performer and a superb popular artist.

Charles is a *popular* artist in the sense that jazzmen no longer are. He has a truly mass audience, and his records sell in the hundreds of thousands. His is a voice of profound esthetic humor, irony, and anguish, functioning in a milieu of grinding triviality and delusion. He discovered his talent when he turned from crooning balladry to blues, and evolved a style strongly influenced by gospel song and expanded by his own skillful, contemporary musicianship. Recordings from those years of discovery are collected on *The Ray Charles Story* (Atlantic

2-900), surely one of the most arresting musical and social documents in the history of American popular art.

Once he had gained his following, Charles seemed perfectly willing to work with any material, in any setting—good and bad and (worst of all) indifferent. His recent ABC-Paramount record, with the tongue-clotting name *Ingredients in a Recipe for Soul* (ABC/S-465), is that sort of mixed bag. But it has an "Old Man River" which, as Charles transmutes it, is a harrowing, breathtaking, and finally beautiful experience. And it has "In the Evenin'," a superb contemporary singer's approach to a classic blues, and, I think, one of the most moving vocal blues performances I have ever heard.

During the past fifteen years there has cropped up the practice of setting words to previously recorded jazz instrumentals. The vocal Lambert, Hendricks, and Bavan (once Lambert, Hendricks, and Ross) have brought the practice to its biggest audience. One can hardly take offense when the point of departure is lightweight material like "Watermelon Man" or "Sack o' Woe," both of which are included on *L., H., & B., at Newport '63* (RCA Victor LPM/LSP-2747). But wording out Lester Young's "One O'Clock Jump" solos, melodies of a profoundly ironic joy-and-pain, as the jabberings of a drunken buffoon is something else again.

A word from my side of the fence about the Victor *Great Scenes from Porgy and Bess* (LSC-2679). Conductor Skitch Henderson wisely chose musicians who understand jazz as the core of his orchestra. And when Leontyne Price goes into jazzlike inflections and embellishments at the end of "Summertime," one is aware of being in for a very special experience. Perhaps one is reminded of the Italian past when an ability to make spontaneous departures was required of a singer. But one might do better to reflect that there is the basis for a truly American musical theatre. We have the instrumentalists, the singers. What we need, alas, is another Gershwin.

Saturday Review, February 15, 1964
Copyright © 1964 Saturday Review, Inc.

Blues Night

By 8:30 P.M the vibrant sound of live music can be heard at the top of a wide staircase on 125th Street near Fifth Avenue that leads down to the Celebrity Club. The piece is a medium blues with the strong flavor of the Southwest and Kansas City, circa 1938.

At the bottom of the stairway, to the right, at the entrance to the club, there is a table that holds a couple of stacks of tickets and a change box. It is recognizably presided over by Victoria Spivey. She has on a tarnished-gold semiformal dress, a matching stole, a pair of high-heel boots, also gold; and she is sporting a new, short-clipped hairdo. The printed tickets on the table in front of her read TRIBUTE TO THE GREAT PIONEER OF THE BLUES, MAMIE SMITH, TO HELP RAISE FUNDS FOR A MONUMENT TO HER ILLUSTRIOUS MEMORY.

Earlier handbills and announcements for the event had said that the evening would feature, among others, Jimmy Rushing, Lucille Hegamin, Hannah Sylvester, Blue Lu Barker, Lillyn Brown, Rosa Henderson, Sam Theard—a heady history of early vocal blues recording and Negro-American cabaret is implied with those names.

Victoria Spivey had a successful blues record in 1929, "Black Snake Blues." She made it when she was sixteen. She had gone to St. Louis from her home in Dallas, her head full of determination to make a record and also full of the conventional warnings about what can happen to unwary young girls at the hands of big-city slickers. When she got there, she walked boldly into the Okeh recording studios, demonstrated her singing and her piano, and soon had a record date for herself.

Miss Spivey also was a leading actress in an early and still celebrated sound film, *Hallelujah*, directed by King Vidor. In good Hollywood fashion, she did not sing in the movie, although almost everyone else in the cast did. She continued recording and singing into the thirties

154

and forties. She and trumpeter-singer Red Allen, then she and guitarist-singer Lonnie Johnson, were successful recording teams for a while. Recently, she has become more active again and made new recordings for Bluesville and for her own Spivey label.

And Mamie Smith. Mamie Smith was the first woman to record a title blues. She did so in 1920—"Crazy Blues." It was an instant success, reportedly selling 75,000 copies in its first month, a phenomenal sale in those days, and it established the recording of blues song for once and all, the line of descent unbroken to this day.

Not that "Crazy Blues" "made" Mamie Smith; she was a highly successful and well-paid performer during the teens of this century. She carried with her a group, Mamie Smith's Jazz Hounds, which, at various times, included such jazzmen as pianist Willie (The Lion) Smith, trumpeters Bubber Miley and Johnny Dunn, tenor saxophonist Coleman Hawkins, and clarinetists Garvin Bushell and Buster Bailey. But when Mamie Smith died in 1946, she was penniless, reportedly deprived of her money by managers and hangers-on. She was buried in an unmarked, triple grave in a Staten Island, N.Y., cemetery.

The female singers on the list—Lucille Hegamin, Hannah Sylvester, Lillyn Brown, and the others—had been able to record their blues, too, once Mamie Smith had made the way.

The Celebrity Club is a large basement room, with a bar the length of its back wall. The main area of the club is taken up by tables and a good-sized dance floor. Against the wall opposite the bar, there is a bandstand that also is good-sized. The side walls are painted with woodland scenes dominated by birch trees, and the various pillars that reach from ceiling to floor around the room are covered in a cloth that looks like birch bark. The lighting in the club is a fairly dim amber or red. The public-address system seems to have its somewhat harsh speakers planted everywhere.

The music one is hearing is indeed southwestern, circa 1938, for it is provided by Buddy Tate's band, a small but often highly spirited ensemble employing two reeds, trumpet, and trombone, plus guitar, electric bass, and drums.

Tate is a fixture at the club. When he isn't playing conventional ballads from conventional stock arrangements for conventional dancing, he may take out his own book of originals and play a blues or a medium- or up-tempo jump tune. Most of these are in good southwestern style, an honorable and, with Tate's group, still robust tradition. Some of these arrangements also make effective use of the band, getting a full sound from a spare instrumentation. This evening, however, Tate is in Toronto with his fellow ex-Basieite, trumpeter Buck Clayton. Reed man Rudy Rutherford stands in his place on the Celebrity Club bandstand.

By this early hour, there are about fifty people scattered around the room at tables. Most of them are the middle-aged jazz fans of New York. And several are long-standing record collectors. Some are thereby staggeringly erudite in discography, and they do invaluable work in the field. Some are deeply responsive to music. But others are jazz antiquarians—or they are simply record antiquarians, more interested in master and take numbers than in vocal or instrumental numbers.

At the door, Mr. and Mrs. Zutty Singleton arrive, greet Miss Spivey, and take their places with a group of friends at one of the larger tables. Trombonist Dickie Wells enters, looking quite young this evening. At almost every entrance there are shouted greetings that burst across the room, accompanied by robust waves of arms and underlined by warm chuckles.

As "Stardust" finishes, Wells takes his place on the stand beside the band's trombonist, Eli Robinson. Ah, he is here to play! Rutherford signals " 'A' Train," and Wells begins in his really beautiful but firm lyricism.

No one seems to be paying much attention to the music now. The audience is waiting for the blues queens and kings, who are seated to the left of the bandstand at a long table, a row of gray heads and interesting, lively faces, nodding from time to time to the music and chatting quietly. Nearly everyone in the room glances at the long table from time to time, in curiosity and expectation.

Directly across from the guests of honor, on the opposite side of the bandstand, there is a young man fascinated not only by them but by the fact that he is in New York listening to live jazz played by American musicians. His name is Karlheinz Kesten, a pianist and the secretary of the Hot Club of Iserlohn, Germany. His presence has a lot to do with the reason for this unusual benefit.

Last fall a group of American blues singers visited Germany on a tour arranged by producer and critic Horst Lippmann. They included Miss Spivey, Rushing, Big Joe Williams, Muddy Waters, and Lonnie Johnson, among others. Miss Spivey met Gunter Boas and his wife, Lore, a German couple whose interest in the blues goes back many years and who are members of the Hot Club of Iserlohn.

Inevitably, the three spoke of Mamie Smith. The Boases were shocked to discover she was buried in an unmarked grave. They wanted to do something about it. In late November they held a benefit concert in Germany with six groups, raised some money, and obtained a tombstone for Miss Smith. The Hamburg-American Steamship Line agreed to transport the stone to the States free of charge, and appropriately they used the SS *Iserlohn*. There was a ceremony when the ship departed, including music by musician members of the Iserlohn club. Kesten made the trip with the headstone.

The Inserlohn docked at New Orleans, and although customs allowed the stone to pass through free, there was a charge for duty, a charge for express to get it to New York City, and a charge, the highest of all, to have Mamie Smith's remains moved from the three-level grave to a plot of her own. Miss Spivey and Lennie Kunstadt decided to hold a benefit on this side of the water to try to raise the additional money, and the Celebrity Club management donated a Monday evening.

There are now about one hundred people at the tables and bar, and there are new arrivals on the bandstand, too. Trumpeter Pat Jenkins takes his place as clarinetist Tony Parenti arrives, shouts a greeting toward the bandstand, and takes his seat with a couple of friends at a nearby table. The rumor that Rushing is here hurries across the room.

The band is into a medium blues again. Jenkins finishes his solo, and then it is Rutherford. He stands there, knees bent, in a neat, conservative blue suit, looking as polished and as prosperous and almost as complacent as a stockbroker who lives quietly in the suburbs and seldom goes out in the evening. Yet he is saying things with his horn that are full of terror and love and joy and beauty. That is the way of the blues if you can play them, and Rutherford can play them. Wells musically instructs the band, setting a riff figure behind Rutherford, and the rest of the players fall in immediately.

It is 10:20 now, and suddenly a familiar voice fills the room, ringing through the loudspeakers: "I want a little girl. . . ." The crowd looks up and there is Rushing, standing in front of the bandstand, holding a hand microphone, a slight, sly smile on his face. He is a big presence of warm and easy charm. Wells starts to improvise behind him now, and suddenly it is 1939, not in a nostalgic and half-realized echo but almost in reality—one half expects to hear a Lester Young solo at the end of Rushing's chorus. As he finishes, there are shouts and loud applause. And then, of course, he goes into a blues: "She's little and low and built up from the ground. . . ."

Seven choruses later the applause is louder still, and then the emcee of the evening, Boots Marshall, is at the microphone proclaiming, "We want you to enjoy yourselves and make yourselves at home; we've got a lot of stars to come. . . ."

At the back of the room Horst Lippmann has entered with his friend, guitarist Attila Zoller. They take their places at the bar where they are greeted by Kunstadt and introduced to several patrons.

The band begins another instrumental blues on a heavy boogie-woogie bass figure. Rutherford is playing clarinet now; he has a big tone. There are three couples dancing, executing a kind of becalmed businessman's Lindy.

"I came to sign up some people for another blues festival for next year in Germany," Lippmann is explaining to a new acquaintance at the bar, as a sudden burst of laughter rises from a nearby back table.

Danny Barker is at the entrance now, his guitar in one hand and his wife, Blue Lu Barker, by his side.

"Danny! Man! What on earth. . . . Where did you get that hair? When did you start wearing that thing?" There is broad laughter from Barker and a friend at the bar over the toupee he is sporting, and Barker protests innocently about "my rug."

It is obviously going to be a long evening, and a couple of unhardy souls give up and head for the front door.

At the bar, several heads turn to note the somewhat unexpected presence of composer-pianist Tadd Dameron.

The band has reassembled now, and, with all the sitting in, it is almost a different group—it is certainly a larger one. The players are laying down some Kansas City-style riffs that probably remind Dameron of his youth and his days with the Harlan Leonard Band.

As the piece ends, emcee Marshall starts acclaiming "that wonderful lady who is responsible for what goes on here tonight, Miss Victoria Spivey. . . ." She marches forward to acknowledge the applause. At least half the room expects her to sing, but suddenly she is gone, and Marshall is doing a fast and loud "Just One of Those Things." ("A trip to the moon on gossamer wings" on *blues* night?)

Dameron has slipped in at the piano now, and Marshall begins to introduce the guests of the evening at the table of honor to his right. "A young lady that can still make high C, Miss Rosa Henderson." She bows from her seat at the table. So does Hannah Sylvester, another who first recorded her blues in the twenties. The crowd is surprised at this, for most of the audience had expected her to sing. Miss Sylvester had recorded again recently, after all, for Bluesville and Spivey records.

Then Lillyn Brown, a woman of nearly white-haired dignity is at the microphone.

"You won't believe this," remarks the venerable actor Leigh Whipper to a young acquaintance standing in the rear of the hall, "but she is seventy-nine years old."

Miss Brown is speaking with clear and fluent energy about how she came to write one of her numbers "a few years ago," and then she is into it, "I'm Blue and Rockin'." Her voice is as big and ringingly precise as that of a woman of thirty, with no aging elderly vibrato or cloudiness. And her musical drive matches its clarity.

As the audience shows its delight after her last verse, Miss Brown seems equally delighted. "I have a little short one now," she says. She was one of the first to follow Mamie Smith on records, but she is not trading on her past tonight—she is singing here and now:

> *If you want me to love you,*
> *Please don't make me cry.*
> *If you want me to love you,*
> *Please don't make me cry.*
> *'Cause if you make me cry, baby,*
> *My love just seems to die.*

As she leaves to return to her table, the audience is again smiling broadly over its applause. And the musicians are smiling perhaps broadest of all.

"Look," says a middle-aged fan at a side table, "that's Louis Metcalf on trumpet sitting in now."

The continuity of guest performers continues. Blue Lu Barker is standing front and center of the bandstand in a blue dress. Danny Barker, looking rather mild in contrast, is on her left, his right foot propped on a chair and his guitar resting across his knee. Suddenly neither of the Barkers seem mild, for they have gone into "Hot Dog! That Made Him Mad!"

During the applause at the end, half the crowd seems humorously bracing itself for their best-known number—and they anticipate correctly. It is, according to Danny's announcement "by very special request," "Don't You Feel My Leg." Broad laughter shatters Lu's opening verses.

Then comes Sam Theard ("I'm a sick comic, you know—sick of being out of work"), who has been doing comedy and songs at least since the twenties, when he started in his native New Orleans, but who is probably best known for having written "I'll Be Glad When You're Dead, You Rascal You" and "Let the Good Times Roll."

"Gimme that E-flat arpeggio," he is tossing over his shoulder in Dameron's general direction. "Ah, that's nice. Do it again."

"I'll be glad when you're dead, you rascal you . . ." he sings, and then goes into an energetic, acrobatic dance across the floor in movements that seem unlikely in the neat, tan, tweed suit he is wearing.

Then clarinetist Parenti. By invitation he borrows Rutherford's instrument to play a slow clarinet blues for the crowd.

"How does he sound to you, compared to me?" Rutherford asks a fan standing to the left of the dance floor.

"Your sound is fuller, I think. But, you know, all of those New Orleans clarinetists have a certain lyric thing. I don't know how to describe it exactly, but they all have it."

"Well you see I asked you because he is using my instrument. But I learned from him too, so . . ."

Parenti's sound is still billowing across the room as a somewhat disappointed patron consults Miss Spivey near the door. "Victoria, Queen, I didn't come here just to watch you take up money for Mamie Smith or take bows," he says with a sort of half-smile. "I came here to hear you sing."

"Well." She looks up, pausing. "My guests come first." Then with a slight laugh: "And we're so far behind now, I may not get to sing at that."

It was nearly 2 A.M. when Miss Spivey finally did sing. By then she had passed out about two hundred admission tickets at the door.

John Bubbles of the old Buck and Bubbles vaudeville team had come by, spoken a song in his recitative style, and danced charmingly.

Lucille Hegamin, the first to record a blues after Mamie Smith, had sung "He May Be Your Man (but He Comes to See Me Sometimes)."

Maxine Sullivan had arrived and had sung her extended version of "St. Louis Blues" with a voice still sounding like 1940 and with several encouragements to the band members to solo between her verses.

Rushing had come back.

And others had sung and reminisced.

When Victoria Spivey stood up at the mike, she did two numbers, and one of them was "Black Snake Blues." As she started it, about half the room probably felt that, for the time being at least, all was right with the world.

Down Beat, April 9, 1964

Early MJQ:

It would not be inaccurate to say that the Modern Jazz Quartet was formed when its members were the rhythm section of Dizzy Gillespie's 1946–48 big band, and actually Milt Jackson, John Lewis, and Kenny Clarke, along with Al Jackson on bass and Chano Pozo on bongos made some sides in about 1948 for an obscure label called "Sensation." But the real beginning of the Quartet as such came in August, 1951, when Jackson, Lewis, Ray Brown, and Clarke assembled for a session as the Milt Jackson Quartet for Dizzy Gillespie's Dee Gee records. They decided they liked playing together very much and wanted to continue to. Percy Heath came in for Ray Brown and a coöperative group was formed with no single man as the leader, but with John Lewis soon taking over as "musical director" out of mutual agreement. Success was gradual, and several of the players took jobs with other leaders while interest in them as a group gradually began to build.

Here, I will confine my comments and my examples to some of the pieces on the first few record dates they did as the Modern Jazz Quartet, pieces that first revealed the character, the potential, and the limitations of the music to come.

The Modern Jazz Quartet started at the very best place to start, as a group of fine jazz players and improvisors, and, as with Ellington's orchestra, its achievements had as much to do with the developing talents of its membership as of its leadership. The group could probably have made first-rate jazz music simply by improvising on blues, jazz standards, and medium and slow ballads. Those earliest records show the group doing just that, and on the surface, the outstanding member was Milt Jackson.

Jackson's rather cold instrument entered jazz warmly of course when

Louis Armstrong liked what he had heard a drummer named Lionel Hampton play on a vibraphone in a recording studio, and encouraged him. Jackson, himself, has superb natural equipment. His excellent ear led him to absorb the rhythmic, harmonic, and melodic language of modern jazz during the forties. Early, he also showed ideas of his own, ideas that were not merely a matter of transferring Parker's saxophone lines or Dizzy Gillespie's phrases to his own instrument. In spite of his apparently cold instrument, he usually projects direct and immediate feeling. With the quartet, the resourcefulness of his playing—in color, dynamics, and range and refinement of feeling—has increased remarkably.

John Lewis' approach to the piano is usually either orchestral or hornlike. His knowing discreet use of his talent as a pianist is an example of careful craftsmanship, and of almost exemplary acknowledgment of his limitations and a willingness to create within them. It has probably taken some effort for a player whose style is apparently introverted by nature to learn to communicate feeling as Lewis does. In its modest emotional tone Lewis' piano is therefore an excellent contrast to Jackson's generous extraversion, but in its way it is no less strong.

In Kenny Clarke, the group had one of the best drummers in jazz; his impeccably smooth yet inspirationally commenting accompaniment can make improvisation seem so easy—perhaps even to the improvisor. However, Connie Kay has been more adept at integrating his drumming with the group textures and forms that were emerging. Bassist Percy Heath has virtually come of age musically in meeting the standards of the Quartet.

As I say, a group of fine players. You can hear that on what are still two of their best recorded performances, "Ralph's New Blues" and "Softly, As In A Morning Sunrise." But there is more to hear on those performances than that. One thing is the accompaniments Lewis improvises behind Jackson's solos. They are not the percussively delivered chord patterns we are used to in most piano accompaniments nowadays. On the "Blues," Lewis begins behind Jackson with a version of the theme that the group has just stated, and then lets it lead him into an original, spontaneous countermelody which beautifully complements Jackson's lines.

Later, at exactly the right moment, Jackson similarly enters behind Lewis' solo—getting a wonderful flutelike sound from his vibraphone, incidentally. Of course, the basis for what Lewis does on "Morning Sunrise" is in the jazz tradition. He is obviously taking the brief repetitive, rhythmic phrases, the "riff" accompaniments from earlier jazz styles, and elaborating them into more complex counterlines. Coming from the materials of earlier styles, these lines also contrast with Jackson rhythmically for they are based on the quarter-note rhythmic ideas that were a part of Armstrong's style, and which we all know quite readily from "swing music," whereas Jackson's rhythm is most often in the eighth-note style of modern jazz. Such things give group-texture, and they give continuity, organization, and larger form to an improvised performance. They also involve the collective, polyphonic improvising that can be so exciting in jazz—or in any music.

Such an effect of continuity and form can come from simple means. On "But Not For Me" there is the fact that Jackson (his sometime sentimental streak—that, for me, is very evident in things like the "Gershwin Medley"—in tow) begins his improvising alone, unaccompanied. The tension and suspense of this truly *solo* improvising is soon relieved by Heath's entrance behind Jackson, and, as this duo builds a different kind of tension, Clarke and Lewis soon make a reassuring appearance behind them.

However, there is another aspect of Lewis' talent and his approach to polyphony that appears—very briefly at its worst and later at its best— on these recordings. On "Morning Sunrise," there is a short introduction, obviously borrowed from European baroque music; it is brief, gratuitous, pointless—and to some it may even seem pretentious. However, "Concord" also owes a debt to baroque music, but the nature of the debt and the nature of the results are quite different. It is a fugue, but its kind of borrowing is not pointless.

In itself, a jazzy quasi-fugue would mean nothing. As a matter of fact, in the pseudo-jazz that is always around (in both arty and popularized versions) the fugue stunt is old stuff. The Quartet's first fugue called "Versailles" was a failure, I think. As Max Harrison has indicated, it reminded one of Bach and of the conservatory practice room; it was a sort of exercise. But on "Concord" both the writing and the group response are obviously finding their way to something rather different and more important, a real, improvisational jazz-fugue. As a matter of fact, the written basis of "Concord" consisted of only eight measures of music; the rest was improvised. The baroque language is being transformed and assimilated. The performance is also excellent evidence of Connie Kay's adaptation to the group, for one of the contrapuntal lines in this fugue is sometimes passed back and forth between Heath's bass line and Kay's spontaneous percussion.

"The Queen's Fancy" is another example, a more limited and I think less successful one, of borrowing, in this case from the Renaissance English composer Giles Farnby. Although he cannot always succeed at it, of course, John Lewis simply *finds* himself with baroque forms, but there would be nothing remarkable, significant, or even interesting about that fact if he did not go further. Like all jazzmen, Lewis borrows whatever appeals to his own creative impulse and whatever suits his own sensibilities. But like the best jazzmen, he borrows in order to create and he transmutes what he borrows into music with an impetus of its own. There is nothing of the pastiche in the Quartet's later fugues, and "Concord" was the first to show that this would be so.

"Django" is probably John Lewis' and the Quartet's finest achievement in both written composition and improvised form. It is, of course, a funeral piece for Django Rinehardt, the French-gypsy guitarist-turned-jazzman. The theme seems to imply all that: an elegy that is French, gypsy, and jazz. The chord sequence for the improvising makes a new section since it is not derived from the them, by the way. But when a performance of "Django" unfolds, we see that something else was in Lewis' mind—the tradition of consolation and rejoicing at death that was a part of New Orleans culture and of early jazz. A simple, traditional blues bass figure (it was used in King Oliver's "Snag It") appears during the first improvised choruses as a countermotif, a countermovement of consolation and a continuation of life. As it reappears, it converts the players from their pensive introspection, and Lewis even hits on another blues countermotif to accompany it. Gradually there is a kind of emotional resolution between these opposite moods as the theme reenters at the end.

The delicate movement and range of "Django" is an achievement in itself; its melodies and motifs are excellent; and the act of holding all these opposites together is a real achievement both for Lewis and for the players. "Django" also has that quality mandatory in a jazz piece of being able to inspire good solos. As a matter of fact, as the Quartet plays "Django" today, the improvising and its emotional tone is quite different from the early recording, but the flexible structure of "Django" is still there.

These early Modern Jazz Quartet records announced the imminent maturity of an important composer and of an important group. Personally, I have been hearing these performances for some time now, and I often still find new details in them. There is Kenny Clarke's switch from cymbals to brushes on his snare drum on "Delaunay's

Dilemma," and its immediate effect on the other players. There is, again, the rhythmic contrast of Lewis' playing behind Jackson on that same piece. There is the beauty and musical logic of Jackson's improvised melody in the second chorus of "Milano." There is the appropriate way Jackson bursts into *invention* immediately in his section of "La Ronde," not bothering with a literal statement or even a paraphrase of the theme. There is the fact that Lewis picks a fast tempo for his section of that piece, although he is no finger-virtuoso as a pianist—and that he makes something of it. And there is the interplay of Lewis and Jackson on their interlude in Clarke's otherwise not entirely successful section of "La Ronde." And there is Jackson's demonstration on some of the slow pieces that the change of a couple of notes or the shift of a few accents and bit of emphasis here and there by a sensitive player can make a sentimental tin pan alley ditty seem melody sublime.

But, as I say, you *begin* with good players.

Kulchur, 1965

Videotaping with Duke

The final rundown and television taping of the show was scheduled for 1 P.M. No one was late. No one, that is, except the man who was supposed to bring Duke Ellington's suit, and he held things up considerably.

By 12:50 P.M. Ellington himself was moving down the hall toward WNEW-TV Studio 1. Inside, technicians were moving lights and cameras and chatting. And musicians were chatting, mostly, as usual, on the quantity and quality of last night's sleep. Tom Whaley, the Ellington orchestra's staff copyist of many years, was present, looking distinguished and carrying a home-movie camera, which he put to frequent use during the afternoon. Billy Strayhorn arrived, loaded down with a beige raincoat and the morning *Times.* Johnny Hodges was strolling around, occasionally twirling the instrument strap that hung at his neck.

The orchestra's chairs were set up, saxes on a raised platform to the left, brass similarly to the right, with Ellington's piano, Sam Woodyard's drums, and Major Holley's bass centered to the rear. The setup made a kind of inverted U, and it would allow the cameras to move in close to the sections and the individual players. Producer Robert Herridge and director Arnee Nocks had five cameras on the floor.

Cootie Williams arrived as several of the brass men were casually taking their places at music stands. But the milling around hadn't stopped yet. Nat Hentoff was talking with Harry Carney near the saxophones' platform. And Herridge was on the studio floor now, inconspicuous except for his clothes—a rough blue denim shirt, a pair of rumpled khaki trousers, and yellow work shoes.

As the early proprietor of *Camera 3*, an experimental television show done by the New York station of the Columbia Broadcasting System, WCBS-TV, Herridge had sought to discover what things would come across effectively on the small television screen and how they could be made more effective. He often presented jazz on *Camera 3*.

Subsequently, as producer of *The Lively Arts* for CBS, Herridge was responsible, with technical advisers Whitney Balliett and Hentoff, for the show called "The Sound of Jazz," a program that had featured Count Basie, Thelonious Monk, Red Allen, Billie Holiday, Pee Wee Russell, Jimmy Rushing, and Gerry Mulligan, among others. Herridge had become convinced that the best presentation of jazz was informal, with a minimum of comment and a close concentration by the cameras on the deep involvement of the musicians as they played—physical involvement that manifested psychological involvement as well.

Later, for CBS syndication to local outlets, the *Robert Herridge Theater* offered a program by Miles Davis with an orchestra led by Gil Evans, a program featuring Ben Webster and Ahmad Jamal, and a ballet on "Frankie and Johnny" for Melissa Hayden with music by Charlie Mingus and featuring Jimmy Rushing.

Currently, Herridge is taping a group of shows, some drama and some musical, for New York presentation—and then for national syndication—on WNEW-TV, the New York City television outlet of the Metromedia Corporation. One of these was to be an hour by Ellington, to be shown Sept. 2 and 6. Again, Hentoff was serving as technical adviser, and one of his first acts was to persuade Herridge and director Nocks to have the Ellington orchestra's second-in-command, Strayhorn, in the engineering booth. Strayhorn would give specific musical cues, signals on what was happening and about to happen, throughout the taping, these to be relayed by headphones on the studio floor.

Things were beginning to settle down on the studio floor. One of the men was attaching a typed sheet of instructions to the side of his camera. A piano tuner was doing a final checking of the concert grand that Ellington was to use. Ellington was not on the floor now, but suddenly Harry Carney's baritone sound cut through the buzz of the room, and Cootie was warming up (using his plunger, by the way, even for this), playing "From Here to Eternity."

Around these two sounds the Ellington orchestra gathered.

At 1:15 P.M., one of the trombonists told a joke that set the whole brass platform laughing. Over in a corner Hentoff explained to a friend that a few weeks before there had been some trouble in getting to Ellington, that is, to get through to him via agents and managers, and to get him to sit down and discuss a purely instrumental hour's presentation of his music for television. Ellington had also agreed, but with some apparent reservations, that the group could dress informally for the show. "All right," he said "the men can wear their own suits, but we'll bring the new uniforms along just in case."

The show was to begin with a full performance of "Take the 'A' Train," featuring Williams. Then four separate musical sections were to follow. And the idea this afternoon was to take things singly, to run through one section at a time and then tape it.

In the first portion would be the current Ellington medley of three of the best early Ellington-Bubber Miley pieces, "Black and Tan Fantasy," "Creole Love Song," and "The Mooche," followed by a version of "The Opener," with solos by Paul Gonsalves, Buster Cooper, and Cat Anderson. In the second section, there would be a version of the extended "Tone Parallel to Harlem."

The third section would be taped last, since its length was the most flexible. It was to include a piece Ellington worked up with the orchestra at the previous day's rehearsal, which he punningly titled "Metromedia," followed by "Jam with Sam," both featuring extended soloing. Finally, they would go back to run down and tape the third section with two Hodges features, "Passion Flower" and "Things Ain't What They Used to Be," followed by the Ellington feature "Kinda Dukish" leading into "Rockin' in Rhythm."

"Danny, baby, up on the lights!" a man in a tweed hat shouted. Stagehands had drawn a pale blue curtain backdrop around three sides of the studio and suddenly everything looked orderly, bright, and vaguely unreal.

". . . just as soon as Duke finishes shaving. . . ." The words drifted up in reply from somewhere in the crowd.

"Fellas in the band"—it was Nocks, the director, now on the floor in the center of things—"we'd like you to be dressed the way you're going to be when we tape. We want to see about the lighting and so forth."

To his left someone was checking the sound on Ellington's voice microphone. "Yeah, I hear you now."

And then Ellington was back in the studio, temporarily in a tan jacket and a blue knit sports shirt and no tie. (So they were still waiting for his suit.) Herridge was leaning over the piano with Tom Whaley at his side. Whaley sat down to roll out an old sentimental ballad to everyone's amusement. Then Strayhorn sat on the piano bench and did the same ballad with some fine, archaic tremolos.

Then a characteristic descending run of notes announced that Ellington himself was now at the keyboard.

The lights went down, and the tension went up. A camera man shouted, "Arty, baby . . ." and a light man heard, "Stand by with me, Danny. I'll cue you."

Ellington started to improvise on the first eight bars of " 'A' Train." Woodyard came in under him. The lights came up quickly as the main camera backed away, taking the whole band. Suddenly over the loudspeaker, a voice from the control room shouted, "Hold it, Duke! Hold it."

"I wasn't rehearsing," he answered calmly. "Is this mike on? You'd better test it."

There was a conference in the center of the floor on lights and camera movements. . . . "You kill the lights except on Duke. He plays. Then you bring them up fast when the band comes in. At the same time, the camera moves back fast to take in everybody."

In the background of all this, Ellington was striking a slow, broodingly impressionistic series of piano chords.

Then: "Okay, fellows. Stand by. Duke, stand by, please."

Everything went as it was supposed to. Ellington approached the finish of his introduction, the lights came up, and the camera backed away to take in the whole band. Williams stepped to the center for his solo. His sound had a burred edge even on open horn. He began in a kind of paraphrase tribute to Ray Nance's old " 'A' Train" solo and then went off on his own. The saxes sounded fine. Williams played his darting coda.

Then the urbane Ellington faced his voice microphone and began to announce the medley of early pieces. He didn't get far—"Hold it, hold it. We lost a light. And if he steps up that way for his solo, he's in the way of the camera."

Another conference of technicians.

In the control room, one monitor screen showed a peaceful shot of Ellington, his head on his arms, resting across the top of the piano.

They began it again, and during the opening chorus of " 'A' Train," the superimposed titled flipped by: A PORTRAIT IN MUSIC/DUKE ELLINGTON AND HIS ORCHESTRA.

"Beautiful opening!" somebody said. Nocks was crosscutting from one camera that was close up on Williams to another trained on the saxes, as the players exchanged phrases. Nocks spoke firmly to an assistant, who in turn spoke to the camera men on the floor through their headsets: "Stand by Camera one! Take one! Stand by three. Take three!" Then he instructed the lighting director, who in turn spoke to his men on the floor through phones. And to the sound man, who instructed his men on the mikes and the booms on the floor. In the control room, it seemed a finely controlled roar of shouts and orders. But none of this technical turmoil reached the players, and the show was coming out orderly on the monitor screen.

Williams began the "Black and Tan-Creole Love Song-Mooche" medley. Then Rolf Ericson came in, also plunger-style. Then Russell Procope on clarinet. All five cameras were trained on him from different angles: his face, his embouchure, his fingers . . . medium shot, full length. Nocks cued the various angles as his solo unfolded. Then there were three clarinets on "The Mooche"—Procope, Carney, and Jimmy Hamilton. ("Hal, are they all on the mike?") Then Lawrence Brown, giving his own kind of lyric elegance to the current role as the orchestra's plunger trombonist. Then Williams ended it, with the clarinets holding a long, impassioned note under him.

"He's going back pretty far for those pieces," someone remarked quietly on the sidelines.

"Well, that's basic American music, man. What else could be? Charles Ives?"

"The Opener"—and Gonsalves, Cooper, and Anderson stepped to the center for swift solos.

So they had run through the opening and the first section.

Ellington stepped over to consult with Cooper about a certain point in "The Opener." Williams, somewhat aloof so far this day, joined in with a point about a change of key.

"Any problems?" a late arrival asked Hentoff.

"No, these men are all pros," he said.

No one seemed to be in charge half the time, and no one needed to be.

"Are we having an across-the-street break?" somebody asked, as if to contradict Hentoff.

"Lock the doors!" he got in mock answer from across the room.

Whaley was at the keyboard again, joined this time by Hamilton and Hodges. Sound men and camera men were discussing what they had seen so far and hoped to capture soon during the actual taping. Ellington and Herridge were in a conference in a corner. Woodyard approached a table that held an endless and constantly renewed supply of coffee and pastries. He looked rather sad when he couldn't find a plain glass of cold water.

Ellington's suit still had not arrived. Well, why not run down the second section now, and then tape both in succession later?

"Let's go! On the stand fellows!"

Soon Ellington was speaking into the rehearsal camera with a sly half-smile: "And now Harlem, or rather our 'Tone Parallel to Harlem.' . . . Harlem is very close to us. . . . A lot of nice people live there. Oh, some naughty people too. But Harlem is such a nice place it even has a minister for congressman. . . . We hear it late one Saturday night and early Sunday morning. We start this by having Cootie Williams pronounce the word 'Harlem' on his trumpet."

Williams picked it up and then began to pass the phrase to the whole brass section. Ellington was at the center of the orchestra, conducting with both arms. Then Gonsalves was soloing, and Ellington held a mike toward his horn. Woodyard, alert to the tricky tempo changes, whipped up the "Latin" section. Then Lawrence Brown, with a felt mute on his horn, stated the Sunday morning theme. Then Procope, Hamilton, and Carney, all on clarinets, wove a variation on it.

"I'm sorry, I'm sorry. Hold it, Duke. Cut!"

There was a pause, as Ellington asked, "What letter is that?" The technicians settled their problems in a moment.

"Duke, can we go back to Lawrence Brown's trombone solo?" Yes. (They learned this score too in the previous day's rehearsal it seems.)

"Yeah, what letter is that?" Ellington asked again.

Brown stood up again and restated his theme. Again the clarinets recomposed it. As they played, Ellington stood at the center, apparently examining a fingernail. Then he was waving and gesturing the group into the finale. Left arm, right arm, left arm, right. Both arms.

"Take five!"

It wasn't exactly a break for everyone, although several players headed for the hall and the bank of telephones against a back wall. There were various conferences about camera angles, lighting positions, and the rest. To the rear of the studio, Whaley took some kidding about his movie camera: "In case their tape doesn't come out, you can always sell them what you're getting, I suppose?"

"You know I took some wonderful stuff on the set when we were working on *Paris Blues*," Whaley said. "And the developer sent back some movies of a kid's birthday party. I wrote and wrote but never did get my film back."

Around the room one could hear: "They're going to take longer than they planned at this."

"When do you think they'll wrap it up?"

"Do you know it's Duke's birthday today?"

"Hey, Duke's clothes came! Now we'll move!"

Soon, Ellington entered in a blue suit, light television blue shirt, dark blue tie, and blue suede shoes.

"Stand by, fellows! From the top of the show!"

Nocks was on the floor for a final word with the camera men.

"Let's make this one——"

"Hold your shot. Is Duke ready?"

"Hal, let us know when——"

"Get ready—wait one second."

"Okay, Arnee? Okay, roll the tape."

Ellington's introduction approaches its end. The camera quickly pulls back.

No lights.

"Dammit!"

"Okay, again. Fade 'em down. Cue, Duke."

The taping brought the music fully to life; no one was coasting now. On the medley, the cameras caught Lawrence Brown in fine detail. One had the movement of his face muscles. Another, his hands, manipulating plunger and slide. Another, the slight but telling movements of his body in time with his phrases.

On "The Opener," Gonsalves croached. Cooper's embouchure worked rapidly. And Cat Anderson was caught by one camera in laughing amusement at his own high-pitched ending, the moment after he finished his solo.

"Beautiful ending!" someone shouted.

"There was only one little thing I didn't like in the whole segment." It was Herridge's voice; he didn't go on to say what.

Inside the studio, the assemblage was still subdued and quiet until someone shouted, "Take five!"

It seemed considerably less than five minutes later when the shout went up in the hall outside the studio door, "Okay, everybody! We're gonna tape 'Harlem' now!"

The musicians reentered the studio and moved toward the stands.

Ellington sat in a spotlight at the center of the group, awaiting his cue that the tape was running. He joked mildly with the band under his breath. Then on his cue, he did his speech about Harlem.

Two cameras catch Cootie's opening pronouncement: "*Har*-lem. *Har*-lem. . . ."

One was suddenly aware of the careful attention to sound the crew was giving this show, a quite unusual thing for television, even on a musical program. There were seven mikes for the music alone.

Ellington conducted with no score, of course, encouraging, quieting, cuing. Woodyard's hard tom-tom produced a strong "Yeah!" from the leader.

Then, as the lyric Sunday morning theme was unfolded, first by Brown and then by the clarinets, one camera caught Ellington, suddenly in repose, with his head resting on his arms across the piano. The Duke won't be in church this morning; he overslept.

At the end, a simple "Okay, Duke," quietly spoken through the loudspeaker, hardly gave an indication of how pleased men in the control room were with the sequence.

"Every shot came off right," Hentoff remarked, smiling, on entering the studio.

At 4:35 P.M. the piano tuner had finished rechecking the instrument, and there was a cry of "Okay, fellows, let's run through the final section now."

Into the cold camera, Ellington explained that "Passion Flower" featured Johnny Hodges, and that Robert Herridge felt that the meaning of a "passion flower" was better experienced than explained. Then he gestured to his right and turned. And saw no Hodges.

"Where are you going to be?"

"Well, I'm over here."

"Oh."

As Hodges segued from "Passion Flower" into "Things Ain't What They Used to Be," Whaley sat in one corner copying out some parts for the new piece, "Metro-media."

When they finished "Rockin' in Rhythm," an inside joke sent up a roar from the orchestra. As it died down, Nocks announced loudly, "Please be in your seats in exactly one hour. Then we will tape this section, time what we have, and then do the third section."

About ten minutes later, most of the musicians had left to eat supper. But Anderson was still around, watching the tape playback on a monitor in the studio. He laughed again at his own ending to "The Opener" and at the shot of himself looking surprised.

"This is even better than the show we did in England," he said. "Of course, they only used three cameras."

"Hey, there's a camera showing behind Cootie in that shot!"

"Herridge doesn't care. He wants it informal, and he doesn't see any sense in pretending to the viewer that there aren't cameras around. So if one camera picks up another, what about it?"

Ellington watched the playbacks on another monitor, seated in a chair in the director's booth. His face was sober and did not give away his feelings much. Behind him, a semicircle of camera men and light men were more vocal.

"Hey, look at that shot George got!"

"Eddie, did you see that!"

"That's good, that's good. . . ."

"Sure I got the cue right. I'm old enough to know that piece for a long time."

By 6:15 P.M. everyone was back, feeling cheery and well fed. "Rockin' in Rhythm" did rock, and they finished the whole show by 8.

Then there was a birthday party.

"How old am I—fifty-five?" Ellington asked, smiling, and lopping off ten years.

It was a surprise party; yet it probably surprised no one. Still, it was not the sort of thing one often sees in a television studio.

But then, an hour of music by a great jazz orchestra, carefully produced, well photographed, and well recorded, is not the sort of thing one often sees in a television studio, either.

Down Beat, August 27, 1964

In Praise of Jack Teagarden

The audience might be composed of the sort of avid fans who would applaud no matter what he played. Or it might be only partly attentive. In either case he seemed to play and sing with complete relaxation and professional poise. Yet if you watched his quietly genial face closely, you might see a fleeting frown or a quick downward turn at the corners of his mouth that would let you know that he hadn't been quite satisfied with what he had just done, that the last solo hadn't come off as well as he had wanted it to.

Jack Teagarden (who died on January 15 in New Orleans) was a professional jazz musician for more than forty years, performing night after night in situations that were sometimes trying or downright harassing. And, by the nature of his craft, he had to extemporize at least some of his music each time he undertook to play it. Yet, on occasion, he remained capable of exacting self-criticism.

Teagarden was one of those exceptional musicians who, by the late twenties, perceived not only what jazz had achieved, but also which part of that achievement seemed most worth preserving and what such music might best undertake next. This means that Teagarden belongs with Louis Armstrong (who towers above the rest), with Bix Beiderbecke, with Earl Hines, with Coleman Hawkins, in the advanced guard of the period. (Sidney Bechet belongs with them, too, yet Bechet, as Ernest Ansermet pointed out at the time, was already a major figure by 1919.) All these men were very good instrumentalists; each in his way knew his instrument as many of his important predecessors in jazz had not known theirs. And Teagarden was a superb trombonist by almost any standard. Teagarden shares with Jimmy Harrison (and possibly Dickie Wells and Miff Mole as well) the distinction of having lifted the trombone from its mournfully effective, sometimes clownish percussive-harmonic role at the bottom of the Dixieland ensemble and raised it to the level of a subtle, flexible melodic voice in jazz. Yet each of these men, certainly Teagarden and Harrison, found his way for himself, independently of the others.

Weldon Leo Teagarden was born in Vernon, Texas, in 1905. His parents were both of German ancestry (and apparently not with any American Indian ancestry as is sometimes said), and both were musical. So were and are their other children: trumpeter Charlie, drummer Clois, and pianist Norma. Jack began piano at five; then he had some lessons on the baritone horn; and finally his father presented him with a trombone. He was playing professional jobs by 1920, when his family was living in Oklahoma City, and he was already developing the largely self-discovered trombone technique that he retained all his life. He spent the early twenties barnstorming through Oklahoma, New Mexico, Texas, and northern Mexico with various dance groups, moving as far away as Kansas City in 1924.

Three years later he was in New York. The word was out among jazz-men about his abilities. He continued of necessity to work with the sort of semicommercial orchestras that were to earn him his bread and butter until the late thirties—groups like Sam Lanin's and Roger Wolfe Kahn's. With drummer Ben Pollack's orchestra, Teagarden, Benny Goodman, and Jimmy McPartland could often share a final chorus or two of jazz, improvising after a grim opening ensemble and quaint "period" vocal chorus. Meanwhile, Teagarden was making his most important early recordings with various casual "pickup" combinations under various leaderships. He remained in commercial dance groups (Mal Hallett's and Paul Whiteman's) until late 1938 when he formed his own big band, which continually struggled with financial unsuccess until 1947. Then he joined Louis Armstrong's newly formed small group, staying with him until 1951. Teagarden led a small quasi-Dixieland group of his own.

If I seem to be making a historical figure of Jack Teagarden by my claims to his role in the twenties, it is very far from my intention. He left a large and uneven heritage of recordings, but the unevenness is not always his fault.

Teagarden was capable of creating and sustaining a very special, personal aura, even in adverse circumstances—even in the company of a man like Louis Armstrong, whose grandiloquent statements are emotionally quite removed from Teagarden's deceptively easy, self-contained moments. There was, for example, a superb evening in 1947 at New

York's Town Hall with Armstrong and Teagarden that virtually renewed the careers of both men and happily was recorded.

Teagarden was able to follow Armstrong's devastating vocal burlesque
on one of his specialties, "Pennies from Heaven," with a half-chorus
solo that is an effortless lyric gem. He makes very little of the melody
line of that piece as written; he invents one of his own that is more
interesting, punctuated by typical Teagarden virtuoso flourishes. Some
of those flourishes come close to decorativeness, and they have a kind of
quiet elegance that one would never hear from an Armstrong. Yet nothing in that half-chorus seems *merely* decorative, and that, I think, is a
good measure of his talent.

On the same stage and the same evening Teagarden did "St. James
Infirmary." In it we have the best example I know of the Teagarden
aura, the calm, almost lazy, deceptively understated, musical demeanor
that is all firmness and power under the surface.

Like Armstrong or Billie Holiday—for that matter, like Leopold
Stokowski—Teagarden returned to the same repertory year after year.
He could do "Beale Street Blues," "After You've Gone," "Stars Fell on
Alabama," "Sheik of Araby," "Basin Street Blues," and the rest night
after night; do them well; and occasionally do them as if this night
were going to be the last. And he could also do them very differently.
There is another good "St. James Infirmary" from 1940, with Teagarden
and the then-Ellingtonians (Rex Stewart, Barney Bigard, and Ben
Webster) that not only offers different musical ideas but a radically
different emotional approach to the piece.

I have said that in "Pennies from Heaven" Teagarden's solo is largely
an invention. So also is his early, celebrated "Sheik of Araby" from
1930 with Red Nichols, wherein Teagarden invented out of the chords
while a lesser trombonist, Glenn Miller, hummed the original theme
behind him.

However, most of Teagarden's best solos are paraphrases of melodies
as written, and they show his taste in knowing what to add, what to leave
out, what to rephrase. I have a particular favorite, the 1956 version of
"My Kinda Love." The piece has a very good main melody, but the
"bridge" or "middle" part of the song is not so good, except that it has
a charming final descending phrase. On the recording, Teagarden has
his solo on that middle or bridge, and he wisely keeps that final phrase.
However, he tosses out the inferior beginning, inventing a new one. It is
a good one, which also leads up to that final phrase more logically and
beautifully.

On "After You've Gone," also from 1956, the trombonist alternates the written phrases from that familiar piece with inventions of his own. If one refuses to care about how the original is supposed to go, Teagarden's version does not fall into disparate pieces, but has a clear and original logic of its own.

Although it seems spurious to me to describe Teagarden as "the king" of blues trombonists, as recent album huckstering does, I am sure that (unlike Hines and Beiderbecke, for example) he was authentically a blues man, that he could play the twelve-bar blues with a real feel for the idiom, and not just play in the form. And I am also sure that, like many another important jazzman, he could use such blues feeling discreetly no matter what sort of piece he was playing. His blues playing was not like any other man's blues. That, it seems to me, attests to the individuality Teagarden was able to find in the idiom, not to a lack of authenticity.

The indigenous twelve-bar form is surely the core of the Teagarden heritage on record. He did "Makin' Friends" vocally and instrumentally on his first important record date in 1928 with an Eddie Condon ensemble. And Teagarden's preliminary solo on the 1929 "Knockin' a Jug" survives even after Louis Armstrong's final bravura statement at the end of the record. Following these, there were the variants of "Makin' Friends" like "Dirty Dog," "That's a Serious Thing" (which, incidentally, forecast Harold Arlen's "Stormy Weather" melody), "Jack Hits the Road," etc., which punctuate his subsequent career in the studios. An exceptional tribute occurs on "The Blues" from a 1939 *Metronome* magazine-poll "all star" recording: Tommy Dorsey refused to solo as long as Teagarden was present, but finally played a discreet background to Teagarden's blues improvising.

The strength in his blues playing also provides an answer to those who have said that a sentimentality in his work accounts for his durability as a popular performer. It also seems to me that any committed sentimentality in a man who performed "Stars Fell on Alabama" night after night would have done him in long ago. I doubt if a sentimentalist could have gotten through the elaborate Teagarden introductions and codas without playing the fool. I have mentioned elegance and his penchant for flourishes, but elegance is not weakness and flourishes are not frou-frou.

An ability to play a simple blues well is a good esthetic test for a man who can obviously perform on more sophisticated melodies and harmonies. Similarly, an ability to rediscover the early jazz repertory and return to the simpler structures of "Muskrat Ramble" or "Panama" or "My Monday Date" is also a test, and Teagarden did all these pieces well with the Armstrong All Stars.

It has been said that Teagarden's voice is almost a version of his trombone; like many untrained voices, it deepened through the years and thereby became even more like his trombone. Conversely, we can hear how much of his flexibility on trombone simply had to be self-taught because it is so personally vocalized. (This also applies to his device of removing the bell of his horn and muting the end of its tubing with a water glass, the only trombone mute he ever cared to use.) He recorded trombone and vocal versions of "Basin Street Blues" many times but a comparison of two of the best versions, from 1931 with Benny Goodman and 1956 with Bobby Hackett, is fine evidence of his durability.

Teagarden had a genuine desire to reach people with his music, but that desire had nothing to do with compromise. He was always well-mannered; he would show you musically how he felt without apology, but he would never grab you by the hair and demand that you be moved. And he was unapologetically himself and true to his talent. Thereby, Jack Teagarden walked with an artistic dignity all his life.

Saturday Review, March 14, 1964
Copyright © 1964 Saturday Review, Inc.

Ella and Others

Ella Fitzgerald, as you may know, is a singer's singer. Her control is sure, her notes are clear, her pitch is precise. Her range isn't wide but her voice has body, perhaps as much body as a popular singer is entitled to. Her rhythm is impeccable. And she swings, still in the manner of her beginning, *circa* 1936. But for all her professional control she can improvise and her final chorus or so may give impressions of a gleeful abandon.

Ella Fitzgerald is also the public's singer. She packs them in at the record shops, auditoriums, and night clubs. But she is not, as you may not know, a reviewer's singer—at least not in some quarters.

Her Verve release, V/V6-4060, is in her series of "songbook" sets and is devoted to the work of that displaced American-Viennese, Jerome Kern. Her accompaniment was arranged by Nelson Riddle, who writes with a good understanding of Ella Fitzgerald, with miraculously relevant taste in scoring for strings, and with the same coy brass figures that he has been using for the past ten years. As her detractors protest, Miss Fitzgerald often does ignore the words to her songs. (So much the better for her, perhaps?) One thing she responds to, in her relatively uncluttered way, is harmony. It is a response that Kern's pieces can only encourage and that Riddle understands, as witness the cumulative, modulative climax he provides for her on "A Fine Romance." Also, without any egocentric connotations, Ella Fitzgerald responds to the quality of her own voice and to the paradox of its precision plus its slight natural hoarseness. Hear her first chorus to "All the Things You Are," or hear the way she undertakes the difficult steps on "Remind Me." She is also a good spontaneous, original melodist; again, listen to her second version of the "release," the middle part of "All the Things You Are." Or notice how agreeable she makes the cutie-pie aspect of Kern when she recomposes "She Didn't Say Yes."

No, Ella Fitzgerald is not capable of tragedy. She is capable of good melodrama ("Yesterdays") and of a kind of nostalgic pensiveness ("Can't Help Lovin' That Man"). To her detractors, all the rest is engaging shallowness. But for me, hers is the stuff of joy, a joy that is profound and ever replenished—perhaps from the self-discovery that, for all her equipment as a singer's singer, she is absolutely incapable of holding anything back.

Nancy Wilson isn't holding back. But what she's putting forth is a good imitation of the late Dinah Washington with glimpses of Sarah Vaughan (or are they the crumbs from Dakota Staton's scraps of Sarah Vaughan?). She performs with a calculated impact on *How Glad I Am* (Capitol S/ST 2155). And the monotonous rock-'n'-roll effects of her accompaniment are even more offensive when they are dolled up in studio strings.

A few years back, at about the time of a Decca album called *By Special Request* (DL 8173), I would have called Carmen McRae the best jazz singer to come along since Sarah Vaughan. Since then, it seems to me that she has gone in almost every direction but her initial one. In any case, she spent a great deal of time taking a Lena Horneish stance, including tossing of head, gnashing of teeth, and forcing of histrionics. *Bittersweet* (Focus 334) discovers Carmen McRae restored once again as a jazz singer, a formidable jazz singer. The album's chic repertory is of the kind that apparently seems profound when half overheard in the boozy, patent-leather atmosphere of East Side bars ("When Sunny Gets Blue," "Spring Can Really Hang You Up the Most," "Here's That Rainy Day"), but that may turn out to be pretty vacuous when carefully listened to beside the phonograph. Yet Miss McRae, in the manner of a great actress, uses these pieces as proper vehicles. She attends to their lyrics, but only so long as it takes her to sift a truly dramatic moment from their implications. This moment her singing expands and explores. Moreover, she affects no peppy tempos, and, with only a quartet behind her, hides behind no loaded accompaniments.

Saturday Review, November 28, 1964
Copyright © 1964 Saturday Review, Inc.

The Rediscovery of Earl Hines

By 1928 Louis Armstrong had begun to attract musical associates equal to the task that he had outlined, that of revitalizing jazz and leading its players out of a declining New Orleans style and into what was to become its "swing" era. The most brilliant among those associates was pianist Earl Hines, and with him Armstrong recorded such small-group classics as "Muggles," "West End Blues," "Squeeze Me," and the trumpet-piano duet "Weather Bird." At the same time, Hines was recording such solo classics of his own as "Blues in Thirds" and "I Ain't Got Nobody."

The 1950s, however, found Earl Hines leading a strident Dixieland "revival" band in San Francisco—an experience that might long ago have embittered a lesser artist. And this relatively obscure musical life was punctuated only by a couple of bookings with a trio into the kind of after-theater clubs that feature self-effacing music, as an unobtrusive accompaniment to the patrons' conversation.

It is not enough to say that Earl Hines plays today as well as he once did, for it may be that he plays better, and he certainly plays with more creative energy and devotion to his idiom than such an immediate follower as Teddy Wilson.

Hines's style has changed little since the twenties. There are momentary harmonic refinements perhaps in his essentially straightforward approach, and he no longer uses the brittle octaves in his right hand— an effort to be heard above the din of an earlier day. His left hand still walks smoothly in tenths, and still breaks them off briefly for complements to his right or for forays into an *oom-pa* stride. His right hand is still apt to enter the dazzling double-time rhythmic mazes for which he is famous. Nowadays, if the dexterity of his fingers may fail him momentarily, he still never loses tempo or momentum. Hines also still knows how to use dynamics teasingly and tellingly. And he still knows how to paraphrase a theme and when to leave it to invent a new one. But a renewed rhythmic vitality was what Hines brought to the music, and the remarkable thing is that after forty years his idiom is still fresh and moving when played by the master.

Those of us who love jazz have come to accept a great deal of carelessness and lassitude. We live with hours of warming up, nights of creative enervation, weeks of coasting, months with young musicians thrust prematurely into celebrity, and years with middle-aged men who infrequently rise to the level of their illustrious younger days. What a sublime pleasure it is to hear a man of fifty-nine play so rousingly, yet with such fine confidence and poise.

My evidence for the foregoing assertions comes, first, from a series of appearances Hines made in March, 1964, at the Little Theater in New York, memorable concerts that were everything that programs of semi-improvised music ought to be, and, second, from a series of recent Hines LP releases. *The Real Earl Hines* (Focus 335) was done on stage in the final concert of the Little Theater series. It offers Hines's charming spoken introduction, inviting the audience to an informal evening of music. It contains a version of "Memories of You," a piece that obviously did not tempt Hines for its quaintness but for its strength, and for the possibility of a bit of mock melodrama. It has "I Ain't Got Nobody" in a performance still full of drive after thirty-six years in Hines's hands. It has "Tea for Two," a tired warhorse in which Hines finds unexpectedly delicate melody, good parody, and commendably timed changes of tempo. And it has an agonizing trill of several choruses on "St. Louis Blues," a moment of winning showmanship to which Hines is fully entitled. The album's only drawback is that in the processing perhaps—the tape dubbing, the equalizing, and the rest—some of the vital "presence" of the music has been lost.

"Fatha," the New Earl Hines Trio (Columbia CL 2320; stereo CS 9120) offers Hines and the same otherwise sympathetic accompanists from the concert, Ahmed Abdul-Malik, bass, and Al Jackson, drums, but here they occasionally seem slightly out of phase with the leader. Hines comes on strong, sometimes as if he were after a hit (a redo of "Frankie and Johnny" boogie woogie style, a bossa nova, and lots of tricky effects), and just weren't going to relax long enough to make his best music. However, there is an excellent reading of "Breezin' Along with the Breeze," a very good one of "Broadway," and there are fine choruses on "Believe it, Beloved" and "Louise."

Spontaneous Explorations (Contact CN 2; stereo CS 2) offers Hines's piano unaccompanied (except for an occasionally audible light foot-tapping) and done, I understand, in an afternoon's work with a minimum of retakes. It is the most consistent and in many ways the best of the albums under review. It is certainly an utterly charming recital, with Hines's sometimes luxuriant and always crucial left hand beautifully audible throughout. There are splendid readings of "Undecided," "I've Found a New Baby," "Squeeze Me," "Tosca's Dance" (a version of one of Hines's earliest pieces, actually), and a soundly showy "You Always Hurt the One You Love." There is also a Tatum-esque "Jim" and a "Fatha's Blues," an example of how much expressive introspection Hines, no down-home blues man, can find in the form.

A reissue Hines album, *The Grand Terrace Band* (RCA Victor LPV 512), is relatively disappointing. It comes from 1939–40 when Hines led a good swing band, but some of his solos might have been done by anyone with a knowledge of Earl Hines, and his hit of the time. "Boogie on the St. Louis Blues" (here offered in a previously unissued "take") is uncharacteristic and virtually anonymous. Also, the band's style had little individual character and was sometimes derivative—at this period the arrangers and some of the soloists had discovered Jimmy Lunceford and obviously were also discovering Count Basie. There is one rather alarming apparent exception: Hines's piece, "Piano Man" (recorded July, 1939), is almost exactly like the Gene Krupa specialty, "Drummin' Man," credited to "Parham and Krupa" (recorded in November, 1939), even to its lyric.

For a while one of Hines's most celebrated followers was the late Nat Cole, and Capitol has now begun to reissue the King Cole Trio (T 2311).

One piano solo after another ("These Foolish Things," "Body and Soul," "Gee Baby, Ain't I Good to You") contains striking ideas, but oh how diligently one must dig beneath the deferentially glossy manner and cool, inhibited surface to hear them. Perhaps no man was ever more destined for mass popularity than Nat "King" Cole—even before he ever sang a note with those strings.

Saturday Review, June 26, 1965
Copyright © 1965 Saturday Review, Inc.

One Cheer for Rock and Roll!

Surely little in contemporary culture is as much deplored as the music currently favored by adolescents. It has been dismissed as the caterwauling of a disturbed generation. It has been called the result of a conspiracy of payola doled out by record companies to disc jockeys who keep their hands under the turntable, palms up. In the more far-out reaches of right-wing politics, it has even been called a subversive plot.

But there seems to be no escape from the Top 40 rock 'n' roll hits; more and more they assault our ears wherever we turn. And it becomes increasingly evident, in British life as well, and in French life, in Japanese life—even in South African life.

Periodically show-business trade papers like *Billboard* and *Variety* declare that the "trend" is dead. But rock 'n' roll has endured for more than ten years now, and it seems more firmly entrenched than ever. Still, scorn for the state of popular music continues, a scorn sometimes accompanied by a vague nostalgia for the glorious, good old days of (let us say) Glenn Miller.

The good old days are not coming back, and rock 'n' roll is not going to go away. All things considered, there may be very good cultural, social, and even musical reasons why it will not go away. In any case, rather than register more outraged complaints about it, we might do better to ask where it came from and why it is so tenaciously meaningful to young people.

One thing that is often overlooked in the self-perpetuating controversy over rock 'n' roll is that the style not only determines hit records, but it also actually provides popular music with vitality and leadership of a sort. Doubters (probably legion at this point) are invited to ask themselves where the leadership in U.S. tunesmithing came from in the past.

Clearly it came from Broadway and its nearby streets and avenues, either directly or by example. It came from our popular songwriters who worked, by and large, in the musical theater—George Gershwin, Jerome Kern, Irving Berlin, Cole Porter, Richard Rodgers, Harold Arlen.

Well then, what sort of leadership does Broadway currently provide? To be entirely blunt about it, none at all. Lerner and Lowe's *My Fair Lady* may be the last Broadway musical to give the American people a collection of tunes it wants to hear on the air, sing in the shower, and try out on the parlor upright.

When Steve Lawrence appeared recently on national television, he chose to introduce himself with the title song from *Hello, Dolly!* But try naming one other song from that show. And try naming even one song from Lawrence's own show, *What Makes Sammy Run?* Or name one song from Irving Berlin's most recent musical, *Mr. President.* Or name more than one song from Richard Rodgers' *No Strings,* or from Lerner and Lowe's *Camelot,* or from Frank Loesser's *How to Succeed in Business without Really Trying* or from *Baker Street.* Or name two songs from *Fiddler on the Roof,* from *Fade Out, Fade In,* from *Golden Boy,* or from *Ben Franklin in Paris.*

If Broadway does not set an example for new music, can one at least find solace by turning to the so-called "good music" stations of FM radio? Not if "good" popular music means, as it seems increasingly to do, the Melachrino strings, the middle-brow Musak of Norman Luboff and his ooohh aahhh choir, plus (in moments of real daring) the quasi-jazz of Peter Nero, Al Hirt, and Henry Mancini.

Situation hopeless perhaps? Well, not entirely.

Although the choices of teenagers have dominated popular music for the last ten years, they have not, as is often contended, shoved all else aside. In the last year or so a singer named Jack Jones has established himself without riding rock-'n'-roll mannerisms. Tony Bennett has built himself a solid career during the last ten years. So has Andy Williams. So have Eydie Gorme and Steve Lawrence. And so—admittedly with the help of Broadway—has Barbra Streisand.

There is also the fact that many young singers who made their initial success only among teenagers go on to a broader success and a more varied repertory, for example, Paul Anka, Bobby Rydell, Bobby Darin, even Chubby Checker. (But on the other hand for some of those youngsters, broader success may mean only that Frank Sinatra is not as hard to imitate as one might think.)

What about the state of our popular music when rock 'n' roll first took over? One of the earliest attacks directed against the style called it "smut." *Variey* for a long time waged a campaign against lewd lyrics, or *leer-icks* as it called them, of rock 'n' roll, its editors suspecting that a line like "we're gonna rock all night" was a double entendre. What they seemed to have overlooked was that Jo Stafford's "Teach Me Tonight," one of the last big before-rock-'n'-roll hits, had an entendre that was somewhat less than double. And *Variety* apparently forgot, when one of its writers attacked a recording of "Love for Sale" by Dinah Washington, that it was only the latest version of a tune that the renowned Cole Porter had written for Broadway in the 1930s.

Other high-culture events in popular music at the time the rock arrived included the ascendency of Lawrence Welk and the fact that thousands of middle-aged American women were panting over the simperings of Liberace. Perhaps the strident energy of the rock is the expectable reprisal to a culture that wants Musak in its elevators.

There are several musical compensations in the rise of rock 'n' roll. It would make matters simple if we could condemn it all out of hand, but the truth is that we can't. It should be fairly common knowledge by now that the first stylistic forebear of rock 'n' roll was Negro rhythm and blues and that the second was a secularized version of Negro gospel music. But a national news magazine recently gave a glowing description of Britisher Petula Clark's "Downtown" with no reference to the U.S. religious idiom from which the piece partly derives. The early popularity of rock 'n' roll drew attention to some exceptional blues performers such as Joe Turner, Big Maybelle, Ruth Brown, and LaVerne Baker.

Very soon R & R was presenting the fine parodies put together by a pair of young composers, Jerry Lieber and Mike Stoller. They wrote for the group called the Coasters, and their songs included "Yakity Yak," on the grumbling responses of a teenage boy being ordered to do his household chores ("put out the papers and the trash or you don't get no spendin' cash!" and "get those clothes to the laudromat!"). And they included the narrative of the class cut-up "Charlie Brown" ("why is everybody always picking on me?") and a youngster's disbelieving responses to the heroics of a traditional movie cowboy as seen on the late show, "Along Came Jones."

Rock 'n' roll also brought Ray Charles, one of the most remarkable popular artists this country has ever produced.

In his earlier days, Charles had been a follower of the even-tempered balladry of the late Nat (King) Cole. But in 1952 when he was encouraged to turn to the blues, he remembered the exultant gospel music of his youth. Through that memory, he arrived at a starkly arresting, sometimes poignant, sometimes humorous blues style. And in this style, Charles has been able to transmute everything from "Swanee River" through the country-and-western "I Can't Stop Loving You" into stark musical experience. From one point of view (a wrong one, I believe), Charles's music dramatizes the cry of the damned, but the remarkable fact is that so uncompromising and unadorned a style, so unmitigated a flow of musical emotion, could have such widespread acceptance and popular success.

Then there is Elvis Presley. Clearly Presley has established his presence as a fact in American entertainment. He will be a part of it probably for the rest of his life—unless he should get bored with it and retire, a millionaire many times over. What is not so evident is the remarkable cultural synthesis that Presley has wrought.

He has musical roots that are striking indeed. First, he belongs with the so-called country-and-western singers, who find their business headquarters in Nashville, Tenn. Actually, these performers are neither country nor western in outlook, and their music is more or less southern in style. It presents the longings of the new-urban man; he is uprooted from the country, where he sang about the hills and true love, and transplanted to the city, where he sings about loneliness and the false love of a cold, cold heart. But the appeal of this musical idiom is widespread and particularly successful in (of all places) eastern New Jersey and western Canada.

As a white southerner, Presley had other roots, however, with other implications. Presley also knew his Negro rhythm and blues and knew them well. One of his early influences (an influence both on his singing and his pelvic wiggle) was the Negro blues bard whose colorful professional name is Bo Diddley.

The music trade papers were quick to recognize the nature of Presley's style and coined the portmanteau term "rockabilly" for him and his imitators. Sociologists were perhaps less aware of the remarkable fact of his music's widespread popularity, of the social implication in this alliance of a Negro and a southern white musical idiom, and of what it obviously might mean for future race relations in the United States.

When Presley first arrived he was treated as shocking and horrendous by everyone except his teenage followers. But now that it seems that he is not going to go away, he is at least tolerated. Besides, he doesn't wiggle as much as he used to.

Perhaps that growing tolerance of Presley is evidence of a larger tolerance toward rock 'n' roll in general.

Take the twist. This dance—or is it only a pseudo-dance?—came along about four years ago and was quickly discovered by certain influential adults. The more relentless midtown Manhattan night-club-goers—a bizarre amalgam of press agents, actors' managers, and what are usually called, probably by default, "socialites" and "celebrities"—took their jaded tastes to a west-side bar called the Peppermint Lounge.

Very soon adults everywhere began to get into the act. "I've never seen anything like it," said Duke Ellington, who has been around since before the Charleston. "No dance has ever captured so many different kinds of people. Society people are doing it. The kids are doing it. The rich people and the poor people, the fancy and the frumpy—everybody."

And now the Beatles. The very same people, from gossip columnists to grandmothers, who thought that Presley was revolting, but who were somewhat titillated by the twist, now find the Beatles utterly charming.

I do not suppose that anyone who has seen their films, *A Hard Day's Night* and *Help!*, could deny that they are (or can be made to seem) talented comedians. To be sure, the Beatles are rather bizarre—and bizarre in curious ways. They stand for irreverence and individuality, but they sport a version of stuffy Edwardian dress and have the long Fauntleroy hair of turn-of-the-century schoolboys—or perhaps of scrubbed-up, midcentury beatniks. They are frolicsome and seemingly self-contained, but at the same time they deport themselves like restless twelve-year-olds, vaguely running away from—well, one knows not what.

However, at least two of the Beatles are talented musically. The rock 'n' roll style to these two seems a matter of a general tone, an occasional tune, and a more than occasional set of mannerisms. Paul McCartney is a rare popular composer, and a great deal of the Beatles' repertory consists of ditties that might have been researched in Elizabethan song books or in collections of English and Irish airs. McCartney's ballad "And I Love Her" has already been recorded by pop singer Keely Smith, jazz singer Carmen McRae, and orchestrator Gary McFarland. Similarly, "She Loves You (Yeah, Yeah, Yeah)" and "I Wanna Hold Your Hand" are being passed around among pop singers and studio arrangers of all persuasions.

John Lennon, the Beatles' frequent lyricist, uses a wildly humorous, punning, parodying verse in his books *In His Own Write* and *A Spaniard in the Works* that has had reviewers comparing him to the most sophisticated literateurs of this century.

Faced with his books' notices, Lennon bought a copy of James Joyce's *Finnegans Wake*, and was quoted as saying, "It was fantastic. Incredible. It took me half a day to get through half a chapter, but it was like finding daddy."

With McCartney, the promise of a refreshing popular tunesmith is at hand and with Lennon, the sartorial conservatism aside, the possibility of a truly contemporary lyricist.

Ray Charles discovered his real musical talents when he switched from lightweight balladry to wailing gospel-influenced blues. Elvis Presley, whether his talent is really musical or not, made a striking synthesis of the country-and-western and the rhythm-and-blues idioms. In Paul McCartney and John Lennon, the Beatles have, respectively, a melodist and lyricist of potentially high caliber, whose ditties have more to do with the tradition of British balladry than with any other musical idiom. Significantly, none of these men in his best work looks to Broadway, past or present, for inspiration or guidance.

With the other shaggy-haired and sweet-faced British groups that have appeared since the success of the Beatles, the story is somewhat different.

Their repertory most often comes from Negro America, sometimes country blues singers, men largely unknown to white audiences, with sometimes colorful professional names: Muddy Waters, Howling Wolf, Bo Diddley, Chuck Berry, and Jimmy Reed. Last year the Rolling Stones invited Waters to their recording session in Chicago and treated him with a respect that amounted to reverence; one wonders how many of the Stones' youthful fans have ever heard of him. Of course, it is worse than deplorable that Muddy Waters and the other blues bards have so limited an audience in the United States and never, or hardly ever, appear on national television.

Is there race prejudice operating here on the part of the fans of, say, the Rolling Stones? Unquestionably there is—and probably some of it is quite unconscious. However, the question would obviously be simpler if such younger U.S. black stylists as Martha and the Vandellas, the Supremes, Mary Wells, Dionne Warwick, and Major Lance had no white following. (It might be interesting to test a junior high school class— preferably a racially mixed class—with alternate, unidentified records by Muddy Waters and the Animals or Bo Diddley and the Kinks and see what the youngsters' comments would be.)

In any case, rock 'n' roll is not going away, and, if only by default, there is reason for it to stay. Actually, there is more to it than the default of our other popular music, and more to it even than the talents of Charles, Presley, and the Beatles.

The music has been maligned as primitive, sensual, crude, as placing its main emphasis on rhythm, and so on. To anyone familiar with the history of U.S. music in the last sixty years, these strictures must sound terribly familiar. In the teens of this century, ragtime was attacked in almost the same terms. Similarly, the jazz of the twenties. One respected American dictionary for years carried an entry on "jazz" that spoke only of rude, blatant, cacophonous nonmusical noises. And the swing music of the thirties was told to go away by the self-appointed arbiters of our culture for much the same reasons.

What did the attackers of these idioms recommend for popular consumption? Well, of course they were always terribly pious about the European classics, but many a guardian of U.S. musical life was pushing pretty hard for the likes of Victor Herbert and Sigmund Romberg, or, to a later generation, George Gershwin—the man who, in the phrase of the twenties, "made an honest woman out of jazz."

Perhaps we were brainwashed by the ideas of late nineteenth-century Germany music instructors who touted Brahms and Schubert but who then smiled with benign indulgence on the likes of Ludwig Englander's *A Madcap Princess*, Gustav Lauder's *The Fair Co-ed*, and, later, Rudolf Friml's *Rose Marie*.

In the first part of this series I noted that leadership in American music once came from Broadway, from Kern, Gershwin, and the rest. Those men learned from their predecessors in the theater, from men like Victor Herbert and Sigmund Romberg, who, in turn had borrowed from the never-never, wish-fulfillment Vienna of Oscar Strauss and *The Chocolate Soldier.*

This country's tunesmiths have thus been heirs to the musical forms and the philosophy, implicit and explicit, of middle European operetta. They have inherited the decadent, love-conquers-all romanticism of Franz Josef and the morality of a dying aristocracy and an encroaching bourgeoisie. Musical theater in the United States was sired by Johann Strauss, Jr., or Franz Lehar with the *Countess Maritza.* Then it was raised, in the phrase of British critic Max Harrison, "in the gutters of Vienna."

Can anyone doubt that the sentimental spinster secretary of Richard Rodgers' "Do I Hear a Waltz?" is the countess' natural granddaughter? No, she no longer marries a prince—she has an adulterous fling with a good-looking Venice shopkeeper. A note of sordid reality has intruded upon the Middle Europe daydream.

The history of popular music in the United States since 1900 has been the history of a clinging to the Viennese tradition, represented by Broadway on the one hand, and an ever more frantic and frenzied effort to break away, represented by jazz and related forms on the other.

If one is faced with a choice between "Love Is Just a Game That Two Are Playing" and "The Leader of the Laudromat," he is perhaps faced with a musical and philosophical dilemma, indeed. On the other hand, the choice may be between the deluded innocence of "Love, Your Magic Spell Is Everywhere" and the recent hit-parade threat of a "World Without Love." Taken together, these two titles may be said to represent a terse history of the soul of twentieth-century man, and it may not be too farfetched to contend that the later piece echoes the insights of T. S. Eliot's *The Waste Land* as they hit the rock-bottom of popularization (pun intended).

Lyricist E. Y. (Yip) Harburg said it recently: "The elder generation was a victim of illusion. They were Pollyannas, prettyfying everything. So now we live with disillusion."

As the writer of the lyrics for "Over the Rainbow," "where troubles melt like lemon drops," and "How Are Things in Glocca Morra?," Harburg should know.

Of course, Cole Porter and Richard Rodgers and Irving Berlin do not sound *exactly* like Sigmund Romberg. One thing that keeps them from merely echoing Middle Europe is a few, fleeting borrowings from jazz.

The story of the influence that jazz has had on all our music—an influence wide but not yet deep enough—is one few Americans know anything about. How many realize, for example, that the major effect on the style of our most durable popular singer, Bing Crosby, was the work of a great jazzman, Louis Armstrong? For that matter, Armstrong has affected every area of our music. Our classicists write differently because of what he showed the trumpet could do; our symphonic brass men play with a vibrato they are not supposed to have because he had one; even our popular songwriters can be dated stylistically as pre-Armstrong (Vincent Youmans) or post-Armstrong (Harold Arlen).

Light borrowings from jazz once entered the vocabulary of popular musicians fairly quickly. But as jazz has become more and more sophisticated and developed, and more specifically an instrumental idiom, the process may take years of sifting down.

Twenty years later it is possible to hear snippets of the revolutionary jazz of the mid-1940s, of modern jazz or be-bop, introducing a comic on a television variety show or bubbling through the theme music of a situation-comedy series. Imitation Miles Davis is now used to sell cigarets on television and imitation Stan Getz to promote jet flights to Miami. (And real Stan Getz to sell cigars.)

As if to confound matters, jazz itself is at the moment entering a new phase, and this fact inevitably alienates its more advanced forms for the time being from any mass following or possibly even direct influence.

While the modern jazz of the forties was still sifting down, popular music had turned to rhythm and blues, actually another and much simpler form of jazz. And in so doing, popular music was once again turning its back on Vienna—or the Vienna of sixty years previous—but this time more firmly than ever and more deeply.

The current ascendency of popular "folk music" is all of a piece with the popularity of rock 'n' roll. The Kingston Trio and the Rooftop Singers are not folk singers but singers of folk songs—that is, to put it briefly, they are singers of almost any and all songs that do *not* derive from the theaters of Middle Europe but come instead from the traditional balladry of England, Ireland, and the United States, from the blues of American Negroes, from almost anywhere except from the entertainments of the Hapsburgs.

Joan Baez, perhaps the most talented of the young folk singers, recently expanded her repertory by recording a selection by Heitor Villa-Lobos, and the effort has been well received. If Miss Baez had chosen Jerome Kern or Rudolf Friml, she would have been a dead duck: the students who asked her to sing at Berkeley, Calif., during the recent campus "free speech" demonstrations would have sensed that she had somehow sold out, and they would have been right.

It has been said that the musicals of Rodgers and Hammerstein represent the beginning of a truly American musical theater. But it is quite possible that what they actually represent is the last flowering of a dying tradition, transplanted in the United States. And it is quite possible that the current wretched state of Broadway music has come about because theater composers are beginning to sense there is no more gold to be panned from the Viennese gutters and have not yet discovered a vine of their own.

In its now-frantic effort to break away from affected innocence, to turn away from an operetta philosophy—where love often came to mean manipulation of another's will, and concern for one's fellow man often meant knowing what's best for somebody else—in all its effort to break away, current popular music has found delusions that are frequently much more frightening than those it rejects. But for all its restless monotony, its banality, and its own special set of delusions, contemporary popular music here and in Europe still holds the promise of a rebirth.

The promise is of a popular idiom that will embrace traditional folk balladry and blues, that will have a firm melodic lyricism and considerable rhythmic sophistication. Its philosophy may well have a reality and an honesty that will make the chic sophistications of Cole Porter and Lorenz Hart seem like clever daydreams of talented schoolboys. If such a musical idiom should come, I have no doubt that it will capture the imaginations of all sorts and conditions of men the world over and be equally important in Trent, Tallahassee, and Tokyo.

In any case, there is no question of turning back. Our popular musical culture will find a way to express the positive sensibilities of this century or it will perish.

I do not suppose that anyone who has listented to the Top 40 lately or watched the faces of our young people as they dance to it could doubt that the time is running out or could doubt that if our popular music does topple, it could easily indicate that all else is about to topple too.

Down Beat, October 7 and 21, 1965

Albert Ayler, For Example

A few months ago, in reviewing an LP by the young soprano and tenor saxophonist Albert Ayler in this space, I said that Ayler might be working out a perfectly valid musical language of his own, but that it perhaps might be best not to intrude until he has things further along. More recent releases by Ayler make me realize that if such a view does not need to be altogether abandoned, it does need to be drastically reconsidered.

A new Fantasy LP called *My Name Is Albert Ayler* (Fantasy 6016; stereo 86016) is a recital of only limited success. But paradoxically it is at the same time a highly enlightening one, and not only about Ayler's talents but about the intentions of the jazz *avant-garde* in general. The LP is an American release of music recorded in Denmark a couple of years ago. The repertory is, on the face of it, conventional, and includes readings of "Bye Bye Blackbird," "Summertime," "On Green Dolphin Street," and the blues by Charlie Parker called "Billie's Bounce." Besides Ayler, the ensemble inclues two Danish musicians, on piano and bass, and a young American drummer. The pianist, particularly, is thoroughly capable and (like hundreds of pianists the world over) thoroughly schooled in the conventions of be-bop or modern jazz; he is also (again like hundreds of pianists) bland, slick, almost thoroughly dull, and to Ayler, apparently, almost thoroughly inhibiting. At first impression, Ayler's playing declares above all else: let me be free of this thoroughly capable, slick, bland, dull, conventional music.

Does Albert Ayler attempt to make music only from a negative premise, then? Well, perhaps that is only one's first impression.

One's second impression is apt to be even more negative, however. Out of Ayler's saxophone come notes that are overblown, honked, twisted, growled, shrieked. Indeed, he sometimes sounds like an amateur who simply has not learned the proper embouchure for a reed instrument or the proper fingering for the saxophone. Yet at other times he perfectly articulates strings of difficult, short notes, fleet runs, and perfectly pronounced saxophone tones. It is evident that Albert Ayler is a very good saxophonist indeed. And putting one and one together, it is therefore necessarily evident that whatever Ayler plays on his instrument, he plays deliberately. Ayler has decided that whatever sound he can cause his horn to make, that sound might become a part of his music. Much as King Oliver decided that the wail produced by putting a pop bottle in the bell of his cornet was a part of his music, and much as Sidney Bechet decided that the growl produced partly in his throat was a part of his music, and much as Rex Stewart decided that the choked sound produced by pushing the cornet valve only halfway down was a part of his music, so Albert Ayler has decided that the honk or whinny produced by a too-loose use of the saxophone reed can be a part of his music.

Ayler plays the melodies of "Bye Bye Blackbird" and "Billie's Bounce" with a kind of antiswing and calculated carelessness—almost as though he did not quite know them or know how to play them. And he approaches the slower ballads, "Summertime" and "On Green Dolphin Street," with what seems at first a deliberate bathos. Does deliberate bathos make for parody? I think not, but I do think that in Ayler's music a kind of bizarre beauty emerges.

Much contemporary art has as a major purpose the deliberate esthetic exposure and destruction of old standards. That is a quality shared, it seems to me, by Picasso, Joyce, the Marx Brothers, and the Three Stooges, as well as earlier jazz. And I believe that with much truly contemporary art one also sees the emergence, however tentative, of new standards. All well and good, but a work may be fully contemporary in tone and still not be very good. The Marx Brothers were superb comedians but the Three Stooges are not.

The test of Ayler's music comes when he is not boxed in by conventional standards and conventional formats. On "C.T.," he is accompanied only by the superb young Danish bassist Niels-Henning Petersen and the very good drummer Ronnie Gardiner, and he is allowed to roam freely. I appreciate the challenge involved; I appreciate the careful and attentive response of the accompanists; I appreciate the passion and the daring of Ayler's improvisation. But I would be less than honest if I were to deny that after a few minutes of the performance, I was no longer engaged; I felt, as I often feel with John Coltrane, that I had attended a search of twelve minutes duration for a reward of three.

A later Ayler can be heard on a record I have mentioned in this space before, ESP-Disc 1002, with the perhaps regretably portentous title of *Spiritual Unity*. Here, with a trio, Ayler explores four thematically related pieces, all built on simple (and, for me, simplistic) compositional ideas. Ayler's solos are frequently orderly and logical developments, especially so on a piece called "The Wizard"—more orderly than many of John Coltrane's but, for me, less imaginative than Ornette Coleman's.

The most recent of Ayler's recordings is something of a reversal. It is a one-sided LP of a single work called "Bells" (ESP-Disc 1010), recorded by a sextet during a concert. The opening portion features some simultaneous improvisation by all the horns, and is perhaps deliberately anarchic. This is followed by a cadenza by Ayler; it is teasingly effective but it prepares us for nothing more daring than music built around simple marchlike themes, featuring an ordinary triad and performed with more than an echo of the shakily intoned, archetypal brass bands of New Orleans!

Any conclusions I would have to offer on Ayler at this point are necessarily tentative; I would say that as a composer he has a sense of form superior to his sense of melody, and that as an improviser he gains stature among players of "the new thing" from that same sense of form.

Saturday Review, November 24, 1965
Copyright © 1965 Saturday Review, Inc.

Jazz in Peek-a-Boo

Limelight's album jackets continue to look as though they were designed by someone with the bankroll of a shipping magnate and the taste of a retired madam. The latest batch features pop-outs with peek-a-boo windows through which one may observe drawings of Aztec warriors or photographs of Milt Jackson standing inside some abstract statuary in the garden of the Museum of Modern Art.

Jackson peeks through the Modern's sculpture garden because his LP (Limelight L/LS 86024) was recorded there last summer, in a concert featuring Jackson's vibes, James Moody's flute and saxophones, and Cedar Walton's piano. Jackson is rhythmically inventive on "The Quota," and Moody's solo on "Turquoise" has the kind of modest strength to be heard in his best flute work. Also commendable is Moody's theme "Simplicity and Beauty" (but not its variant, which he calls "Flying Saucer"). More typical of the recital is "Montelei." It is obviously the work of major musicians but it has a decidedly perfunctory air. However, I would recommend the LP to anyone who still insists that Milt Jackson is inhibited by his usual role as a member of the Modern Jazz Quartet.

The occasion for the Aztec icons is an album by Dizzy Gillespie featuring a long work in six parts by Lalo Schifrin called *The New Continent,* performed by the trumpeter with a large California studio orchestra conducted by Benny Carter.

As usual, Schifrin proves himself knowledgeable, professional, and skillful—and, heaven knows, he went to music school! To put it another way, he is fanciful but not imaginative. In a section called "The Chains," Gillespie bursts through with a basically simple solo at medium tempo with a tambourine-dominated shuffle rhythm and a little cumulative riffing behind him. It is a beautiful episode, and it makes most of what has preceded, and most of what follows, sound like musical posturing.

The peek-a-boo in Gerry Mulligan's new Limelight album shows silhouettes of some rather awkward-looking rock-'n'-rollers. The set is called *If You Can't Beat 'Em Join 'Em,* and the idea, you see, is to offer jazz versions of some recent Top 40 hits, done by Mulligan and a quartet featuring Pete Jolly's piano and Johnny Gray's guitar. On the whole, I would say that it takes more of Mulligan's musical imagination than comes through here to beat 'em, and it takes more energy than comes through here to join 'em. However, the set might be worth a try as an introduction to jazz for youngsters. (Incidentally, I was half hoping for versions of the Beatles' "And I Love Her" and "Yesterday," two good songs that might be well suited to Mulligan, and when I saw "King of the Road," I anticipated a good opportunity for counterpoint from Mulligan but didn't get it.)

Emarcy, Limelight's companion label, is more modestly packaged and is often devoted to reissues. *Out of the Herd* (MGE 26012) is devoted to recordings from the mid-forties by small ensembles, largely drawn from Woody Herman's orchestra of the time. What has always struck me as remarkable about that orchestra was its singularly eclectic approach—it featured bits of Lunceford, Ellington, Henderson, Basie, plus a veneer of be-bop that is sometimes rather thin, delivered with a kind of tense, strident energy that only the young can produce and perhaps only the young can fully enjoy. That same strident enthusiasm was what held together all the disparate parts, of course, and somehow, twenty years later, it still does. Recording on their own, the Herman side-men sometimes tried out more extended balladry, like trombonist Bill Harris' "Characteristically B.H." or his "Mean to Me," than they got with the big band. Or they attempted more orthodox bop, like Neal Hefti's pastiche, "I Woke Up Dizzy." I might argue with some of the selections here: "Cross Country," very characteristic of these players and their music, is not included, but Red Norvo's "The Man I Love," which is more indebted to Goodman than to Herman, is included. However, "The Man I Love" has a solo by Teddy Wilson that is a thing of beauty, and one of the few moments on this otherwise lively and agreeable LP that make one want to dredge up the word *art*.

(Incidentally, Columbia's three-LP set, *The Thundering Herds*—C3L-25, monaural only—gathers much of the material recorded by the Herman big band and the "Woodchoppers" smaller ensemble for that label between 1944 and 1948.)

Le Jazz Hot (Emarcy MGE 26004) is a collection of titles by Django Reinhardt that were made in wartime Belgium and have never before been released on this side of the Atlantic. The various accompaniments are small, large, and very large; some of the individual players are good, but abilities in general range from acceptably competent to—well, somewhat less than acceptably competent. At this period, Reinhardt's playing was repeatedly at its fullest development. On this LP it is as if Reinhardt, in the spring of 1942, were able tastefully to elaborate and embellish his earlier self. Surprisingly, one of the best performances is a reinterpretation of the guitarist's "Nuages" with a large orchestra including strings. Reinhardt's ornamentations are a delight and the accompaniment is discreetly sympathetic in orchestration and performance.

Reinhardt was deeply (and obviously) indebted to American jazzmen, but he did not merely imitate them. Therein lay his strength as an exceptional improvising musician—a fact that, considering the derivative quality of so much jazz, is not so celebrated as it might be.

Saturday Review, December 25, 1965
Copyright © 1965 Saturday Review, Inc.

Mostly About Morton

The reputation of Ferdinand "Jelly Roll" Morton as a jazz composer, leader, and pianist should be firmly established, for his work is one of the glories of pre-Armstrong jazz. But it is not, partly because some commentators will not admit that pre-Armstrong jazz had any glories. And partly because Morton—personally a braggart and blowhard, an all-around colorful character—was something of his own worst enemy. And partly because only Morton's best work does him real credit.

For that latter reason particularly, I don't think that a new Vintage reissue *Hot Jazz, Pop Jazz, Hokum & Hilarity: Jelly Roll Morton* (RCA Victor LPV-524) can do his reputation much good. The album begins with very good Morton in "Wild Man Blues." It includes an interesting but only partly successful piano solo, "Freakish," in two different "takes" (both of which, contrary to the commentary in the liner notes, have been previously issued). It offers a fine little arrangement called "Hyena Stomp," damaged because Morton, basically a humorless man who was sometimes determined to be comic, introduced into it a few "animal imitations," as the label puts it. And it has a bristlingly effective piano solo by the leader on a piece called "Tank Town Bump." For the rest we have monotonous efforts by Morton to adapt himself to the then developing "big band" style (or to modify his small band approach along similar lines), or we have good accompaniments to bad vocals, or we have selections on which Morton functioned almost anonymously as a sideman to clarinetist Wilton Crawley. It is rather as if we put together a Shakespeare anthology that started with *Coriolanus* and *A Comedy of Errors*, followed by *Timon of Athens, Pericles, Titus Andronicus, King John*, and *Henry VIII*.

There is a difference of course: Shakespeare's reputation, real and academic, would survive. Morton's, as I say, must suffer.

Perhaps Vintage has scraped the bottom of its Morton barrel, and issues this LP in the interests of completeness or to satisfy the curiosities of antiquarians and jazz scholars? Not so. Still unreissued, for example, are the better version of Morton's masterpiece, "Dead Man Blues," or his two best trio performances, "Wolverine Blues" (recorded in two almost equally interesting and quite different takes) and "Mr. Jelly Lord," or Morton's most successful big band score, "New Orleans Bump."

Victor-Vintage owes us a careful anthology of Morton 1926-28, plus an enlightened selection of Morton 1929–30. The appearance of a catch-all set like *Hot Jazz, Pop Jazz, Hokum & Hilarity* can only mean that once again that debt will be postponed.

To switch from Jelly Roll Morton to pianist Ramsey Lewis is to leap forward in time, and perhaps public success, but not in artistry. *Hang on Ramsey!* (Cadet 761) is a kind of follow-up to Lewis' recent hit recording "The 'In' Crowd." On the surface, Lewis performs his basically Ahmad Jamal-derived style quite ably and pleasantly, and while listening I frankly found myself wanting to get up and dance more than once. But after the three hundredth tremolo and five hundredth blue note had gone by, and after the second minute into a pointless ostinato, I had the feeling that with Ramsey Lewis everything is made pleasant, everything from joy to anguish. It gets pretty monotonous.

Nina Simone is a singer who accompanies herself on piano and who takes an occasional piano solo. She apparently has a large following, large enough so that she records prolifically and so that she has had a successful evening of her own at Carnegie Hall. Yet, as far as I know, her records are seldom played on the air, and if she has ever made an appearance on national television, I am unaware of it.

Nor are these the only puzzles involved in Nina Simone's popularity. I do not think that the appeal of Tony Bennett, for example, is particularly musical, but his popularity does not surprise me and I think I understand it. But I confess I have no idea what Miss Simone's appeal is.

I will, for whatever it's worth, apply a few jazz standards to her newest record, *Let It All Out* (Phillips 200-202; Stereo 600-202), and not unfairly, I think—she has been called a jazz singer and she certainly has done a deal of borrowing from jazz and blues singers and players.

As a pianist, she does not swing, she has few ideas, and she has the precious habit of interpolating her youthful study-pieces into her act. As a singer, she affects up-tempo hipness (on "Mood Indigo," of all inappropriate pieces), she affects close-to-the-microphone lushness, she postures torchy and she postures cute. She wears the mask of Billie Holiday for "Don't Explain" and the mask of blues shouter Big Mama Thornton on her *double-entendre* "Chauffeur." I will say that she undertakes a variety of tempo and of attitude on this LP, and that it is an aspect of her presentation which some more professional singers might learn from.

Pianist Phineas Newborn, Jr., has recently been called "the greatest living jazz pianist." I must say that I think that pronouncement raises comparisons that are quite unfair to Newborn's talent; that is, if greatness in an improvisational idiom has to do with originality, with emotional depth, with melodic organization, and logic.

Newborn does have a prodigious digital technique and fleetness of touch. More technique than *any* jazz pianist? Well, one can mention only a few in the same sentence—Tatum, Solal, Peterson, Peiffer, and Hank Jones. . . . One should also mention Bud Powell, for he is obviously Newborn's prime stylistic instructor, and, after Powell, Newborn is the only virtuoso pianist with a *rhythmic* grasp of modern jazz.

If the sheer virtuosity of difficult runs that are intelligently selected and cleanly played with a deft touch and perfect time can be its own reward—and it can be, particularly if one expects nothing else—then Phineas Newborn, Jr., can be a rewarding pianist. And "The Sermon," "Blue Daniel," and "Hard to Find" on his new LP *The Newborn Touch* (Contemporary 3615) are highly rewarding.

Saturday Review, March 12, 1966
Copyright © 1966 Saturday Review, Inc.

The Comic Mask of Fats Waller

Thomas "Fats" Waller was a pianist, singer, and song writer, but his first love was the organ. He would play the instrument whenever he could, alone and deeply absorbed, for hours at a time, performing all kinds of music on it and particularly Bach. "But," he would remark, "who wants a colored organist?"

The answer is that a few hundred ambitiously middle-class Negro churches around the country would have wanted one—such churches as undertake baroque chorales rather than gospel songs—these churches would have wanted one, provided the organist were content to live in modest obscurity. But obscurity was not for Fats Waller; both by destiny and by choice, success and fame were. In gaining that fame, Waller paid a price that involved not only sacrificing the organ but sacrificing perhaps half of his talent.

To be sure, the successful Fats is pretty nearly irresistible. This is the Waller who entered a recording studio with his "Rhythm" (usually a sextet), to be handed some inane current ditty and who proceeded to record it with frequently hilarious vocal parody and general good musical spirits. We are reminded of this Fats again and again on RCA Victor's new Vintage reissue of sixteen Waller numbers (LPV-525), most of them recorded during 1935 and 1936, and on the Waller Vintage release of a few months back (LPV-517).

Waller's pseudo-operatic histrionics in undertaking a Bobby Breen specialty called "Let's Sing Again" are side-splitting. His mock misery in reheating the "Sugar Blues" did the sort of permanent damage to subsequent performances of that piece that the Marx Brothers did to *Il Trovatore*.

The effect of Waller's vocal mugging is immediate, winning, complete—and it all sounds easy. It *was* easy, I think, and, for most of the musical aspects of Waller's talent, it was also limiting. Only a complex man could have held experience at arm's length by means of such good comedy, to be sure, but a complex and musically gifted man like Waller might have done a lot more.

Waller was so good a composer that, given a chance to record some piano originals, he might walk into the studio virtually unprepared and simply knock off a couple of pieces. They would be respectable and probably good—or good enough. Of course, if Fats Waller were not capable of excellence, it wouldn't matter too much. But Waller was capable of excellence, and he showed it often enough to make the totality of his musical output a joy, a frustration, and finally a tragedy.

A respected younger musician wondered recently if any of Waller's music could be said to survive. I confess I was shocked that he would even pose such a question. In the first place, the bursting joy with which Waller's piano could interpret a line like "Why Do I Lie to Myself About You?" or the pensiveness he brought to "Thief in the Night," or his technical jubilance on "I Got Rhythm" are enough to make one want to hear him.

Second, Waller wrote at least three superb and somewhat neglected melodies: "Squeeze Me," "Black and Blue," and "Honeysuckle Rose" (and incidentally, himself recorded only the latter in an adequate version). These to me are the great Waller compositions and not the post-ragtime piano pieces, of which we have examples in "Valentine Stomp" and "Goin' About" on the Vintage releases.

Then there is Waller's sense of structure as an improviser, a quality in which his predecessors and teachers like James P. Johnson and Willie "the Lion" Smith gave him good lessons. There is a fine example of this in the Vintage series in the blues he called "Numb Fumblin' "; he alternates robust percussive choruses with highly lyric episodes back and forth, building each in complexity, until the two moods come together in choruses of shimmering virtuosity at the end.

Personally, I am still waiting for the LP appearance of several of Waller's best solo recordings, including his superb variations on "Keepin' out of Mischief Now," his pensive reading of "Georgia on My Mind," his "Tea for Two," and his solo version of "Honeysuckle Rose."

Waller did burlesque and cajole the poor tunes he was handed to record, but it was not often given to him to work a change by spontaneously rewriting such ditties as Billie Holiday did. Nor was it given to him to fuse together his penchant for comedy and his musicality, as a successor like Thelonious Monk has done. On occasion Waller did use his talents as a clown to hold his audience while he also offered them the gifted and reflective musician who lay under the surface, but, alas, it was all too infrequently.

If Waller had managed against odds that were admittedly great, to bring together all the elements within him—the fine pianist, the irresistible clown, the exceptional composer, the introspective after-hours organist—he would, I think, belong with that handful of geniuses that jazz has so far produced.

As it is, he does belong in a place of his own, very carefully labeled "Thomas 'Fats' Waller." And in that place Waller the clown shines in spite of everything we say. His antics on "Somebody Stole My Gal," "Dust Off That Old Pianna," and "If This Isn't Love" might almost be taken as definitive of Negro American humor and its attitudes. And those attitudes include a penetrating and unexpected parody of the kind of "shiftless darky" humor that White America has expected of Negroes. Such comedy, done as well as Fats Waller did it, has its place in the scheme of things—as the gods surely will agree.

Saturday Review, March 26, 1966
Copyright © 1966 Saturday Review, Inc.

Ornette Coleman in Stockholm

In 1958, when Ornette Coleman's first recordings appeared, many listeners were puzzled; his music sounded, they were apt to put it, "too far out" for them. Some musicians were puzzled too, but they were more apt to find his work simple, or even to voice a doubt as to whether Coleman knew what he was doing.

Two new LP releases of *The Ornette Coleman Trio at the Golden Circle, Stockholm* (Blue Note 4224 and 4225) are the alto saxophonist's first new recordings in several years. They may answer the earlier reservations of both audiences and fellow players. Coleman's original talent, his refreshing approach to jazz rhythm, jazz melody, and improvisation have been around long enough to be familiar. No, his ideas have not yet found their way into an Andy Williams record but there was some would-be Coleman during a recent TV background score. By now, most listeners can go directly to the music itself, rather than be stopped by its surface unfamiliarity. And a musician will surely note the clarity and precision with which Coleman now articulates every note, every inflection, every phrase. There seems no question about it, Ornette Coleman knows what he is doing, he means it all, and he now plays with almost the careful deliberateness of a sculptor whose small mistake may destroy a larger design.

The question that remains for a listener is how much he likes what he hears. A musician of course may have the additional question of how fruitful he finds Coleman's approach for future of the music.

By the time these "live" Stockholm performances were taped, the Coleman Trio had developed praiseworthy individual and collective virtues. Bassist David Izenzon had begun to swing more, and he has a particularly well organized solo on "Dee Dee" in Volume 1. Drummer Charles Moffet had elaborated his basic, down-home style (a style appropriate to Coleman, who is basically a bluesman) so that it became capable of an appropriate variety of textures (again, hear "Dee Dee").

"Faces and Places," also in the first volume is characteristic, finely developed Coleman—a swift and frequently ingenious monologue built on melodic permutations of one direct rhythmic idea. "European Echoes" is a lightly humorous waltz in which Coleman's solo grows out of an enunciation of the basic waltz count, 1-2-3. Perhaps the most successful piece is "Dawn," a lovely group invention in which each member contributes equally and almost simultaneously.

One of the most striking performances in Volume 2 is also descriptive—"Snowflakes and Sunshine"—and this judgment, I should add, comes from one who usually distrusts the idea of program music. It is a tissue of shimmering impressionistic sounds on which Coleman plays some functionally successful violin and trumpet. There is also a slow, prayerful but optimistic "Morning Song," a variant on the dirgelike mood of which Ornette Coleman is a master. "The Riddle" is a wonder and a real contribution to the jazz language, a riddle of tempo that moves in and out of several speeds with such natural musical logic that one barely notices. Similarly, on the deliberately meandering "Antiques," there are casual changes of tempo.

These records show Ornette Coleman's music at such a level of development that, if one doesn't know his work at all, Blue Note 4224 and 4225 are an excellent place to begin.

Coleman's style allows for free melodic improvisation, not on the outline of a succession of chords, as in earlier jazz (the "harmonic variation" of classical parlance), but on an harmonic pedal-point or "drone." Coincidentally, I am sure, Miles Davis used a similar approach on certain of his pieces, and after recording these pieces with Davis, John Coltrane developed the idea on certain of his ("Impressions" on Impulse A-42, for example). Such an approach is at once relatively simple and highly challenging. The soloist has only one chord or one "drone" to deal with instead of several, but he has to make that single point of departure yield a long stretch of eventful melody.

I am sure that Ornette Coleman found his way to such "modal" improvisation on his own. Perhaps it seemed to certain New York musicians as if Coleman had already staked out a personal claim in territory where previously they had only panned some nuggets. In any case, it should come as no surprise that John Coltrane was attracted to Coleman's music. Atlantic now has issued concrete evidence of that attraction, an album recorded six years ago with Coltrane on tenor and soprano saxophones, Don Cherry on trumpet, Charlie Haden or Percy Heath on bass, and Ed Blackwell on drums—in effect, Coleman's group of the time without Coleman.

Perhaps six years is too long a time to have waited. Coltrane is certainly more adept at "free" improvisation now than he was then, and his style has become richer both technically and emotionally. Admittedly, "The Blessing" and "Invisible" are early and tamer Coleman, but on Cherry's piece, "Cherryco," unless I am missing the point, Coltrane seems stuck for ideas. He is at his best on the more conventional Thelonious Monk piece "Bemsha Swing." I am disappointed, too, that the most interesting of the three Coleman compositions included, "Focus on Sanity," is truncated. The original (on Atlantic 1317) uses several ensemble passages, several changes of tempo, and shifts of mood. This version virtually cuts it down to a medium-tempo section followed by a faster one. Throughout the LP, Cherry offers one fanciful melodic turn of phrase after another, generally with a technical precision not heard on his previous recordings.

Saturday Review, June 11, 1966
Copyright © 1966 Saturday Review, Inc.

More of the Ellington Era

Columbia's *The Ellington Era, 1927–1940*, Volume 2 (C3L39) is, like its predecessor, Volume 1 (Columbia C3L 27), a collection of three LPs drawn in this case from forty-four old 78-rpm titles. To say that it is not quite so good a collection over-all as the earlier one is perhaps not to say very much. In Duke Ellington we are dealing with one of our greatest musicians, and his failures may interest us as much as the successes of lesser men.

I shall not attempt exhaustive comments on the new volume, for it seems to me that in 1966 it would be more appropriate to try to put in perspective this man's whole recorded career to date rather than dwell in detail over a part of it. Let what follows, therefore, stand as some appreciative jottings by one listener on some of the music at hand.

The album necessarily begins less auspiciously than the previous one, for that set already gave us versions of "East St. Louis Toodle-oo,"

"Black and Tan Fantasy," and "The Mooch," the early collaborations with trumpeter Bubber Miley that had so much to do with the affirmation of Ellington's talent and direction as an orchestrator and leader. But here the first titles do show Ellington trying out his soloists (and the second piece, "Take It Easy," indicates what good ones he had by 1928) ; or they show him trying out various textures and effects and discovering an ensemble character for his orchestra; or they show him, on "Move Over," cautiously experimenting with unusual structures; or they find him significantly testing several personal moods within the basic blues form. However, the first LP in the album ends with the expanded, 1932 version of "Creole Love Call," an appropriate juxtaposition of themes from Miley and Rudy Jackson, and "Creole Love Call" is perhaps the best of all the early pieces, in part because of the appropriate modesty of Ellington's own contributions in scoring.

And here is Ellington in his 1932 version of "Rose Room" providing his soloists with encouraging background figures strictly to the chordal contours of the piece. Any other arranger of the time would probably have plowed through with riffs on a harmonic makeshift, and hoped for the best.

Ellington's own "Showboat Shuffle," from three years later, is a gem of momentum, in theme, in variations (written and improvised), in orchestration, and in technical execution.

The 1935 "Reminiscing in Tempo," originally issued on four ten-inch 78s is almost unique among Ellington's extended works. It is not an alliance of several themes like the earlier long works, nor is it a suite, like most of the later ones. "Reminiscing in Tempo" is a sustained exploration of one main theme, plus some complimentary motifs. There are solo moments, but Ellington's real vehicle in the piece is the orchestra, its resources and textures. "Reminiscing in Tempo" is the sort of instructive piece of American music that might be in the repertory of every "stage" band in our high schools and colleges. (Ah, but will it ever replace the Stan Kenton *kitsch* which so many of our faculty band instructors inflict on their charges? Apparently these men accept the press-agentry about Kenton's "innovations" and "artistry," in which case they cannot know Ellington's work.)

"Azure," neglected perhaps because it is so simple, is one of Ellington's most affecting slow, introspective mood pieces. It has a weak release but its main strain is superbly scored. And its melody is neither too "vocal" in character—as, say, "In a Sentimental Mood"—nor too sentimental—as "Lost in Meditation." A ritual sentimentality can be the curse of sophistication, and an urbane sophistication is the cornerstone of Ellington's genius in its successes and its failures alike.

So, I have used "genius," a word that is easy to use, but a quality not so easy to demonstrate, and impossible to "prove." If I were to pick one title from this set for such a demonstration, I think it would be the cryptically titled "Old King Dooji" from 1938.

On this work Ellington provided a continuously varied theme and presented it with written and improvised variations. Most of the jazz composers around him at the time would have broken such material into snippets, orchestrated it much more simply, spread it out, and made several pieces out of it, depending for their effects on the force of repetition of two-bar riffs. Yet Ellington's logical little work is neither disparate nor overloaded.

In a sense I am carping to say so, but it seems to me that there are better ways to present Ellington's career than the one Columbia is using. It would be more enlightening to have his music documented year by year, and record date by record date, than to keep going over the same thirteen years with each album. Probably some listeners will feel that Columbia is simply putting together all the Ellington material it happens to have on hand in good 78 copies as each set comes due. I doubt it, and it may be that the company feels the procedure it is using makes the material more marketable. (For all I know, it does.)

In any case, it is not time to stop. Still pending are the 1937–38 versions of "East St. Louis" and "Black and Tan," two instances in Ellington's career where a return to former glories, and using different soloists, brought about superior versions. There is the 1939 recording of that marvelously titled piece, "Doin' the Voom Voom." Compared with the original version of ten years earlier, it is a revelation of the technical evolution of jazz ensemble playing, particularly in the rhythm sections, and of Ellington's evolving ideas of sonority. It is also succinct evidence of the master's influence. For over the years "Doin' the Voom Voom" was raided, literally two bars at a time, by swing-band arrangers as source material for their "originals."

And just in case Columbia should run out of studio-made records, there is, say, the sound track to Ellington's 1935, all-musical movie short, comprising his first important suite, "Symphony in Black," the rights to which should not be difficult to clear for LP. No, it is not time to stop.

Saturday Review, July 30, 1966
Copyright © 1966 Saturday Review, Inc.

Rehearsing with Monk

"What time does a ten o'clock rehearsal start?"

"Well, I think Jerome Richardson will be here soon. And Steve Lacy. They picked up their parts yesterday to take them home."

The speaker is Hall Overton. He is dressed in a rather baggy white shirt and dark trousers, standing next to a two-burner gas stove in the kitchen area of his midtown New York loft studio, three steep flights above its Sixth Avenue entrance, and as he finishes speaking he offers his visitor some coffee.

Out in the rather rugged two-room studio, two photographers are busy setting up their lights, attaching them to pipes and to the sides of the several bookcases that line one wall or placing them on the tops of the two upright pianos. Overton has a floor-through, which means the front windows would overlook Sixth Avenue if they were not largely covered by blinds against the morning sun. The two rooms are one in effect, since they are separated only by a wide arch. In the center of the rear room there are set up two rows of four chairs, plus as many music racks and stands as are available.

At 10:15 A.M. the first two players arrive. Thad Jones and Phil Woods are neatly dressed, and both look bright and wide awake. After greetings, Jones and Woods take chairs, get out their horns, look over their music, meanwhile exchanging stories about somebody's embouchure and somebody else's pet dog and cat.

Overton continues to prepare and offer coffee in the kitchen alcove. He explains, "We are going to do 'Thelonious' and 'Monk's Mood,' which are not too hard. We will be doing 'Four in One' at the concert, but we can't rehearse it today because I don't have the score yet. And we have another tough one, 'Little Rootie Tootie,' though it's not quite as hard as 'Four in One.'"

"Didn't you do that at a Town Hall concert a few years ago?" Jones asks.

"Yeah. Monk misplaced the score, and I had to do it all over again. Of course, our instrumentation this time is different."

As Overton speaks, trombonist Eddie Bert arrives, quietly, as is usual with him.

The reason for the Thursday morning rehearsal is revealed in a poster on the side wall of the studio: "THELONIOUS MONK Orchestra at Carnegie Hall. Saturday, June 6 at 8:30 P.M." It is to be Monk's second concert of the season, a kind of follow-up to his much-praised evening at Lincoln Center last December.

Again, Overton has done the scores for the orchestra, working not only with Monk's themes but also with written variations based on Monk's recorded piano solos on a couple of the pieces—these are what make up the difficult portions of "Four in One" and "Little Rootie Tootie."

It is the third such collaboration of Overton and Monk, the first being the 1959 Town Hall concert that Jones remembered.

As planned, the Carnegie concert is to open with a Monk solo. Then Monk's quartet is to play several pieces—the quartet currently consisting of Monk, tenor saxophonist Charlie Rouse, bassist Spanky DeBrest, and drummer Ben Riley. The orchestra is to appear in the second half, and the evening will end with a second Monk piano solo.

It its now about 10:25, and Steve Lacy has arrived.

"Of course, a ten o'clock rehearsal starts at eleven," somebody says.

Woods is playing the piano. Overton is explaining how jealously Monk guards his own scores: he usually asks for them immediately after a concert performance and puts them away at home but often can't find them again when he needs them.

At 10:30 Richardson enters, offering hearty and boisterous greetings to the others.

Overton is now going over a part with Bert. Nick Travis arrives, looking mildly genial as usual, and is soon in joking conversation with Jones. From time to time the phone rings, and Overton speaks quietly into the receiver, "Well, right now we're about to. . . ."

Rouse has still not arrived, but at about 10:35 the six horn men assemble in their chairs by unspoken agreement to begin the rehearsal. It turns out that the saxophones need a little more light on their parts, and some lamps get moved around.

"Hall, have you got a piece of sandpaper? This reed is a little . . ."

It is Richardson. Lacy has a piece and passes it over.

Overton faces the group and indicates that they may as well start with the hard one, "Little Rootie Tootie."

"Let's try it at this tempo right here," he says crouching slightly and patting his right foot. "I'll give you a measure and a half."

They begin the train whistle effect that opens the piece.

"Hold it! Steve, come down. Phil, I'd like you to accent the G-flat and the A."

They start again. Halfway through the chorus Overton stops them again, saying:

"Phil, right there—you got the right sound. But hold it a bit and give it a little vibrato."

"Put a little crescendo on it?"

"Yeah, maybe like a dotted quarter."

The phone rings. "Hello. . . . He's not here. . . . I'm not sure—he should be here any minute."

They begin again: "One, two, three, four. Cut off at three. But get the swell."

"At the fifth measure of B," Overton says indicating a section of the score, "baritone, two trumpets, and trombone. Got it? Okay."

The four horns execute a fat chord.

"Now, all of it again. We are missing the tenor, an important sound here, of course."

They are also still missing a rhythm section, but an ensemble swing is definitely developing.

"That was right, but let's try it at B once more—in the sixth measure. That G should be louder. Now once more at B."

They have the opening chorus down now, and it is time to move to the hard part, the closing ensemble choruses based on Monk's solo. Overton indicates the section, saying, "Okay, let's get started at E."

Spontaneously, Jones and Travis begin the chorus with no cue from Overton, using the previous tempo. The others join. The phrases link together. There is laughter at one passage, caused by its difficulty—and its unexpected musical logic. Hall shouts "diminuendo" over the ending.

The group has awakened to a musical challenge. "Can we go back to I or J?" Richardson asks.

"Right now let's get this part here—you have to accent every one of those triplets," Overton says to the group generally.

A few minutes later Thad Jones is asking, "Let's start back at E again."

Overton agrees now. But before the group begins, Jones and Travis are running off one of the most difficult passages together.

"That was crazy!"

"It is kind of ignorant, ain't it?" says Jones, laughing broadly.

As they go through it again, Overton goes to the piano and stands at the keyboard, reaching down to add the continuing train whistle responses to the ensemble.

"Hey," Richardson says at the end, "it's moving! It'll walk by itself now!"

Rouse enters, to general greetings and a "Hey, Roustabout!" from Jones.

He takes his place between Richardson and Woods, and Overton asks if Woods can lend his instrument case for a substitute music stand.

Once more Jones and Travis begin the closing variations, and the group joins them. They have set the tempo faster this time. A mistake breaks up a couple of the players, but the music continues.

"Is that where you're going to put it?" asks Richardson about the new tempo.

"No," Jones replies. "Just to try it."

"Nothing wrong with it," Richardson responds. "Feels good up there too."

"Hey, let's tune up," says Overton going to one of the pianos to sound an A. After the general din, he takes his place in front of the group again, saying, "From the top, now that we've got everyone here."

Afterwards: "Once more, from the top. But didn't we get a train whistle sound on this introduction before?" He is addressing Woods, who had played "Little Rootie Tootie" at the Town Hall Concert. His answer comes from all sides, as various of the players try wailing and bending their opening notes. Then there is one more run-through, and it comes off well.

"How about this way, Hall?" Jones asks, and then runs off a slightly revised and reaccented version of one of the trumpet phrases. He has made the passage less pianistic, pronouncing it the way a brass man would.

"Fine—now at the end of your part," Overton continues to the group methodically, "I have written out four chords. We can use these for backgrounds. You play each three times, like the opening. Let's try the first one." He gives a downbeat. "Now the second." Another downbeat, followed by another triple wail.

"Man!" somebody interjects, "that's a weird sound."

At the end of the fourth, the sudden clanging and wailing sound of a fire engine swells up from the street below.

"That's the whistling sound we want!" says Richardson over general laughter.

They are about to set aside "Rootie Tootie" for the time being.

"Hall, can we have some coffee or something?"

"Sure." There is a break while coffee is prepared.

"Got anything to eat? I didn't get any breakfast."

"I think there's some cookies."

"That'll do fine."

"This music is hard to phrase right," Overton muses in the kitchen alcove.

"Yeah. So many of Monk's things are traditional, but he uses them in such an original way. If you play them the old way, they don't sound right at all."

At about 11:30 drummer Riley arrives with his set, apologizing for his lateness. He moves a little stiffly and explains that he caught a cold early in the week and then aggravated it by going out in the rain to pick up his daughter after school.

A couple of minutes later, Jules Colomby, who is to produce the concert, enters. With him are Spanky DeBrest and Thelonious Monk. Monk walks in, staring rather vaguely in front of him and not looking at anyone in particular. He returns Thad Jones's greeting and twirls around in a kind of dance movement. Lacy approaches him, and they exchange greetings. Then for a moment he looks out of the back windows of the studio. Soon he speaks to Overton: "How's it going?"

"So far pretty good. There are some problems with the horns. . . ."

Monk is still in his hat and raincoat, which is buttoned all the way up tightly around his neck, the collar turned up.

DeBrest warms up by reading his part. Riley sets up his drums.

"Thelonious," Overton is saying, "I scored out some chords at the end of 'Rootie Tootie.' When you hear them you might want to pick a couple for backgrounds for the solos."

Monk nods.

The coffee break is about over, and the group is reassembling in the chairs as Overton tries to set future rehearsals: "Let's have another tomorrow morning."

"I can't come," someone says. "I have to teach, and I have a job tonight that will keep me out late besides."

"Neither can I—I have a show to do," Bert says almost shyly.

"Maybe we could get substitutes for you two—wait a minute!" Overton remembers. "I can't either. I forgot I have something I can't break. Well, it'll just have to be Saturday morning before the concert. Here. Ten o'clock?"

There is general nodding.

"Then we'll have to get to the hall early to set a balance. We can get Carnegie during the afternoon for rehearsing, too, if we want."

"No, let's not rehearse in the afternoon. Our chops will be worn out before the concert."

"We ought to do 'Thelonious' and 'Monk's Mood' today," Overton says. "Shall we do them and then go back to 'Little Rootie Tootie'?"

Monk is walking, pacing the room, skirting the musicians, dancing a little, waiting to hear. He still has his coat on, and his collar is still up.

They run down "Thelonious," Monk's intriguing theme built around one note. At the end, Overton turns to Monk and says, "That goes faster than that, doesn't it?"

Monk moves to the piano, apparently to give the question a complete answer, and begins to play the piece himself, a bit faster, very force-fully, and with fascinating harmonies and successions of sounds pivoting off that one note.

At the end, Overton asks, "Are you going to take all the blowing on this?"

"Anybody can blow it if they know the chords."

"Well, did it sound okay?"

"Was everybody in tune?" Monk asks. "Yeah, it sounds okay."

Overton turns to the group again and says, "Let's decide about the solos later. Now we'll try 'Monk's Mood.'"

As the players get out their parts, Overton confers with Monk.

"We'll do it this way," he says finally. "We'll begin with a solo chorus by Monk. Then the band. Then Charlie Rouse. Then Monk. Then the band again, and out."

As they go through "Monk's Mood" again, the composer moves to the rear of the group to listen and probably to have more room for his rhythmic pacing as well.

"Try for a feeling of triplets right here," Overton instructs. "Okay, from the top again."

Some of the players move their feet in a kind of suggested 6/8 time to get the proper feeling during the triplet passage.

"Is something wrong with your part there in the first eight?" Overton asks. "Let's see your copy, Charlie."

One more run-through, with Bert's trombone again opening up the theme and the group picking it up. They now have rehearsed their ballad for the evening, "Monk's Mood."

"Okay, let's go on to 'Rootie Tootie' again," Overton says. "Monk, I'd like you to hear those chords now. Maybe you could think about how you would like to use them for background?"

Monk nods. And paces. And turns. His tread is becoming heavier and more varied.

"Okay, here we go, chord number one."

A piercing collection of sounds.

"Now number two. Three times again. Number three. Number four."

Overton looks up at Monk, who continues stepping and turning.

"I think number one and number four work out," Overton says finally. "Maybe we can use them in the background. Okay, now from the top of 'Rootie Tootie.' "

They run through it once, and it goes well. As they are about to begin again, Overton says, "Hey, Thelonious . . . ," gesturing toward the piano.

Monk seems uninterested. He still has on his coat and hat and is perspiring, especially around the collar. Jones and Richardson start off again, with no signal from Overton, who crosses to the piano to play the continuing train whistle responses to the orchestra's figures. He is backed by accents from Riley.

At the end, Monk says, "Everybody ought to hold that last note."

"But fade it out gradually, right?" Overton asks.

"Yeah."

"Now for backgrounds to the solos. The last time we did it this way. For the first eight, we play A once. For the second eight nothing. Then play the bridge. Then lay out for the last eight. Then do it the other way."

"In other words," Woods says, "alternate eights."

"Yes, but first one way, then the other. See what I mean? Let's try it. Thad, you blow two choruses."

Jones starts to blow with the group for eight bars, then off on his own for eight, back with the group for eight more, and so forth. Jones is just riding along for rehearsal's sake, of course, but he sounds good.

"Don't use the last eight," comments Travis at the end, "because it's up an octave. Use the first there."

Monk's movements, feet complemented by flying elbows, are developing into a kind of tap dance. At the same time, he still seems to be executing counterrhythms and special accents to the piece as they play it. Overton crosses over to him for a quiet discussion—a discussion on cigarettes, one might think from the concentration with which both of them are smoking.

Moving back to the front of the group again, the orchestrator says, "We've got exactly a half hour left. We don't have the parts on 'Four in One.' How would you like to spend it?"

"Let's work on 'Tootie,' " Jones says. "At E."

There is general agreement. But the musicians spend a short moment to chat and joke a bit beforehand; it is as if the group were gathering strength for a difficult task.

Then after a couple of minutes, Overton says, "Okay, here we go at E. One . . . two . . . one, two, three, four."

The choruses go well, but there are still rough spots.

"I want to take it at H."

To the rear, Monk is decidedly tap dancing now, in an unorthodox but effective way. The collar of his raincoat is quite wet. His face is still expressionless—or perhaps a bit solemn. And he seldom looks directly at anyone unless he is speaking to them—as if he were too shy to but not quite admitting it. He is listening, and his movements still seem to be a way of participating in the rehearsal—encouraging, feeling if it's right. From time to time, one or two of the players will turn to watch him briefly after a particularly heavy stomp or tap or a triplet.

"Could I have J, slower?" Overton asks, moving beside Riley, humming the band part and gesturing with his right hand to indicate snare accents.

"That's not the problem, playing that part there," suggests Richardson. "It's getting that accent right at a faster tempo."

"Once more this way, and then we'll do it fast."

As they go through it again, Overton lays his conductor's score aside and crosses to the piano. He sits down this time to play, and as he bends over the keys in playing Monk's part he almost takes Monk's piano position.

At the end, he turns to Woods and asks, "What do you think, Phil?"

"It's coming. Can we do the whole thing?"

"Good. Let's do it all, and, Thad, do two choruses solo, with the background. Then into E. Okay, right from the top. And Phil, you cut it off at the end, because you'll have to at the concert. They can all see you."

They play "Rootie Tootie" from the top, and suddenly the piece seems whole—from the opening ensembles, through the backgrounds through Jones' chorus, blowing into the variations at the end. The only thing missing is Monk.

"Hey, Phil," someone chides. "That wasn't a very classy cut-off."

"Don't listen to him—that was fine, Phil."

"Thanks a *lot!*"

"Okay," says Overton, smiling lightly at the banter. See you on Saturday at ten o'clock, here."

To the rear, Monk's percussive steps and patterns continue.

Down Beat, July 30, 1966

In Memoriam, Bud Powell

Pianist Earl "Bud" Powell died the night of August 1 in Kings County Hospital, New York. The obituaries mentioned tuberculosis, malnutrition, and alcoholism, but it might be said that Bud Powell died of something—a demon perhaps—that pursued him most of his life and that manifested itself in symptoms that were sometimes physical and sometimes psychological. Or perhaps Bud Powell died of the scarred, unreachably tragic nature of his own being and of the terrible buffeting that life had given him.

By the mid-forties, it was fairly common among insiders to say that Powell on piano was to the modern jazz of the time what Dizzy Gillespie was on trumpet and Charlie Parker on alto saxophone. Musically, he had followed a lead that they provided, to be sure, but to put it that he was "Bird on piano" is to overlook his pianistic heritage, which included an assimilation of (among others) Art Tatum and Teddy Wilson. It is also to overlook his own contributions; his most immediately obvious debt to Parker and Gillespie was that he had absorbed them rhythmically, but clearly he spoke their language with accents and punctuations of his own.

Within a few years some of his ideas had received the idle flattery of middle-brow popularization by George Shearing. But Powell also received the deeper compliments of a more legitimate following among a whole generation of younger pianists. "They cut him up like a gathering of anxious medical students working on a corpse," remarked one player in the early fifties, and many of them took what they could and played it the best they could. Certainly no one equaled the master. Horace Silver was one who understood that it was best not to try, but rather to take what one could and make something of one's own.

Powell sometimes played like a man running before a threat, and perhaps a part of him knew from the beginning that time would run out for him. There was an urgency in his playing that was sometimes almost extra-musical and sometimes not, and there was an emphatic precision in his touch, even at the fleetest tempos, that was, and has remained, entirely his own.

Powell's style belonged to the mid-forties, as does his heritage, and the best of his recordings were made by 1953. The great Powell is not the faintly pretentious composer who wrote "Glass Enclosure" out of Prokofiev, or who translated his youthful exercises into "Bud on Bach," or who came up with an effective Latin-esque novelty in "Un Poco Loco." Nor is it the Powell of slow ballads—the shadow of Tatum lingered across his keyboard all too often in such moods. The great Powell is the Powell of medium and fast tempo pieces from the modern repertory such as "Ornithology," "A Night in Tunisia," "Little Benny" (which in his version is called "Bud's Bubble"), "52nd Street Theme," "Parisian Thoroughfare," or the Powell of standard melodies at similar tempos such as "I'll Remember April," "Somebody Loves Me," "All God's Children Got Rhythm," or "Indiana."

Intricate structures to him weren't all-important; he found inspiration in both sophisticated outlines ("How High the Moon") and simple ones (the blues, and "I Got Rhythm"). His reharmonization of, say, "I Want to Be Happy" is both unassuming and ingenious, but what usually mattered in Powell's playing was his finding a basis, almost *any* basis, for his own inventive, linear energy, an energy that seemed both unabated and, one might say, insatiable. Melodies simply seemed to cascade out of him. But under inspection they prove to be logical melodies.

There is an astonishing moment on his first version of "A Night in Tunisia" where his right hand winds through a sustained linkage of notes for a full eight measures, unbroken by a single rest or bar line, but there is nothing of a technical stunt involved in that passage. Nor is there anything greatly exceptional about it, and, symbolically at least, the moment is characteristic Powell. It is also so musical that (as with many another of his improvised lines) if it were transcribed, slowed down, and played quietly, it would prove to have a natural lyricism that is both surprising and fundamental to its character.

Powell made, as time has already witnessed, too many records, and some of them are painful to attend. When he was ill, the otherwise precise, galvanized coordination of his hands was not there, and he seemed not to know it. And, toward the end, he made some recordings where the separate techniques of each hand had deteriorated. But throughout the fifties and into the sixties there were brief, heartening, but ultimately frustrating recoveries, when the old technique and creativity came back to him.

The best Powell is contained in two Blue Note albums called *The Amazing Bud Powell* (1503 and 1504); in his Roost album, *The Bud Powell Trio* (2224); and two Verve albums, *Bud Powell: Jazz Giant* (8153) and *The Genius of Bud Powell* (8115). (Those latter two especially had best be got while the getting is good, for the company has recently declared them out of print.) Powell as a member of a Charlie Parker Quintet is spread across two Savoy LPs (12001 and 12009). And he can be heard working in solo and accompaniment with various other of his fellow modernists on Savoy 12011 and Prestige 7248.

Saturday Review, August 27, 1966
Copyright © 1966 Saturday Review, Inc.

New Music on Blue Note

When Blue Note Records was founded twenty-seven years ago it was one of about three independent labels exclusively devoted to jazz. The company was at first the part-time project of Alfred Lion, together with his associate, Frank Wolff. Its earliest sessions included Sidney Bechet, on recordings that are still in print, and boogie-woogie piano solos by Mead Lux Lewis, Albert Ammons, and Pete Johnson. Those latter recordings are, unfortunately, no longer in print, but it was their popularity that made Blue Note a full-time proposition.

Blue Note recorded guitarist Charlie Christian when Christian was easily the most advanced instrumentalist in jazz. But it was not until 1947, a few years after modern jazz began to reach records, that Blue Note began working with modernists such as trumpeter Fats Navarro, composer Tadd Dameron, and pianists Bud Powell and Thelonious Monk, in sessions that, now transferred to twelve-inch LPs, are among the glories of the Blue Note catalogue.

Similarly, the label has approached the new thing, avant-garde music of the 1960s, with a bit of caution. It had an able second-generation modernist, Jackie McLean, under contract, and when MacLean moved into freely modal experimental areas, Blue Note recorded the results. As the label continued to sign promising young talent, it inevitably recorded the new music as played by younger men such as pianist Andrew Hill, trombonist Gracham Moncur III, vibist Bobby Hutcherson and others. By 1966, however, Blue Note had signed such leaders of the movement as pianist Cecil Taylor and alto saxophonist Ornette Coleman. Coleman's first Blue Note releases, as already noted in this space, are excellent, but so far there are no releases by Taylor.

Three recent Blue Note albums are by musicians directly associated with the ensemble of Miles Davis. *Spring* (Blue Note 4216) is led by Davis' young drummer, Anthony Williams. *Speak No Evil* (4194) is by his current tenor saxophonist, Wayne Shorter. The pianist on both of those albums is Davis' man Herbie Hancock, and on *Maiden Voyage* (4195) Hancock leads the Davis rhythm section—former Davis saxophonist George Coleman, and trumpeter Freddie Hubbard.

But the question of side-men does not end the matter, for a great deal of this music stems directly and indirectly from the more experimental pieces in the Davis repertory of the past few years, pieces such as "Milestones" (on Columbia CL 1193), pieces like those on the enormously influential *Kind of Blue* LP (Columbia CL 1355) by Davis and featuring John Coltrane, and pieces like those contributed by Shorter and Williams to the more recent (and I think less successful) Davis recording *E.S.P.* (Columbia CL 2350). The familiarity of those Davis records, and the subsequent exploration that Coltrane, particularly, has given to some of their ideas, gives some of the music on these Blue Note LPs an air of *déjà entendu.*

For me, much of it also has the air of calculated experiment without complete artistic success. Wayne Shorter, for one, is clearly Davis' best saxophonist in many years and a dedicated musician, but—at least on records—he has never realized the talent and potential that are clearly implicit in almost everything he does. There is one particularly heartening moment on his LP, however, a slow ballad called "Infant Eyes," which shows Shorter undertaking a mood that some young saxophonists seem almost afraid of.

There is a great deal to say about young Anthony Williams and I have said some of it in this space before. For now I will mention only that, while still under twenty, he had an astonishing resourcefulness and originality on his cymbals that, in itself, should grant him leadership among jazz drummers. Freddie Hubbard is unquestionably a fine trumpet player, but the most encouraging thing about his performance here is the evidence, asserted most clearly on a piece called "Survival of the Fittest," that he has broken away from his influences and is forming, particularly in rhythm, a personal and truly contemporary trumpet style. Hancock is a skillful pianist, and in the past some of his recorded performances have been conceived with real daring, but I confess that for me the results are sometimes bland. Perhaps in him the "new thing" has found, if not its Ahmad Jamal, then its Billy Taylor.

By far the most interesting of the Blue Note releases under review is *Complete Communion* (4226) by Ornette Coleman's ex-partner, cornetist Don Cherry, with Argentinian "Gato" Barbieri on tenor saxophone, Henry Grimes on bass, and Ed Blackwell on drums. The LP offers two long, four-part works, "Eliphantasy" and a more successful title piece, "Complete Communion."

Cherry has used his four instruments resourcefully and imaginatively. Each of the horns, as in Coleman's music, is allowed to interpret even a written passage so that in a "unison" ensemble the enunciation of a theme may be simultaneously varied. Cherry also uses counterpoint, written and improvised; he uses both the bass and the drums melodically, and the players respond marvelously. His themes and his improvised sections change tempo and flow logically one to the next; little phrases from each part of the work echo through the rest of it. The solos are frequent but relatively brief, and some of them do rush toward their climaxes a bit prematurely. But in "Complete Communion," Cherry, one of the prime movers on his instrument in contemporary jazz, has offered one of the new music's most interesting efforts at extended composition, a work of many delights, indicative, I hope, of more delights to come.

So far I have been speaking of recording from a label that has maintained its independence for over a quarter of a century. But it was recently announced that that independence has come to an end and that Blue Note has been bought by the expanding West Coast label, Liberty. Blue Note insists on its continuing autonomy in policy. One therefore can hope for the best, the best being that it does hang onto Coleman and Taylor and the others, and record them as they wish to be recorded. For, some day, the results will probably be among the established glories of the catalogue, just as those mid-forties modern sessions are now.

Saturday Review, September 17, 1966
Copyright © 1966 Saturday Review, Inc.

The Trials of Cecil Taylor

These days it might be difficult to find an American intellectual under fifty who does not at least give lip service to the proposition that jazz music is an art. Yet no publication in this country that considers itself highbrow—either among political weeklies or literary quarterlies—gives the music regular "live" coverage. That situation does not hold in England, by the way, for some of the best jazz commentary now appearing is written by Francis Newton for the *New Statesman*; over here one is apt to read more about jazz in one issue of some men's bosom monthly than in several years' issues of the *New Republic*. On the other hand, if you ask an intellectual to name, say, ten publications that he would consider middlebrow, he would surely include *The New Yorker*, *Harper's*, *The New York Times*, and *SR*, all of which give regular coverage to jazz.

In a manner that I trust to make clear in a moment, the foregoing was set in motion by the appearance of the first LP by the avant-garde pianist and composer Cecil Taylor under his new contract with Blue Note records, and also by the appearances of Whitney Balliett's *Such Sweet Thunder* (Bobbs-Merrill), and of A. B. Spellman's *Four Lives in the Bebop Business* (Pantheon).

Balliett's book is his third published collection of jazz reviews and profiles drawn largely from *The New Yorker*; it contains two concert reviews on Cecil Taylor. Indeed, Balliett's first *New Yorker* jazz piece (in 1957, and later collected by Dutton in *The Sound of Surprise*) was on Cecil Taylor. Taylor's work has also been covered and praised in *SR* and covered, if not always praised, by John S. Wilson in *The New York Times*.

Spellman's *Four Lives* includes Cecil Taylor, along with Ornette Coleman, Herbie Nichols, and Jackie McLean, and his book offers some of the most remarkable and penetrating biographical writing ever done about jazz musicians. The author maintains an unflinching fidelity to his subjects, including his subjects' ideas of themselves.

Whatever may have been written about him, Cecil Taylor has an avid following. He has not acquired a large audience or large success, and that is a subject on which Taylor has much to say in Spellman's book. But the arrival of his first Blue Note LP may remind one of the experience of organist Jimmy Smith, whom I discussed in this space recently. Jimmy Smith made one relatively unheralded LP for the same company and woke up not long thereafter to find the world beating a path to his keyboard with the price of admission in its hand. Here is Taylor's Blue Note release, *Unit Structures* (Blue Note 4237), made under his first contract with an established company, and one cannot help wondering what the public response will be. In any case, here is the response of one who has long attended, often admired, and on occasion been much moved by Taylor's music.

Cecil Taylor is the first jazz musician to make sustained, serious, and direct use of his knowledge of the most advanced European composers of this century. Taylor knows those composers first hand, whereas in the past, most jazz musicians have gotten their Ravel, say, from David Raksin and Pete Rugolo. But the result is not a tricky *pastiche* of Stravinsky, Bartók, Schoenberg, Ellington, and Monk; nor is it an interesting hybrid (a description of thinly disguised contempt, in any case). Taylor's music is his own, but if one has to categorize, jazz is his category.

Unit Structures offers four pieces, three of which are performed by a septet; the fourth is a Taylor piano solo. With the large ensemble, Taylor is everywhere. His commanding keyboard energy seems to instigate every note, bring forth every sound, bolster every idea, begin every wave of emotion that courses through the ensemble. The result is both an astonishing musical feat and a perfect plan for the kind of semi-composed, semi-improvised music that Taylor has to offer.

But after several hearings my feeling is that on at least two of the pieces, "Steps" and the three-part "Unit Structure," I have been listening to a passionate demonstration rather than a finished work. I except "Enter, Evening" and "Tales." The former is a lyric piece and the latter is the Taylor solo, remarkable both for its variety and its ultimate unity. But if I am justified in my estimates of "Steps" and "Unit Structure," I think it is possibly because of the breakneck tempos both pieces employ. Taylor, an exceptional player and musical thinker, performing and directing his own music, can sustain twenty minutes at a mad dash, but his side-men understandably may fall into banalities; it is very difficult to think that fast for that long, and perhaps it is a mistake (albeit a bold mistake) to ask most side-men to try.

Taylor, incidentally, provides his own program notes on the back liner. He writes a kind of quasi-poetry, and, although I do think I understand him, I question whether one art (or quasi-art if you will) provides the best commentary on another.

I will take the occasion to add that Taylor's best LPs are his *Looking Ahead* on Contemporary 7562 and his half of *Into the Hot* on Impulse A-9; anyone interested in what is going on in the new jazz will find essential music on those two Cecil Taylor LPs.

To return to Balliett for a moment, one might say on the face of it that a man would be entitled to the position of critic if he has shown that he can write a respectable essay on the work of a major musician. It is appalling how few jazz writers have performed that task, indeed, have even undertaken it. Balliett has not only undertaken the task but has done so in a highly individual way, sometimes using little more than a record or concert review as his point of departure. And I can recommend his remarkable description of Cecil Taylor at the keyboard, which begins on page 235 of *Such Sweet Thunder*, as essential reading for anyone who has never seen Taylor in person.

A final note: Capitol has reissued its two-record set by guitarist Django Reinhardt as a pair of single LPs. Volume 2 (T 10458), which includes an exceptional recording date by Reinhardt with three Ellington sidemen, is particularly recommended.

Saturday Review, March 11, 1967
Copyright © 1967 Saturday Review, Inc.

Words for Sarah Vaughan

Sarah Vaughan has one of the most remarkable voices that any of our popular singers has ever possessed. No, it's not quite fair for her to say that, because to find comparable voices one needs to turn to the opera or concert stage, and even there he will find few of them—perhaps none. Her voice has range, body, volume. More important, her control of her voice is phenomenal. Her pitch is just about impeccable, and she can jump the most difficult intervals and land true. No other singer has such an effortless command of dynamics; I know of no one who can move from a whisper to full volume in the course of a few notes and make the move sound less affected than Sarah Vaughan. When, as a young singer, she discovered her vibrato, she indulged it distressingly, but today her use of it—terminally, say, to end a sustained tone—should be the envy of every singer alive.

But her control goes quite beyond that which is required of any other *kind* of singer. For Sarah Vaughan is in several respects the jazz singer par excellence, and therefore she can do things with her voice that a trained singer knows simply must not be done. She can take a note at the top of her range and then bend it or squeeze it; she growls and rattles notes down at the bottom of her range; she can glide her voice through several notes at midrange while raising dynamics, or lowering, or simply squeezing.

To listen to Sarah Vaughan is to gain some idea of what singing must have been like for the great performers in the eighteenth century, when spontaneous embellishment, paraphrase, and perhaps, outright melodic improvisation were requisites. However, she is an American singer of this century, and that means that she is also capable of the great wealth of resources that jazz musicians and singers have discovered that musical expression can encompass.

And yet, and yet. It would be possible to name dozens of exceptional records by Bessie Smith, or dozens by Billie Holiday. With Ella Fitzgerald the general level of performance is very high, but seldom really excellent and seldom poor. With Sarah Vaughan, one would be hard put to come up with a dozen records that are truly excellent, although one could name many dozen brilliant failures without giving the matter much thought.

A few years ago, she was living a sort of double aesthetic life. Half the time she was holding back her powers and going after the "big hit." The other half, she was aiming for the jazz audience and giving the material all she had. The result with the former was that she didn't give us enough, and with the latter that she tended to treat each song like a kind of expanding suitcase into which she put nearly everything she could think of—or so it seemed.

There were always exceptions. In 1950, she did a version of "Mean to Me" (last available on *Sarah Vaughan in Hi-Fi*, Columbia, mono only, CL 745) in which, for most of her second chorus, she did something that perhaps no other jazz singer has ever done. That is, like a good instrumentalist, she improvised a totally new melody, and a quite imaginative one. Only a couple of years later, when she had discovered much more about the size and range of her voice, she gave Harold Arlen's "Come Rain or Come Shine" a discreet, self-contained but powerful reading, with very few embellishments and all of them good ones. (It is also on *Sarah Vaughan in Hi-Fi*).

From that point on, as she discovered more and more of the phenomenal nature of her voice, it seemed that fewer and fewer popular songs could contain her. There is, for example, a gloriously dramatic version of "Dancing in the Dark" in which every note seems to be bursting out of the confines of that song, and it is not exactly a simple one. The performance, nevertheless, should not be missed; it is part of a two-LP set, with the unlikely title *Great Songs from Hit Shows* (Mercury MGP-2-100), which is also not to be missed. We have jazz singers who, with spontaneous departures, can save bad songs and help good one, but Sarah Vaughan is a singer who can save overwrought arrangements, and she demonstrates it time and again on *Great Songs from Hit Shows*.

If I had to narrow the selection of Sarah Vaughan records down from a dozen to three, however, "Ain't No Use" would be one of them; it is on an album which, borrowing its billing from another Sarah, is called *The Divine One* (Roulette stereo, RS 52060; mono, R 52060). She teases that song, she cajoles it—to miss her sly but guileless humor is to miss her art—and she uses or implies almost all her vocal powers in doing so.

The Sarah Vaughan performances that do not satisfy usually seem diffuse and undisciplined. Sometimes diffuseness is deliberate, to be sure. On the new LP, *Sassy Swings Again* (Mercury 61116), she turns Joe Williams's specialty, "Every Day I Have the Blues," and Tony Bennett's specialty, "I Left My Heart in San Francisco," into wild vocal tours de force, and while they last they are marvelous.

The version of "All Alone," however, is apt to stay with us. There her embellishments and departures are few and discreet—or they seem so— and we may conclude that her problems of discipline are technical and vocal ones. Her first couple of choruses on Richard Rodgers' "The Sweetest Sounds" stay with us too, yet there her departures and improvisations are anything but simple. So perhaps the problem isn't really one of vocal discipline.

Perhaps her failures are dramatic failures; perhaps her diffuseness is emotional, not technical. She undertakes "All Alone" as a humorous plea for company, and sticks to that emotional point. And until a kind of floor-show bravura possesses it, "The Sweetest Sounds" is a nostalgic meditation.

In any case, it is good to know that this superb voice *can* express itself through small popular ditties, because it's very unlikely that we have a composer who will write her what she deserves. Ah, but if we did, there would be an improvisational oratorio or opera for Sarah Vaughan.

Saturday Review, August 26, 1967
Copyright © 1967 Saturday Review, Inc.

Legacy of John Coltrane

The sudden, unexpected death in July of tenor and soprano saxophonist John Coltrane robbed the younger generation of jazz musicians of one of its most respected and influential figures. Even those of an older generation of fans and musicians who sometimes shook their heads in puzzled disapproval at his later work knew that he had followed his muse faithfully and honorably. And both generations knew that, cut off prematurely as it was, his music left behind many technical and aesthetic problems for jazz—problems that perhaps only Coltrane himself could have resolved.

Most of us first heard him some twelve years ago as a member of the Miles Davis Quintet, and he was then already an original musician, original in the most important way for a jazz man, in rhythm. For, much as Charlie Parker subdivided the jazz that had preceded him rhythmically, Coltrane seemed to want to subdivide it even further. If one can say that, roughly, Charlie Parker thought rhythmically in eighth notes, Coltrane seemed to be trying to think in sixteenths.

Otherwise Coltrane was a kind of contemporary Coleman Hawkins. Most tenor saxophonists who had assayed Parker's idiom had admired Hawkins' big sound and harmonic precision, but they preferred Lester Young's linear inventiveness, and his dancing rhythmic variety, to Hawkins' more or less regularly delivered arpeggios. But Coltrane, like Hawkins, was a vertical player.

Coltrane was also an assertive player, with a strong and almost brittle edge to his saxophone sound, unlike anything that jazz had heard before him. But there was a shyness and reticence to him also that showed itself in his early solos in an occasional fumbling of notes, particularly in terminal phrases.

It was prophetic that one of Coltrane's best solos from his stay with Miles Davis should have been on Thelonious Monk's piece " 'Round Midnight," for it was during a subsequent stay with Monk that all the powers implicit in the saxophonist's early work asserted themselves. He became a prodigious harmonicist, but, guided by Monk pieces like "Trinkle Tinkle," he was an orderly soloist at the same time. And the lessons learned while he was with Monk showed themselves on Coltrane's own LPs as well. The title piece on *Blue Train* has an eeriness and mystery that stayed with him in much of his subsequent work. "Locomotion," from the same LP, has his rhythmic sense at perhaps its fullest development.

But at this point, Coltrane was a leader only in recording studios. Otherwise he had rejoined Miles Davis, and one of his best solos with him was again on a Monk piece, the blues piece called "Straight, No Chaser."

"Coltrane," Davis said to him, "You don't have to play *every*thing!" The statement is perhaps apocryphal, but it is nevertheless indicative. For Coltrane was still thinking vertically, and he seemed prepared to gush out every conceivable note, run his way a step at a time through every complex chord, every extension, and every substitution, and go beyond that by reaching for sounds that no tenor saxophone had ever uttered before him.

Then came the Miles Davis modal pieces like "So What" and "All Blues," which virtually reversed the course of modern jazz and the techniques that had occupied its players since the mid-1940s. It was as if Davis had said, "Let's stop playing on complex chords and fancy harmonic substitutions. Let's see how interesting we can be on just a chord or two. Or let's forget about chords as such and just play around with a scale or two." On those pieces John Coltrane was interesting indeed, and the approach to jazz improvisation that they suggested occupied him in one sense or another for the rest of his life.

He left Miles Davis and went out on his own, and a rather unexpected thing happened to him. He encountered a popular song that had the same sort of structure he was interested in, a folklike simplicity and incantiveness, and very little harmonic motion. Coltrane recorded Richard Rodgers' "My Favorite Things," and it became a best seller.

So John Coltrane found himself a success. But for the crowds who came to the jazz clubs to hear him, "My Favorite Things" was apt to occupy a half hour of furious, unfamiliar interplay between the leader and his brilliant drummer, Elvin Jones. "Impressions," from a "live" recording session at the Village Vanguard in 1961, is a revisit to the same Dorian mode that Miles Davis had used on "So What"; and "Chasin' the Trane," from the same session, is basically blues and has become one of the most influential of Coltrane's recordings. Both performances show that changes were taking place in Coltrane's music. The knowledgeable vertical player had become a horizontal, linear improviser. Little melodic phrases, motives if you will, are not so much developed and resolved as they are repeated over and over. Coltrane's approach had become frankly incantatory.

Listeners are apt to be of two minds about such performances for the very basic reason that one man's incantation may turn out to be another man's monotony. But Coltrane did have moments of contemplation, relative serenity, and perhaps resolution. There is his admirably straightforward reading of Duke Ellington's "In a Sentimental Mood," in a duet with the composer; there is his long devotional piece, "A Love Supreme," which became his second best seller; and there is the remarkable progression of pieces on the "A" side of the LP called *Crescent* —the title piece, followed by the "Wise One," and "Bessie's Blues."

Coltrane did, indeed, follow his muse faithfully and honorably, and if the changes in his music in the scant twelve years he had in the public eye are true signs of growth, then John Coltrane challenged himself and grew and developed perhaps more than any other hornman in jazz history. He already has his followers and imitators from each two- or three-year period of his work. Some of them, of course, merely decorate the middle portions of the latest release by our pop singers, but even they know the challenges of a superb saxophone technique. To the more talented and serious of his heirs, there are the challenges implicit in such later Coltrane LP's as *Ascension.*

For the rest of us, even if we find many of the later works frustrated and unresolved, we should acknowledge that the dangers and the frustrations and the torments were real, and that they were a part of the deeper frustration of the times which it was Coltrane's destiny to articulate musically. As I wrote of him in *SR* last year, "I think that a performance like *Ascension* might be heard, felt, and reflected upon by every politician, police official, psychologist, social worker, editorial writer—perhaps every American. . . . If a listener is at first confused or repelled by it, perhaps he should hear it again. . . . Coltrane's jazz, like much good jazz, looks deep into the inner beings of all men." Coltrane's reading of " 'Round Midnight" with Miles Davis is on Columbia CL 949. His stay as a Monk sideman is documented on Riverside 490, with "Trinkle Tinkle" and "Ruby My Dear," and the Miles Davis "Straight, No Chaser," is on Columbia CL 1193.

Coltrane's *Blue Train* LP, which also includes "Locomotion" and "Moment's Notice," is Blue Note 1577, and *Giant Steps* is Atlantic LP 1361. The original "My Favorite Things" is on Atlantic 1361, and a new version has recently appeared on Impulse A-9124.

Impulse A-10 has "Chasin' the Trane," but "Impressions," recorded at the same session, is on Impulse A-42. The Coltrane-Ellington recital, with "In a Sentimental Mood," is on Impulse A-30. The *Crescent* LP is Impulse A-66. And the successful *A Love Supreme* is Impulse A-77. The more recent *Meditations,* Impulse A-9110, is offered as a sequel to *A Love Supreme.* And *Ascension* occupies both sides of Impulse A-95.

Saturday Review, September 16, 1967
Copyright © 1967 Saturday Review, Inc.

Monday Night at the Village Vanguard

Seventh Avenue South in New York City is Seventh Avenue below 14th Street, a truck-and-taxi-laden street that courses through Greenwich Village. On the west side of Seventh, just below a street that is now marked Murly Square, there is a canvas canopy leading from the sidewalk's edge to a neat, white double door. Above the canopy is a modest neon sign that announces "Village Vanguard."

Through the white doors, a steep stairway descends to the cellar, and at the foot of the stairs, a second door opens to a small, triangular, dimly lit basement room. This is the Vanguard, one of the best-known and longest-surviving night clubs in New York.

Inside, a slight, studious-looking young man is collecting $3 from each arriving customer. It is Monday, and Monday nights are special at the Vanguard. For the $3 admission, plus whatever else one may want to pay for drinks and food, one gets to hear the Thad Jones-Mel Lewis Orchestra live, and its most ardent admirers will tell you that the Thad Jones-Mel Lewis Orchestra is the best large jazz ensemble there is.

To the right and the left, the club's deep-red walls, decorated with scattered photographs and some ancient tubular instruments, lead one's eyes toward the point of the triangle, where sits the club's bandstand. Ordinarily, a quartet can look pretty crowded up there at the end of the Vanguard, but tonight somehow, there are fourteen chairs and music stands up there plus drums and piano.

It is 9:30 P.M. There are approximately six couples seated at the club's tiny circular tables in the center floor, or at the small rectangular ones against the walls. It's early as things go on a Vanguard Monday; the insiders know there is no real point in arriving until about 10.

Over the PA system, a recorded pianist is playing a Charlie Parker blues; the volume is turned low. A young girl seated against the east wall is saying to her date, loudly for some reason, ". . . off base *again!*" and topping it with an energetic giggle. The lights are dim, but clearly she is a redhead. By the entrance a waiter is explaining a complex chess move to the young doorman.

Pepper Adams, resembling a cheerful, businesslike owl, arrives, crosses to the bandstand, puts a Manila folder on one of the front-row music stands, and disappears to the rear.

The "rear" of the Vanguard is at the lower east point of its triangle, an enclosed area behind the bar that somehow manages to contain the kitchen, the men's room, and a "backstage" area with a small table and a couple of chairs for the musicians for use between sets.

To the rear, a trumpet (or is it Jones's cornet or a fluegelhorn?) warms up, clashing with the pianist on the loudspeakers. Another trumpet joins him—isn't that Richard Williams? The bartender briefly adds to the cacophony with a shaker full of mixed booze and ice.

Adams, laden with his baritone, heads for the bandstand. He is followed by Billy Mitchell with tenor saxophone and clarinet. The buzz of conversation is louder now, louder and expectant. A couple in their late fifties, in the company of a younger man and woman, arrive. The group is neatly and conservatively dressed, like most the other customers.

As they are seated, a lean young man carrying a bass crosses the bandstand and introduces himself to trombonist Wayne Andre, who is opening his instrument case. The bassist is Miroslav Vitous, a young Czech of high reputation, substituting tonight for Richard Davis. As they leave the stand, drummer Lewis arrives, earnest and hurried, and rushes to the stage, where he removes a raincoat and starts setting up. Thad Jones, now on the bandstand checking things out, stops to talk over an administrative point with his co-leader.

In a few minutes the musicians begin to head for the front of the clubroom. One or two drop by the bar or at tables to greet friends and regulars.

"Gimme a drink before the fight starts," someone says. The room is about two-thirds full now, and many of the customers are eyeing the entering musicians, intently or self-consciously. To the rear, one of the waiters, a white-haired man with a middle European accent is confiding to someone at the bar, "I opened this place, you know. Yeah, been here steady since the first night."

The first night for the Village Vanguard was in 1934, thirty-three years ago. The club was started by Max Gordon, who still owns it and runs it and still comes in about every night. Gordon, a short and usually pleasant man, whose round, sometimes cherubic and sometimes intent face is decorated above the ears by what remains of his curly white hair, will explain that he came to New York from Portland, Ore., and got his first job washing dishes in a cafeteria. When the Vanguard opened, it was at first a place where one might have heard Maxwell Bodenheim or Harry Kemp read their poetry, while young painters argued about Georges Braque. A couple of years later, the entertainment was provided by a then-unknown group called The Reviewers: Judy Holiday, Adolph Green, and Betty Comden, with a young pianist named Leonard Bernstein.

Subsequently, the Village Vanguard offered folk music, from Leadbelly's southern U.S. songs to the Duke of Iron's Caribbean calypso; or it had cabaret songs with Eartha Kitt or Harry Belafonte; and comedy by Pearl Bailey and Wally Cox. And there were the Weavers, Robert Clary, Orson Bean—the list is long, and the subsequent successes are many. The club was a tourist attraction that was still considered a hip and "inside" place by New Yorkers themselves.

Fairly consistently, jazz was a part of the bill. Willie "The Lion" Smith worked with the calypso men. Drummer Zutty Singleton brought in a group. Jimmy Hamilton was featured. My own earliest memory of the club is seeing Roy Eldridge there for the first time in 1942 (and wondering when somebody was going to realize I was underage and throw me out).

About ten years ago, Gordon reversed his policy, putting jazz at the top of the bill and letting the folknicks (like the Brothers Four or the

Clancy Brothers) and the comics (Mort Sahl, Mike Nichols and Elaine May, Lennie Bruce, Woody Allen, Irwin Cory) fill it out. Thus the Vanguard booked Miles Davis, Horace Silver, Thelonious Monk, Gerry Mulligan, the Modern Jazz Quartet, Jimmy Giuffre, Anita O'Day, Charlie Mingus, Bill Evans (a regular), Stan Getz, Carmen McRae.

The Monday night sessions with the Jones-Lewis band began about a year and a half ago. Gordon and disc jockey-entrepreneur Alan Grant heard that such a band was out there somewhere rehearsing and went to hear it. The band has been playing, usually to packed houses, on the club's off night ever since, and even for a few weeks as the "regular" attraction.

Jones sits doodling now at the piano. "Snookie Young!" someone greets the lead trumpeter to the rear of the stand. Jerome Richardson, a forceful man in any context, enters with a rack of horns and heads for his seat. Tom McIntosh sits at the end of the line of four trombones. In the house, some musician visitors are beginning to arrive, as they usually do on these Mondays. Joe Henderson is leaning against a back wall. Guitarist Atilla Zoller sits near the end of the bar, smiling as usual.

On the bandstand, the numbers of the sequence of tunes for the first set are being voiced around. "I think the competition got us this evening," says Richardson, nodding at the few empty tables to the rear of the room.

Sudddenly there is the din of a wild tune-up, as Jones stand in front of the ensemble clapping both for and order and to give a tempo.

"It's two hundred twelve and *then* sixteen!" someone is loudly explaining to his neighbor through the sound. Then out of the chaos, all is order as the first piece has begun. All eight brass are playing forte, and the small room is full of sound, yet somehow it is not loud, only exhilarating. Thad solos, telling his story with an easy fluency. The band comes back in. Figures, well up, spread across the ensemble and then subside. The group shouts, and whispers with the same conviction, and the music seems constantly to move forward with a kind of graceful relentlessness.

"Well, all right!" comments Richardson while the last note is still subsiding. Jones thanks the audience for its applause and the microphone fades and crackles on him a bit as he announces that the piece had been "Low Down." Next, he says, will be a ballad, "All My Yesterdays," to feature trombonist Garnett Brown. Brown grins, shakes his head, and points energetically to Andre on his left.

A young man says to his date at a back table, "That's him! See him?"

He is indicating one of the saxophonists. "He's here this time. But no matter who shows up, the band still sounds great."

During the ballad, a couple comes through the entrance. He looks to be about thirty; she looks to be sixty; both look like middle-class suburbanites. The crowd, its attention as usual centered on the band, shows a scattered annoyance as a waiter shows them to a table and asks if they want to order anything.

Five minutes later, the band is into a medium-tempo piece. Jones is rocking from one foot to another, clapping softly—he is conducting, dancing, encouraging, and enjoying himself, all at once. Then tenorist Lou Tabakin is into an energetic Coltrane-esque solo, which has the enthusiastic attention of the audience and the bandsmen. A bit later, behind Jones's solo, all twelve horns are executing a figure that kicks along but doesn't blast.

The cornetist-leader announces that the final selection will be a blues. Richardson begins it entirely alone, with several fast choruses. On Jones's signal, Vitous' bass joins him and then Lewis' drums. Each entrance paradoxically relieves the tension and then sets up a tension of its own. The ensemble enters. Then, suddenly, trombonists Brown and Andre are trading phrases. Then Brown solos. Andre rejoins him. Brown drops out again. The relay effect is stunning.

Richardson returns, and the trombones back him with a tonally oblique figure that sets trumpeter Young to grinning broadly. The dynamics duck way down for Chick Corea's piano solo, but the crowd still listens.

Then Brown is up for still another solo. He manages to bean Richardson with his slide. It gets a laugh, of course, from the band and the patrons alike.

The piece ends with some fine trumpet shakes on top, and the applause is enthusiastic and sustained. Clearly this band has its following, probably the most attentive following to be found in any club today.

The musicians leave the stand, but even now they look quite ready for another set. Jones joins some friends at a table. Adams and Lewis chat with a couple of fans. Over by the bar, Zoller is explaining a fine point of amplification to Max Gordon. Through the door comes trombonist Eddie Bert, horn in hand, ready to play the next set with the group.

A middle-aged fan, seated at the end of the bar nursing a beer, is holding forth, "Now the Fatha Hines band of the mid-forties—that had Bird and Dizzy, you know. Bird was playing tenor. That was quite a band. Then there was the Eckstine band. He had *everybody*—Dizzy,

Fats Navarro, Kenny Dorham, even Miles, who was pretty young then, and Bird, Dexter Gordon, Lucky Thompson, Art Blakey. That was quite a band. Then there was Dizzy's band. . . ." He trails off momentarily, but then turns to the bartender abruptly, saying, "But *this* band! . . ."

Down Beat, November 30, 1967

Big Bands and Miles

I don't think the big bands are coming back. Their work was largely done by the early 1940s. By then, they had spread the word and popularized a musical idiom pretty thoroughly, and there was little left for them to do but repeat themselves. Those that survive either had something special to say in the first place, and still do (Ellington); or they have something to add in the second place (Basie, Herman, Hampton); or they repeat themselves so well that it would probably be difficult to do without them (Goodman).

But to say that the big bands aren't coming back is not to say that there isn't room for more big bands than we've got, and the past couple of years have seen the formation of a number of large jazz ensembles which have been getting along reasonably well and may well find permanent success, or at least be able to stick it out.

One of the most successful is led by drummer Buddy Rich, and its second LP, called *Big Swing Face* (Pacific Jazz stereo, ST-20117; mono, PJ-10117), has appeared. Rich's ensemble is young, spirited, and by now highly polished. He has good players, obviously, but his soloists by and large offer the clichés of a few years back. The arrangements are professional but they tend to be somewhat formless, and they are also given to the clichés of a few years back. The band attempts to come to terms with a few rock 'n' roll devices; the idea is all right in itself but some of the figures, like those on "The Beat Goes On" or "Wack Wack" or "Norwegian Wood," get pretty monotonous when they are ground out for four minutes by an ensemble of sixteen pieces.

Always and everywhere, there is the presence of Buddy Rich. Rich is one of the most technically well-equipped drummers in jazz. His style has expanded over the years, but of course he still "thinks" rhythmically in the manner of the late 1930s. Rich also has an enthusiastic capacity to play *with* an ensemble that is a wonder to hear, and that capacity is much in evidence on the best score on the LP, Pete Meyer's arrangement of "Love for Sale."

It is my own feeling, however, that Buddy Rich has a sizable incapacity to *let* the music happen—that he is always trying to make something happen—and sometimes he seems unaware that something already is happening. On the one hand, he is like a would-be Edward G. Robinson coercively trying to boss the mob. On the other, he is like an anxious dowager who is giving a successful party but doesn't know it, and who moves restlessly about with a fixed smile, chattering away, breaking up perfectly agreeable conversations to introduce guests to other guests they really don't need to meet, and interrupting raconteurs with a forced laugh before they have got to the point.

The young trumpeter Don Ellis is the leader of a large jazz ensemble that has received much favorable press, particularly since its appearance at the Monterey Jazz Festival in 1966. Frankly, I had grave misgivings about a band that proclaims itself in the avant-garde, that features such gimmicks as electronically augmented instruments, that has three bass players and five drummers, and that was given to time-signatures like 7/4, or 7/8 plus 9/8, or, as the heady title of the ensemble's new LP has it, *Live in three and two-thirds over four Times* Pacific Jazz stereo, ST-20123; mono, PJ-10123). I was expecting a kind of pretentious, Kentonesque posturing on the one hand, and Brubeckian stiltedness on the other. But this ensemble performs with a relaxed and frequently winning sense of fun and an unpretentious feeling of adventure as well. The arrangements had a gratifying overall sense of form. And the young soloists are very good. True, some of the tricky rhythms are carried by the percussion while the soloists skate gracefully over them using a more conventional jazz accentuation. And also true, Ellis, an excellent brass player, is basically a Gillespie-inspired musician, which is to say that his accents fall pretty much in the manner of the mid-1940s. So I do not think the music is quite so avant-garde as it may seem.

Johnny Come Lately (RCA Victor, LPV-541, mono only) is a collection of sixteen titles from 1942–45 by the master, Duke Ellington. There are some relatively ephemeral vocals and novelties included, like "Hayfoot, Strawfoot," or "A Slip of the Lip Can Sink a Ship." But there is also, for example, "Sherman Shuffle"—a very good Ellington instrumental—and there is an arrangement of "Caravan" which in my opinion quite surpasses the original reading of that piece.

The album is not intended as a memorial to composer-arranger Billy Strayhorn, having been put together before Strayhorn's recent death, but in a perhaps significant way it might serve as one. Strayhorn came to Ellington as a writer of quasi-sophisticated songs, pieces like "Something to Live For," "Lush Life," and "I Don't Mind," which is included here. Ellington encouraged him to write instrumental works like the fine title-piece, "Johnny Come Lately." In such pieces Strayhorn discovered a strength which, I am sure, will long outlast the adolescent ballads.

Finally, let me give a somewhat belated notice to the Miles Davis LP, *Miles Smiles* (Columbia stereo, CS 9401; mono, CL 2601). The album is directly in the tradition of the "experimental" Davis recordings, the tradition established by *Kind of Blue* (stereo, CS 8163; mono, CL 1355) in 1959—an album whose implications jazz musicians are still exploring—and continued by *E.S.P.* (stereo, CS 9150; mono, CL 2350) of 1965—an album which seemed to me much less successful. *Miles Smiles* is an exceptional recital, Davis's best album in some time, and clear evidence of his continuing dedication as an improvising musician. I was particularly taken by Davis's solo on his own ballad, "Circle," and by the way he reemploys some of his favorite phrases on the Jimmy Heath piece "Gingerbread Boy." Davis's saxophonist, Wayne Shorter, both a writer and player, contributes some of his best work so far. Pianist Herbie Hancock plays with a firm strength I do not hear on the LPs he has been making under his own name. As for bassist Ron Carter and drummer Tony Williams, their superb contributions are beyond the words I could muster for so brief an account as this one.

Saturday Review, September 30, 1967
Copyright © 1967 Saturday Review, Inc.

Steve Kuhn, Piano

In the 1940s there was published a book of casual humor, anecdote and interview by H. Allen Smith called *Low Man on a Totem Pole*. Such a volume may seem an unlikely place for an historian of American music to be doing research, but there is a chapter in it about a small child, the son of an avid jazz fan with a sizeable collection of swing-era recordings. The infant boy, barely able to talk, was very fond of the records and able to tell one group from another. He is described at one point as pointing to the phonograph and gleefully identifying "Benny Gooman, Benny Gooman!"

That listening prodigy was Steve Kuhn, and he remained something of a prodigy for years thereafter. While still a teenager and a high school student in Boston, he was working with the likes of Coleman Hawkins, Vic Dickenson, Chet Baker, and Serge Chaloff. Out of the prodigy class, he subsequently worked in New York with John Coltrane, Kenny Dorham, Stan Getz, Art Farmer, and Charles Lloyd.

Steve Kuhn was born in Brooklyn, and as indicated, he began his acquaintance with jazz at a tender age. As soon as he was physically able, he was putting the records on the turntable and playing them for himself. And by the time he was five, he knew that he wanted to be a musician. On the advice of his father, who had been taught violin in his own youth, he undertook piano as the best place to start, a place from which he could move on to other instruments if he wanted to. He has never wanted to.

As Kuhn remembers it, he found it very difficult to play the classics that were an inevitable part of his instruction without doing some tampering. "Apparently I could improvise some even then, and it was hard for me not to when playing the little Bach and Mozart pieces I was assigned. My teacher knew about my interest in jazz, so as a reward for a good lesson, he would bring in some of the Pine Top Smith and Meade Lux Lewis boogie woogie transcriptions that had been published and let me play them."

In 1947, the elder Kuhn's business took him to Chicago for three years, and then to Boston in 1950. It was in Boston that Kuhn began working as a sideman accompanist to the aforementioned visiting stars, or with local men like Ruby Braff, as a kind of house-pianist at Storyville and its downstairs branch, Mahogany Hall. He also became an irregular regular at the Stable with Herb Pomeroy's sextet.

Kuhn also continued his studies, now with Margaret Chaloff, the renowned classical piano teacher who loves jazz and has been a friend to jazzmen (Charlie Parker used to refer to her as "Mama" and she is very proud of that fact). Her son was of course Serge Chaloff, the baritone saxophonist. Chaloff became a major influence on the young Kuhn and gave him ideas about comping and how to play behind a soloist, ideas about soloing, and a general approach to the problems involved in getting up in front of people and making music.

"We took all kinds of jobs in little clubs around Boston for about eight or nine dollars a night. And often Serge would be yelling out to me the changes he wanted to hear in the piece we were playing, but I never felt he was doing it insultingly. I would come off the stand drenched in perspiration time after time, but I really felt as if I'd done something up there. It was hard work too, because we usually had to work without a bass player," Kuhn recalls.

Another influence on Kuhn was Dick Twardzik, the Boston pianist who died in France in 1955 while touring with the Chet Baker group. "I admired Twardzik very much, particularly harmonically. He listened to all the modern European composers and was quite advanced.

"He would play relief piano at the Stable, and he was supposed to be on for about twenty minutes. But he would get so involved that he might play on and on, usually working on the same piece. Finally, Herb Pomeroy gave him an alarm clock, and when the bell would go off, Dick would stop exactly where he was, pick up the clock and leave the stand.

"He once paid me a compliment on my playing—I was still very young then—and of course I've never forgotten it."

By this time, Kuhn's modern jazz influences were beginning to emerge. He still loved Fats Waller, for one, but he had begun to admire Erroll Garner, Horace Silver—particularly for his feeling—Lennie Tristano, Tommy Flanagan, and above all, Bud Powell. It was only after he had begun to learn from Powell's work, by the way, that Kuhn began to appreciate Art Tatum.

It was not until some time later, during his last year in college, that Kuhn began to appreciate Bill Evans, a player to whom he is sometimes compared. "When he got it together, to me, it was as though he had done something that most of the good jazz pianists had been contributing to, and reaching for, for several years," Kuhn says.

Meanwhile, still in high school, Kuhn had begun to work around Boston on his own in a trio with drummer Arnie Wise, and, at first, bassist John Neves, later Chuck Israels.

In the summer of 1955, incidentally, Kuhn was scheduled to perform a Prokofiev piano concerto with the Boston Pops Orchestra, and he and Margaret Chaloff worked on it for a year. But it turned out the orchestra didn't know the piece and couldn't take the time to rehearse it.

The following fall, Kuhn was at Harvard as a music major, and work with the trio continued. In 1957, he, Israels, and Wise made a trio recording for United Artists, but the session came at a time when UA was losing interest in jazz and it was never released.

In the summer of 1959, Kuhn was a scholarship student at the School of Jazz in Lenox, Mass. It was an important session for that school in several ways, and one of these was the presence of two other students named Ornette Coleman and Don Cherry. "I was put into the same group with Ornette, and we were playing his music. It was the best group, and I was flattered to be in it. At the same time, I was confused about what to do. Max Roach was the faculty instructor of the group and John Lewis was also around a lot of the time. I asked John how he thought I could best fit into the music. I knew what Ornette was doing. I have absolute pitch and I could hear the quarter tones and micro-tones of his music."

Kuhn did find a way to fit in, and in the final school concert he played a relatively simple melodic solo on Coleman's "The Sphinx." Many another pianist with Kuhn's technical equipment, but with less discretion and taste, would surely have thrown caution to the winds and been all over the keyboard showing off his prowess.

Schooling done, Kuhn headed for New York to seek a career as a jazz musician. In the fall of 1959, he became a member of Kenny Dorham's quintet—Dorham had also been a faculty member at the School of Jazz —along with baritone saxophonist Charles Davis and bassist Butch Warren. They worked in Brooklyn, did jobs in Washington, Montreal, and elsewhere, and had a stay at the Five Spot in New York.

"Then I heard that Coltrane was leaving Miles Davis and looking for a band. I called him up, saying that I didn't know if he knew who I was, but could we get together and just play a bit. I knew it sounded funny and that it wasn't the usual way of doing things, and I said so. He said he'd let me know. He called me back—I suppose he must have been asking around about me in the meantime—and said we'd rent a studio and play some. We played for about two or three hours. Then we went out and had dinner. He was kind of quiet about things, as he always was about everything. We drove back to his house on Long Island and played some more, about four or five hours this time. Afterward, he and his wife rode me back to Manhattan, and when they let me off he said he'd call. Two days later he did call. He simply named a salary and asked me if it would be all right. We opened at the Jazz Gallery with bassist Steve Davis and drummer Pete LaRoca.

"He was all music—everything was music for him. I had never met anyone in jazz so completely intense and dedicated about the music before Coltrane," the pianist said.

"As for my work with him, I figured, I could do *anything*. But with

the freedom I was allowed, I ran too much of the spectrum, and the result wasn't really together. Finally, he gave me notice, saying that he
had to and couldn't really tell me why. To tell you the truth, I was just
about to give *him* notice, because I knew it wasn't working musically.
But the event was still hard for me to swallow. I simply hadn't found
myself stylistically. I was not supporting him, really. In a sense I was
competing. He wanted McCoy Tyner, and when I heard them together,
I knew McCoy was supporting him.

"I would see Coltrane afterwards, of course. I remember once I ran
into him on the street, and he said to me quite seriously, 'Steve, show
me something new.' Imagine! Me show *him* something new. He never
stopped searching. His total dedication never let up."

Asked whom he would name as the epitome of swing, incidentally,
Steve Kuhn unhesitatingly answers, "Coltrane."

Early in 1961, Kuhn joined Stan Getz through the intervention of the
late bassist Scott LaFaro. Kuhn greatly admires Getz's technique, faci-
lity, and harmonic imagination. "He is a marvelous player, and his ballads are masterful."

When he left Getz, Kuhn felt that perhaps now he could really get together his own trio. To that end, he rented a studio and made a record
of his own, hoping to place it with an established company. He didn't
succeed.

Before long, Kuhn was working with Art Farmer's quartet, after the
departure of guitarist Jim Hall and at the suggestion of bassist Steve
Swallow. But during that time there was a trio album for a small label,
Contact.

For the past two and a half years, Steve Kuhn has also been a part-
time piano teacher. His students have represented all levels, from begin-
ners through amateurs to professionals. "I was against doing it at first,
but now I feel that as my own playing schedule permits, I want to maintain as many students as I can for the rest of my life. I learn a lot from
it."

Otherwise, Kuhn has held out for the past two years for work as a
leader of his own trio, taking on an occasional gig, perhaps, but no regular jobs. He has also made a very well-received album for Impulse,
The October Suite, a collaboration between Kuhn and composer Gary
McFarland, another fellow-student from the 1959 session of the School
of Jazz. Kuhn feels that the music on this album, although it involves a
string quartet on some selections and a woodwind group on others, is

also representative of the kind of music his trio makes. "I think that in the last ten years, I have learned all that I'm going to learn from the jazz tradition. My influences are assimilated and my own style has taken shape. I listen to a great deal of classical music, including Chopin and Liszt, but especially from Debussy to the present. But in my own playing, I think jazz is where my feeling is. If my music represents a kind of converging of two idioms, all right, but for me there is no question that the jazz feeling is the strongest.

"We play selected standards, a couple of originals by Carla Bley, and, more and more, my own originals. We need some point of departure, some frame of reference, and so does the audience, but we treat the pieces without preconceptions as to tempo or chord changes. We may pick a standard—a new one, say, like one of Burt Bacharach's pieces— but we might use only parts of its melody, its opening phrase or opening couple of phrases, as a basis for what we improvise."

Kuhn feels strongly that communication with an audience is the crux of the matter for a musician, and he believes that the concert stage presents the best future milieu for his group. Not just the big halls in the large cities, but the hundreds or thousands of smaller halls throughout the country, particularly those on college campuses.

"The auditoriums are there, and so are the potential audiences—appreciative audiences, I think, for jazz of all kinds. Someone has got to get it together, set up the circuit and start the booking. We'll play clubs too. There's one advantage to playing in clubs, you know. You don't often come away feeling the evening has been too short."

Down Beat, February 8, 1968

"Bash It!" A Jaki Byard Recording Date

The Impact studios are on West 65th Street and they are, therefore, in what is now called the Lincoln Center area of New York City. But Impact's narrow building was there long before Lincoln Center was a gleam in a real-estate speculator's eye or a twitch in a culture-monger's pocketbook.

Impact is a second-floor walk-up, and en route one might assume that its building is otherwise deserted. The studio is a favorite of Don Schlitten, jazz producer for Prestige records, and Schlitten had booked it for 1 P.M. on a day this spring to record pianist Jaki Byard "with strings." "The strings" were to be Ray Nance's violin, Ron Carter's cello, Richard Davis' bass, and George Benson's guitar. Also set was Prestige's favorite drummer, Alan Dawson, doubling on vibraharp. There were to be some formal arrangements by Byard and some head arrangements to be worked up on the date.

By 12:55, Carter, Davis, and Benson, with the help of Impact's Eddie Heath, were set up inside the studio. The small room now seemed a mass of waist-high baffles and sounding boards and an intricate tangle of stereo microphones, booms, and wires. These somehow managed to leave enough space for a piano, drums, vibes, and strings, and perhaps even the musicians to go with them.

Benson entered the control room to the rear of the studio, and spotting a particular mixer against the left wall, remarked that this was the kind he intended to add to his own equipment. Within a few minutes, Nance had arrived and greeted the other players. He quickly had his violin out, took a look at his music, and asked Heath for a music stand.

Impact's engineer, Richard Alderson, was checking dials and tapes when Byard and Dawson entered at 1:10. Byard announced himself to one and all with a broad, mock-serious, "Well!"

He was dressed in a tweed jacket and flannel trousers, and he wore a tie.

He entered the booth to chat with Schlitten and then soon got down to business. His voice conveyed a combination of energy and eagerness, with a bit of nervousness.

"I'm going to use 'Exactly Like You' to jam a little," he said.

"Why don't you play 'Take the "A" Train' at the same time?" Schlitten remarked, proposing a counterpoint of two familiar tunes on closely allied chord changes.

"Oh, I've got something better than that," Byard answered cryptically.

In the studio, Alderson moved a few mikes and formed Carter, Benson, and Davis into a kind of ritual circle of strings. Carter began a riff, and Nance and Davis soon joined him. They were running over the introduction to the first piece.

"Fellows, make those even eighth-notes," said Byard entering the studio. His voice was authoritative and friendly but somewhat edgy. Then he tossed over his shoulder to Schlitten, "It'll be good when I get in there and play with them."

He crossed to the piano and said, "Okay, let's try the intro to the first piece."

It turned out to be the "Girl Watchers" theme—from television commercial to pop hit to jazz vehicle—and the most difficult arrangement of the day.

"Try it again," Byard said. "Bash it, Alan."

At the end, Byard stood, moved toward the other players and said, "Good! How'd it feel?"

"I can't play it that fast," Nance protested.

"Okay, *he's* got the changes," Byard said, pointing to Benson. "Just do something lyric on the changes."

Byard rehearsed the piece section by section. The introduction. The first chorus. The fugal interlude, which featured Carter and Nance. The ending. As usual, the individual musical parts had a few copyists' errors and some occasional dubious notes.

"Four before C," Carter said at one point. "Is that note B flat or A natural?"

After a run-through, Byard had some new ideas on his score and asked, "Want to do me a favor? Repeat those two bars there. I want to vamp that. But make that an E flat."

"Of course, I can read," someone was protesting a moment later. "But not on Tuesdays. This is my day off."

"We will be here," Schlitten emphasized behind the glass, "until we have finished the album."

Perhaps it was time to change the subject. Perhaps the musicians needed to relax a bit. At least that seemed Byard's idea when he asked the room in general, "What do you all want to jam on?"

There was no response. The musicians seemed to want to get the "Girl Watchers" right after all, and they went back to it. Byard omitted one section that wasn't sounding too good anyway and announced, "We've got five more minutes, and we're going to record it."

"Famous last words," someone muttered.

"Well, don't worry about the fugue—we'll do that and splice it in later," Byard said.

Twice more on a difficult section and Byard jumped up, announcing, "Good!"

"But how much do I play?" Benson wanted to know about his solo.

"For one whole chorus after the *DE doten de da, DE doten de da.*"

After another run-through, Byard changed his mind, saying, "Good! Take another one, George. Make it two for you."

Carter had an idea. "If we could cut out some of those notes in there," he said, pointing to his score, "it would go a little smoother."

Byard's response was aesthetic practicality itself: "Play what you want to."

Alderson entered the studio, moved Benson's amplifier and shifted Nance's chair and mike. He seemed satisfied, and that meant that everyone was now ready to record.

"Stand by," Schlitten announced on the tape. " 'Girl Watchers Theme.' Take one."

Immediately, the players got busy, and their energy filled the studio. Nance bowed at that odd angle he uses. Carter looked studious. Davis looked dead-pan, but as if he might offer a hilarious musical joke at any moment.

About halfway through, Byard stopped the take, announcing that he goofed, and that, anyway, they had better hear a playback in the studio for balance. "In here, I can't hear the cello or guitar."

Ten minutes later, Carter stopped the second take, waving his bow in the air and announcing, "I goofed." But it was a sort of ensemble goof only a discerning ear could have heard.

"Would it help you, Ray, if I give you an amplifier in the studio?" Alderson wanted to know. Nance said it would, and as Alderson installed the amplifier, Carter and Benson strummed a background to their own quiet conversation.

Take 3 was a false start, and to begin the fourth, Byard counted off firmly. "One, two, three, four," onto the tape. Benson threw himself into his solo, eyes tightly closed, forehead occasionally in a momentary, intense frown that seemed to spur him on.

"Good—do another one!" Byard encouraged quickly at the end. Nance seemed to sprawl in his chair as he played, but he was obviously in control of what he was doing. Automatically, he dried his left hand along the length of his trousers at every rest.

One final version of the introduction to splice in the beginning, and Byard was satisfied.

"Good, thank you fellows," he said, and because he knew it was time for some solos all around he announced, "Now. Everybody know 'Exactly Like you'?" There was general nodding or silent assent around the studio. But Byard had more up his sleeve. "Ray, you play 'Jersey Bounce.' You know that? George, you do 'Darktown Strutter's Ball.' I know you're not that old, but you might know it. Richard, you know—what's that thing [he hummed a few notes]—Stan Kenton isn't it?"

"Intermission Riff," somebody called from across the room.

"Alan, you play 'Ring Dem Bells.' Ron, you play that bossa nova thing [again he hummed a couple of bars]."

"Desafinado," someone offered.

"And I'm going to play 'A' Train," Byard said. "I'll play the bridge." And then, "These things all have the same changes," he added as an afterthought. "Ray, take the first chorus, Ron, take the second, George . . ." Byard continued to assign the order of improvising.

In a few minutes, he had passed out a written introduction, and Schlitten was announcing onto the tape, "Exactly Like What," Take one."

A couple of run-throughs and false starts later, they were really into it. The introduction, intriguingly oblique, skittered by. The opening ensemble, which promised melodic chaos, proved to be complex but lucid. Nance set a groove in his opening solo, and Davis, as his sole accompanist, responded. When Benson came surging in for his solo, Davis was joined by first Carter and then Dawson. Each man took two choruses. Byard's energy was climactic. It was going to work.

"What is Jaki Byard going to do next?" Alderson wondered admiringly in the booth. "You never know."

Byard was not quite through with this arrangement. "For the last chorus," he announced, moving from his keyboard to the center of the strings, "everybody play harmonics in C. Al, play up high. And everybody go for himself on the bridge. Try it."

They did, and the effect was stunning—the only way to end a performance that had begun like this one.

"How would it be," Nance asked before a take, "if I bow the opening? Because I'm having trouble playing pizzicato, and I'm not with them, anyway."

"Try it," Byard offered and, at the end said, "Thanks a lot, Ray. That was a good suggestion."

On the final take, Nance again took the opening solo, and again his superb swing set the groove. The groove set, he began to soar, and the others soared with him. The ending still worked.

Just before the playback Byard announced, "Take a break, gentlemen. But be taking a look at this ballad."

He entered the engineer's booth to hear the playback, and after he had confirmed his satisfaction with "Exactly Like What," Byard reentered the studio with a broad smile and said, "Well, we'll continue making history."

The next document for history was the date's ballad, Byard's "The Falling Rains of Life." By 4:50, he was announcing, "Okay, gentlemen, here we go for a run-through." The leader had the gentle theme on piano, Nance an obbligato, Davis a mysterious, double-time walk.

"Improvise, Ron!" Byard shouted at one point.

At the end, Nance joked, "I ran out of music before the rest of you did."

Byard again left his keyboard to speak to the strings: "It's perfect the way you all did it. After this, don't worry. We'll just play for Alan's vibes solo. But it needs *passion!*" He gave some mock-serious gestures with his arms and then squeezed his fists under his chin and added, "*Romanticism!*"

After another run-through, Schlitten entered the studio. "What's wrong?" Byard asked.

"Well, it's fine but it's getting a little long," the producer said.

By the time the second take was going onto the rolling tape, Dawson had a half-chorus, and Byard's sustained ending was enhanced by Nance, who knew just when to enter on top of it and just how much to play when he got there.

By 5:20, Byard had distributed a new piece among the players. By 5:35, he had expressed dissatisfaction with the way it was going, and he took up the music parts. He turned to Schlitten behind the glass panel and invited suggestions.

Schlitten entered the studio and said "Let's jam 'How High the Moon' and begin it as a ballad for Ray. Later how about some fours between Ron and Richard?"

Byard and the other players seemed to agree.

"That's what jazz is all about anyhow" said Schlitten reentering the booth.

Pharoah's Tale

Pharoah Sanders is twenty-seven years old and somewhat surprisingly, that is young enough so that among his earliest musical idols were John Coltrane, Eric Dolphy, and Ornette Coleman.

Sanders was born in Little Rock, Ark., in 1940, and although his given name has sometimes been confused in print, it is Pharoah.

"My grandfather was a school teacher; he taught music and mathematics. My mother and her sisters used to sing in clubs and teach piano. For myself, I started playing drums in the high school band. Then I played tuba and baritone horn, clarinet and flute. In 1959, I started playing tenor saxophone, still in the school band," he says.

"At the same time I was listening to Jimmy Cannon, my band teacher, who played jazz. Richard Boone, the Count Basie trombone player—he's from Little Rock, too. He would sometimes sit in with the concert band.

"In my own playing I was more or less into rhythm and blues. I liked Earl Bostic a lot."

At the same time, Sanders had become interested in art and wanted to be any kind of artist, painter or commercial artist, just to do art work.

"When I finished high school in 1959, I was supposed to take either a music or an art scholarship. I didn't want to stay in Little Rock so I left for the West Coast. I went to Oakland Junior College for a couple of years, and then moved over to San Francisco. I majored in art. But I was getting some rock 'n' roll gigs playing tenor. I also played alto, flute, clarinet, and baritone whenever possible, but I had fallen in love with the tenor.

"On those blues jobs, I played mostly by ear, but I had some private lessons in Oakland which taught me about harmonics.

"By this time I was listening to Sonny Rollins, who was a big influence at first; John Coltrane, who was a later big influence; and Ornette Coleman, Eric Dolphy, Booker Ervin, Hank Mobley and Horace Silver's group. I loved Benny Golson on 'Moanin' ' with Art Blakey.

"When I heard Coltrane's 'Blue Train' LP, I really didn't know what he was doing. I had never heard anybody play tenor like that before, with that range. Most of the guys played just in the middle register.

"When I first heard Ornette's music I liked it—*really*, it was something! It seemed so natural, as if he weren't limiting himself, as if he

247

wanted to let himself just go to the music. I remember talking to Ornette in 'Frisco. I don't know whether he remembers me from then.

"By that time I had begun to try to play that way myself. Sonny
Simmons, and a lot of people I was playing with in Oakland at the
time, were playing a lot freer. They had been playing that way before I
came to California. They heard me and invited me to come down and
play sometime. I was kind of skeptical about it because up to that point
all I had been playing was rhythm and blues. What they played had a
good feeling, but I was wondering, what are they doing? Were they
crazy? But it felt good. So, I just fell in with it, too," he said.

"Later, I started playing jazz more conventionally and studying the
basics—getting my chords and my scales."

The mention of the basics sets Sanders to reflecting. "Actually I have
never had a jazz gig of my own long enough to see what I can really
do on conventional tunes. I would like to get one for at least six nights
a week so I could try to express myself fully 'inside' and see both sides
of it. I still take different kinds of jobs. I play rock 'n' roll for dances,
usually in Brooklyn. It's a big help financially, and my profession is
music, so it's my business to be able to play any kind of music."

Returning to his days in the Bay Area, Sanders remembers, "Once
when John Coltrane came out to San Francisco, he was asking around
about mouthpieces. So I told him that I had a bunch of mouthpieces,
and that he could try them. I also said I would take him around to the
different places in town if he wanted to try some more. I never thought
he'd take me up on it, of course—he was a giant to me then. But he
showed up one morning, saying, 'Are you ready, man?' I was really
shook up! At the time, my own horn was in the repair shop and he offered to pay the bill so I could get it out. All day long we went around
to pawn shops and more pawn shops, trying out different mouthpieces."

Sanders arrived in New York in 1962. He had driven across the
country with a couple of musician friends in a car that constantly broke
down, but somehow they made it. He had absolutely no money. "I slept
in the subway—the police didn't bother me—or in tenement hallways
under the stairs. And I pawned my instrument," he recalls.

"I think my first gig in New York was one in a coffee house in the
Village called the Speakeasy, with C Sharp and Billy Higgins . . . .
We made eight dollars a night. The job lasted almost a year. I used to
live on wheat germ, peanut butter, and bread—I still carry a jar of
wheat germ in my instrument case. It's good food.

"I began seeing a lot of Billy Higgins. We would play together, talk, eat; might be together all day long. If he wasn't playing on his drums he would play on the table, or glasses with spoons, or whatever else he found.

"I took some other jobs. Once I was a combination cook, waiter, and counterman, and all I got was what I ate. Then I caught on that I should be paid, and I split. I was just trying to survive, and it is harder to survive in New York than in Oakland or San Francisco. If I wasn't thinking about trying to survive, I was thinking about music. I didn't think much about commercial art by this time.

"A friend of mine who lived in Brooklyn, someone I had known in San Francisco, invited me to stay at his place. That's where I met Don Cherry, and we began rehearsing and playing together. We got one job at Pratt Institute in Brooklyn. There was an exhibition of student art work and they wanted some of our kind of music along with it. I had to get my horn out of hock for that one, and the other guys in the group helped me by putting up the money.

"When I play, I try to adjust myself to the group, and I don't think much about whether the music is conventional or not. If the others go 'outside,' play 'free,' I go out there, too. If I tried to play too differently from the rest of the group, it seems to me I would be taking the other musicians' energy away from them. I still want to play my own way. But I wouldn't want to play with anybody that I couldn't please with the way I play.

"Anyway, Don Cherry seemed to like what I was doing. I was getting different sounds out of the horn then. For my part, I was just trying to express myself. Whatever came out of the instrument just came out, as if I had no choice.

"Naturally, you have elements of music and musical skills to work with, but once you've got those down, I think you should go after feelings. If you try to be too intellectual about it, the music becomes too mechanical. It seems that for me, the more I play 'inside,' inside the chords and the tune, the more I want to play 'outside,' and free. But also, the more I play 'outside' the more I want to play 'inside,' too. I'm trying to get a balance in my music. A lot of cats play 'out' to start with. But if I, myself, start off playing 'inside' and then let the spirit take over, wherever it goes, it seems better to me.

"I'm not trying to do something that is over somebody's head. My aim is to *give* people something. When I give them something they can give me something, the energy to continue.

The first time Sanders played with John Coltrane was at the Half Note in New York. "We had become pretty close and had been talking a lot. He would call me and we would talk about religion and about life. He was also concerned about what he wanted to do next in his music, about where he was headed.

"We got pretty close and sometimes he would say, 'Come on down and play something with me tonight,' almost as though we were continuing the conversation. So I would just come down and start playing.

"By that time, I thought of him not just as a great musician but also as a wise man. But I was still a little self-conscious and wasn't sure what to do with him musically. I thought maybe I was playing too long, and on some numbers, I wouldn't play at all. And sometimes I would start to pack up my horn. But he would tell me not to. Anyway, I'd never play as long as he did because, you know, he might play for an hour on one tune."

Sanders says he was never asked officially to become a member of Coltrane's group. He would just play with Coltrane from time to time, whenever he was asked to. Then later, he might say, 'I have a job down in Washington for a week. How about coming on down with me?' Or, he'd say he had a record date coming up and would I like to play on it, too.

"Always, it was like a communication through music, like he knew some things that I wanted to know that he could express musically, and that I maybe had some things to contribute, too. It's hard to talk about it, except in spiritual or religious terms, actually.

"Still, he had a lot of things on his mind musically. He wanted to decide what he should turn to next, and he needed time to find out. He was a perfectionist, and he wanted to grow, always. Whatever he did, he wanted it to come from inside himself, and he did not want to hold anything back, or hide anything he found there. Good or bad, it had to be expressed. Once he asked me what I thought he should do next, what he should work on—how could he create something different. I told him maybe he should try to better some of the things he had already done, go back and try again on older tunes. I don't really know if that was any help to him; I don't know whether that was what he was looking for or not."

Returning to the subject of his own playing, Sanders says, "In a group, I like to play with anyone who really wants to play, who really wants to put out the energy. If the players don't put out the energy it takes away my own."

If he is asked about the meaning of his music, Pharoah Sanders replies, "I don't like to talk about what my playing is about. I just like to
let it be. If I *had* to say something, I would say it was about me. About
what *is*. Or about a Supreme Being.

"I think I am just beginning to find out about such things, so I am
not going to try to force my findings on anybody else. I am still learning how to play and trying to find out a lot of things about myself so I
can bring them out."

Down Beat, May 16, 1968

Henderson, Armstrong, and Noone

There are two current points of view on the music of Fletcher Henderson. The older of them concedes that it was the Henderson orchestra,
under the arranging tutelage of Don Redman, that first evolved a jazz
style for a dance-band-size ensemble in the 1920s. And it holds that,
certain earlier successes being granted, the Henderson style did not
really find its full expression until the mid-1930s.

The second and more recent point of view, suggested in Gunther
Schuller's excellent *Early Jazz* (Oxford), holds that the Henderson orchestra's real contributions had been made by 1932; and there is more
than a hint in Schuller's comments that he feels that the subsequent arrangements had reduced these achievements to a polite formula, beg-
ging to be popularized, but creatively stultifying for soloists and arrangers alike.

Both positions might be tested in two recent releases in Decca's continuing "Jazz Heritage" series, Fletcher Henderson: First Impressions
1924-1931 (reprocessed stereo DL 7227; mono DL 9227) and Fletcher
Henderson: Swing's the Thing, 1931-1934 (reprocessed stereo DL
7228; mono DL 9228).

The years 1924 through 1931 are sketched—sometimes well sketched,
but sketched—in these albums. And the year 1934 receives heavy coverage with the likes of "Big John's Special," "Down South Camp Meeting," and "Wrappin' It Up,"—the very pieces, the very arrangements,
and, in some cases (in Red Allen's trumpet solos, say), suspiciously
close to the very solos that Benny Goodman and his sidemen were playing to national acclaim a few years later.

"Copenhagen," from the first set, finds Redman in 1924 adapting the materials of an earlier style and patterning them with exceptional skill and insight. But suddenly there is Louis Armstrong's solo, leaping out of the ensemble and speaking a musical language that knew all about the past and also said enough about the present and future as to send the most skillful arrangers and the most accomplished soloists scurrying after him.

The story from 1924 on seems, in retrospect, the story of that scurry. In the 1931 selections that close the LP, the arrangements and the ensemble show us how far along both the arrangers and the ensemble had come in catching up to Armstrong's lead. And outstanding solos, such as those by Rex Stewart, Coleman Hawkins, and Benny Morton on "Just Blues," show how honorably these men had come to personal terms with the fact and presence of Armstrong's genius.

The second volume offers an interesting subject for comparison in a 1934 arrangement of "Shanghai Shuffle," a piece which in its 1924 version is a part of Volume 1. Otherwise *Fletcher Henderson: Swing's the Thing* is, as I indicate above, a set for all those by now middle-aged fans of the swing bands of the 1930s to own, hear, and ponder for its social implications as well as its musical ones.

Two 1924–25 Fletcher Henderson selections begin the set called *Young Louis the Sideman* (Decca-reprocessed stereo DL 7233; mono DL 9233). In several of its titles, the LP offers a measure of Armstrong's striking development during those four years. For no matter how marvelously he brings to life the stodgy ensemble on Perry Bradford's "Lucy Long," no matter how excitingly he improvises on "I Ain't Gonna Play No Second Fiddle," no matter how brilliantly he bursts through the skilled ensemble playing of Erskine Tate's Chicago orchestra, these things are but preludes to his grandiose statement on "Wild Man Blues." I should point out, however, that the contrast is made particularly dramatic in the context of the LP, for Armstrong is somewhat subdued on several of the intervening selections, frequently charming selections though they be, with frequently fine titles such as "Georgia BoBo" by Lil's Hot Shots, and "Easy Come, Easy Go Blues," and "I'm Goin' Hunting" by Jimmy Bertrand's Washboard Wizards.

The session that produced "Wild Man Blues" was under the nominal leadership of clarinetist Johnny Dodds. Another of its participants was pianist Earl Hines, and Hines as a sideman to another clarinetist on *Jimmy Noone and Earl Hines At the Apex Club, Volume 1* (1928) (reprocessed stereo DL 79235; mono DL 9235).

Noone's group achieved an interesting and often delightful modification of the New Orleans ensemble style. The lead melody, which had traditionally been carried by cornet or trumpet, went to Joe Poston's alto sax, while Noone continued the clarinet's classic harmonic and, more important, contrapuntal functions—and Noone was above all a fine ensemble clarinetist. The resultant textures can be heard on "My Monday Date," "Sweet Lorraine," "Every Evening" (here included in two takes), "Sweet Sue, Just You," and, perhaps best of all, "Four or Five Times." But Noone against Poston is not the only juxtaposition, for Hines and Bud Scott's banjo make a positively memorable experience out of a piece with a negatively memorable title "Blues my Naughty Sweetie Gives To Me." Hines has fine solos on "Four or Five Times," "Sweet Lorraine" (also offered in two "takes"), and his contributions to the ensemble on Noones "Apex Blues" are just about exemplary.

There is some dross, to be sure. Poston is sometimes offensively schmaltzy, and a Noone showpiece such as "I Know That You Know" shows how he might alternate the most pat and banal clarinet runs with the most interesting and influential musical ideas.

In the final analysis, however, I expect that the Apex Club group stands or falls on the quality of its ensemble work. Collective improvisation is, of course, a commonplace practice in 1920s-style jazz, and it has appeared with occasional success in subsequent styles. But it is a deceptive undertaking. Easy to do, it is enormously difficult to do well. Indeed, really good simultaneous improvising, done by men who reflexively understand each other's playing, is as rare as it is delightful. The Noone ensemble provided some of the best examples of it that we have.

Saturday Review, November 16, 1968
Copyright © 1968 Saturday Review, Inc.

Catching the Advanced Guard

The jazz avant-garde, like the advance guard of any activity in any period, feels neglected—it is not being properly recorded and properly heard. Probably it is not, but it *is* being recorded. For a few months now, I have been setting aside about twenty LPs by younger jazzmen to treat them collectively.

Some are by the more successful popularizers of the idiom, such as Charles Lloyd. Some are by the respected names, known to musicians and the public alike, such as the late John Coltrane. But I also have LPs by Roscoe Mitchell, an alto saxophonist and clarinetist; by Lester Bowie, a trumpeter; by Bill Dixon, a trumpeter-composer; Pharoah Sanders, a tenor saxophonist and fluist; by Joe Harriott, a British alto saxophonist; by Don Heckman, an alto saxophonist, composed, and jazz critic(!); by Albert Ayler, a tenor and soprano saxophonist; by Sun Ra, a composer who leads an orchestra; by Joseph Jarman, who plays alto saxophone—even by a Johnny-come-lately to the idiom, clarinetist Rolf Kuhn. If I neglect to mention some of these musicians here and in subsequent columns, it should not be taken to mean that I found their music not worth discussing. It is simply that the stack is a high one and soon it will be higher still.

New and Old Gospel (Blue Note stereo, 84262; mono, 4262) is led by alto saxophonist Jackie McLean, who has worked his way through all contemporary jazz styles and approaches during the last fifteen-plus years, and who sounds like it. For his other horn, McLean chose Ornette Coleman. Coleman, however, is heard on his second instrument, trumpet.

The first side features a four-part suite by McLean, *Lifeline*, in which the third section, "Vernzone," seems to me an exceptional example of the sort of mutually inspiring, creative momentum which only a jazz ensemble can offer in contemporary music. The same applies to the performance of Coleman's "Strange as It Seems," which ends the second side.

The notes describe the remaining piece, Coleman's impressionist "Old Gospel," as exuberant and inspired, and undoubtedly it is. But I felt decidedly let down by Coleman's otherwise functionally effective trumpeting. In the notes, McLean remarks: "It is amazing how far Ornette has gone on that horn in the last three years. I'm not about to compare him technically to anybody, because that isn't the point. . . . The point is how much he plays and the fact that what he plays is entirely him!" That has been my own feeling about the matter, but on "Old Gospel" I was constantly annoyed by notes he was reaching for, but *didn't* play.

It would be interesting to have the opinion of a classicist on *The Music of Ornette Coleman* (RCA Victor stereo, LSC-2982; mono, LM-2982), which has *Forms and Sounds,* played by the Philadelphia Woodwind Quintet with trumpet interludes by Coleman, *Saints and Soldiers,* and a brief "Space Flight" by the Chamber Symphony of Philadelphia

Quartet. I expect the first opinion might be that a great deal of the music sounds like student Bartók. That was my own first reaction. But it was not my second.

I particularly admired the pacing of the various sections on *Saints and Soldiers*, and the developmental portions, particularly of the opening motive. Similarly, the second section of *Forms and Sounds* is a melodic-rhythmic delight and a fine example, it seems to me, of how to utilize jazz rhythms in terms that our concert players can understand and employ. Again, however, I felt let down by some of Coleman's trumpet fluffs, particularly since most of the things he reaches for are good.

"Space Flight," on the other hand, is rather lightweight stuff. But that is perhaps a comment on the unpretentious and musicianly way Coleman approached the other two pieces, and on the altogether remarkable fact that this man, who not too long ago was thought of as a musical ignoramus and false prophet in some circles, should find such works within his creative range and musical inclinations.

A little over a year ago, cornetist and composer Don Cherry offered a Blue Note LP called *Complete Communion* (stereo, 84226; mono, 4226) on which there were two extended works for a quartet, the title piece and one called "Eliphantasy." Both were interesting. But in the title piece, "Complete Communion," Cherry produced perhaps the most successful effort so far at extended composition in the new jazz idiom of the 1960s. His themes and his improvised sections moved easily from one tempo to another, flowed logically, one to the next.

Cherry's new release is called *Symphony for Improvisers* (Blue Note stereo, 84247; mono, 4247). It is a longer work; it covers two sides of an LP and has eight parts (which, however, run together without a break), and it features, besides the leader, six other musicians on eight other instruments. I do not think the new piece quite succeeds; the performance doesn't hang together as well as the earlier one (although Ed Blackwell's fine drumming goes a long way toward maintaining continuity), and some of the piano work seems a bit questionable. But in this longer work for more instruments Cherry is surely to be commended for having undertaken the *Symphony* when, particularly after *Complete Communion*, he might easily have been less ambitious this time around.

Saturday Review, May 25, 1968
Copyright © 1968 Saturday Review, Inc.

Columbia, Epic, and Crosby

The recorded works of Harry Lillis Crosby are getting the treatment at Columbia Records. The parent label issued *Bing Crosby in Hollywood* (mono only, C2L 43), which collected versions of the songs from his first seven feature films, picture by picture. Then followed a *Paul Whiteman and his Orchestra* set, featuring Crosby, on Columbia (mono only, CL 2830). Now Epic has issued the first volume of a comprehensive series, *The Bing Crosby Story* (reprocessed stereo, E2E 202; mono, E2E 201).

The latter set has two LPs, comprising thirty-two titles, covering the years 1928-32. If it does not add every other available Crosby record from those years, it is nevertheless compiled with a thoroughness that should please the most avid Crosby fans—and considering the quantity of by-now quaint and dated music involved, perhaps *only* the most avid Crosby fans.

We begin with Crosby as a member of the Rhythm Boys, the jazzy, novelty-vocal act, fresh from the vaudeville stage and featured with Paul Whiteman's band. And we end with the "romantic" ballad singer of pieces like "(She Takes Me To) Paradise," who was already into the kind of world fame that he sustained for the next thirty years.

We begin with a young baritone, singing higher than his natural range (the popular singers before him were mostly tenors) and, probably for that reason, at relatively low volume. We end with him lower, and more often slower; he was into his range, and shorn of the melodramatic affectations he had borrowed from his predecessors—singers like Whiteman's Skin Young—but still singing at a low, crooner's volume.

The Crosby style, having been set, has proven remarkably durable. Though Frank Sinatra made his break with it in the late thirties and set up his own "school" of pop singing, Crosby-style singers still appeared and flourished. The forties had Perry Como, the fifties Dean Martin, and the sixties John Gary. Crosby himself hasn't *sung* the style since the early forties, but he still sing-speaks it, and they still listen.

The Rhythm Boys must have seemed a pretty hip group in their day, and Crosby perhaps the hippest of all. The Epic set begins with a Crosby

"Mississippi Mud" that includes some minstrelsy that ought to be a sociological embarrassment to everyone involved—except perhaps Bix Beiderbecke, who has a good solo on it. But the variational ideas and scat-sung patterns on "Wa Da Da" and " 'Tain't So, Honey, 'Tain't So" show, beside the jazzy clichés of the era, that the young Crosby knew a lot about what the jazzmen, and Beiderbecke particularly, were up to. The Rhythm Boys' scat-singing on "My Suppressed Desire" (!) has some Louis Armstrong-derived licks—this by late 1928! On the exceptional 1932 collaboration with Duke Ellington's orchestra on "St. Louis Blues" (here given in two rather different "takes"), Crosby shows an acquaintance with the devices of the blues singers of the era, particularly Ethel Waters. And on a previously unissued 1932 duet with pianist Lennie Hayton on "Sweet Sue" both men show good knowledge of Beiderbecke and Fats Waller.

But there was more involved in Crosby's destiny than the popularization of the ideas of leading jazzmen—although, make no mistake about it, the frequently subtle influence of jazz permeated all he did or was to do.

The initially surprising thing about the post-Whiteman sides, say from 1930 onward, is their apparent understatement, the almost boyish coolness with which the verbally ardent love songs are delivered. Perhaps one should postulate that Crosby's popularity depended on an almost asexual manner he carried in matters of the heart—filling in the traditional male role, but doing it without a threat, and accommodating himself to the more aggressive "new woman" of the time. But no. Crosby is not really disengaged. Listen again. He means it, and the understated message comes through. If he was a new and gentler kind of public male idol, he was male nevertheless.

One thing that Crosby helped accomplish, a thing his natural talents prepared him for, was the carrying of popular music into the electronic age. Bing Crosby sounds like a singer *using* a microphone for some of his most telling effects. He was not a singer overheard by the microphone. To say that he is effortless, natural, intimate, as is often said, is to say that he uses the mike to reach the members of his audience more directly. He could be as emotionally effective as the next singer without raising his general volume level—or perhaps more effective simply because he did not raise it. But personal statements like "Paradise" and person-to-person gossip like "Sweet Georgia Brown" therefore work far better for him than pseudo-grandiloquence like "Without a Song" or "Lord, You Made the Night Too Long."

Crosby is a naturally gifted actor, and it was the quality of natural intimacy that enabled him to become not just a remarkably likeable performer, but one of the finest film actors we have had. Electric recording is his kind of intimate medium; film is his kind of intimate medium. Put Crosby's kind of acting on a stage, and it wouldn't carry past the sixth row. Put it on film and he is superb at low-comic banter; he is excellent in light romantic farce; and, in his more mature years, in *The Country Girl* say, he comes close to convincing film tragedy.

That, I think, is the really durable aspect of his talent: Crosby the actor. The records, I expect—even the best of them—are important as they illuminate the actor, and are otherwise properly the property of cultural historians.

Still, until I watch the next Crosby rerun on the Late Show, I could replay the *Bing Crosby Story, Volume 1*, and I probably will.

Easy as a Conversation

Until fairly recently terms like "Chicago Style" or "Chicago School" meant to a jazz enthusiast a group of young men, most of whom attended Austin High School in the 1920s and all of whom were inspired by the great New Orleans players to become jazzmen—men like cornetist Jimmy McPartland, like falling-star clarinetist Frank Teschmacher, tenor saxophonist Bud Freeman, pianist Joe Sullivan, or the brilliant drummer Dave Tough.

Today, however, "Chicago School" is more apt to refer to a gathering of younger players, including trumpeter Lester Bowie, saxophonists Roscoe Mitchell and Joseph Jarman, bassist Malacki Favors, pianist Richard Abrams, and others. Abrams seems to provide inspiration and leadership, and the group has formed an Association for the Advancement of Creative Musicians. They have been recorded by two Chicago-based labels, Delmark (7 West Grand Street, Chicago 60610) and Nessa (5875 North Glenwood, Chicago 60626).

The results show a kind of catchall, or even something-for-everyone avant-gardism, in which some things that "classical" players tried out (and discarded) thirty years ago vie with the approaches of Ornette

Coleman, John Coltrane, Cecil Taylor, and others. Thus various styles and approaches alternate without really clashing—and also without really settling into any over-all new Chicago style.

Lester Bowie's LP also features Mitchell, Jarman, and Favors, and offers two extended performances called, with ultimate frugality, "Number 1" and "Number 2" (Nessa stereo N-1). On the former, improvised instrumental sounds follow on one another, idly and vaguely at first and out-of-tempo. A thunderstorm arises, a train hurls itself through the ensemble, gongs clang portentously, trumpets flutter, reeds shriek and agonize. "Number 2" has a more overt humor and some simultaneously improvised textures that are interesting. On the whole, it all sounds as easy as a conversation among friends—and, I think, about as significant.

On Richard Abrams' *Levels and Degrees of Light* (Delmark stereo DS-413) the atmosphere of a jazz happening continues. On "Bird Song" someone reads a long poem in the rain-barrel atmosphere of echo microphones. Self-consciously "weird" sounds drift by, hinting that we may be hearing an audition of next season's sound track music for *Star Trek*. One passage suggests that every bird in the city of Chicago is chirping away over a tune-up of strings. But then there comes an absolutely stunning passage, a gathering of joyous, unorthodox instrumental sounds by the horns. Alas, it goes on for too long.

On the title-piece to Roscoe Mitchell's *Sound* (Delmark stereo DS-9408), we again have long, languorous, random patches of sound, during which one man momentarily comes so close to painful sobs that one wonders why he bothered to use a saxophone. But Mitchell's "Little Suite" is frankly comedic; a good, lightweight, sometimes raucously funny performance.

On Joseph Jarman's *Song For* (Delmark stereo DS-9410) there is a rather self-conscious, LeRoi Jones-derived recitation called "Non-Cognitive Aspects of the City." There is "Adam's Rib," which has good, eventful improvised textures but which, like some of John Coltrane's late work, seems a suspended prologue to music unplayed. And there is "Song For" itself, on which more science-fiction jingling accompanies some well-paced saxophone improvising and some interesting patters from drummer Steve McCall.

Now. Let it be said that each of these men seems to be a good instrumentalist—he knows his horn, he knows what he is doing, and he probably knows conventional procedures or he probably could not break them with such authority. And let it be said that there is plenty of evidence here that each man knows how to make interesting spontaneous music with a minimum of protections, a minimum of the sort of built-in outlines and preset patterns that jazzmen have traditionally employed—and that ability, of course, is a primary requisite in the new jazz.

There are moments in almost every performance that will bear me out, but my primary evidence comes from three titles I have not mentioned so far. On the Abrams LP, there is a rather Albert Ayler-like "My Thoughts Are My Future." On Mitchell's album there is a frankly dedicatory "Ornette." And on Jarman's a "Little Fox Run" that is busy, lively, and, under its rather wild surface, well organized.

Besides having group textures and solos that are largely sustained, these performances have an admirable, unpretentious momentum to them. No, they do not necessarily "swing" in the traditional sense, and both the hornmen and percussionists phrase with a looseness and rhythmic freedom that is one of the best qualities of the new jazz. Still there is always a healthy respect for tempo on these selections, even when tempo is subject to spontaneous alteration, and that aspect is probably the key to their success—and perhaps the key to the success of all jazz future as it has been to the success of jazz past.

The New York Times, August 18, 1968
Copyright © 1968/1969 by the New York Times Company.
Reprinted by permisson.

Will Charles Lloyd Save Jazz for the Masses?

Tenor saxophonist Charles Lloyd has won a "Jazzman of the Year" award from the readers of *Down Beat* magazine, has been written up in several slick magazines, and has represented American culture abroad in a tour of the Soviet Union. He is also destined, according to one observer, to carry contemporary jazz to mass audiences, including rock audiences—even to save jazz from hopelessly esoteric forms and practices.

Lloyd certainly puts on a show of sorts. With wildly bushy hair, military jacket, and garishly striped bell bottoms, he looks like a kind of show-biz hippie. He usually sounds like a kind of show-biz John Coltrane.

True, the Lloyd to be heard on *Nirvana* (Columbia CS 9609) is not exactly contemporary, for the set seems to be made up of left-overs, seven short selections from a recording session done a few years back when Lloyd was a member of Chico Hamilton's Quintet, and two long ones from another done under Lloyd's own name. There are no credits or personnel given on the back-liner.

However, there is one aspect to Lloyd's popularity that is certainly significant—although more significant socially than musically. Lloyd is a black man. And like Cannonball Adderley before him, he is a black man popularizing black innovations in jazz. The role of popularizer in the music no longer falls to white men, it seems.

Lloyd's current pianist, Keith Jarrett, is not present on *Nirvana*, but he has his own recital on *Life Between the Exit Signs* (Vortex 2006). Jarrett is a talented young man. But in his playing he is still not quite past letting us know who his favorite players are. They are chiefly Bill Evans and Cecil Taylor—and perhaps also those twentieth-century classicists who contributed to Taylor's style in turn. Thus he virtually alternates modified Evans and modified Taylor from one piece to the next.

The modified Taylor seems a more promising direction, for Jarrett's touch and general sensibility are very different from Taylor's. However, "Church Dreams" and "Lisbon Stomp" bring the influences together and approach a Keith Jarrett style, particularly the "Lisbon" title. The latter piece also has a fine bass solo by Charlie Haden, who is never less than very good on this LP.

Stan Getz (to shift abruptly to somewhat more conservative music) is a very good man with a ballad. Not a truly great one perhaps—greatness in paraphrasing ballads is defined by, let's say Louis Armstrong and by vibraphonist Milt Jackson of the Modern Jazz Quartet—but a very good one. And Getz is a popular man; there are people who can't abide the sound of a tenor saxophone but who love Getz's initially unruffled sonority and easy phrasing.

What The World Needs Now (Verve V6-8752) has Getz and an orchestra interpreting the ditties of Burt Bacharach, that clever and tricky manipulator of time-signatures and phrase lengths. It is a pleasant and enjoyable LP, the kind of record that one may turn to often for pleasure, but which, if it were to disappear, one might never miss. As might be expected, on the better songs, the title piece, "Wives and Lovers" and "Walk On By," Getz does his better playing. On some of the others he strains a bit, or he enters that area of boyish weepiness that is surely Stan Getz's own. Richard Evans' arrangements are generally adequate, but for that trite introduction to "A House Is Not a Home," he might consider writing his listeners a short letter of apology.

In the liner notes to *The Don Shirley Trio in Concert* (Columbia CS 9684) the pianist declares, "I make a difference between the artist and the entertainer. The entertainer is interested in pleasing the people and in a big pay check. . . . But the artist is a much more complex personality. . . . He must be true to himself and the tradition of his art form. I try to do this . . . art must come first."

Anyone who is not intimidated by such abject modesty, and who plays the LP, will hear a classically trained and prodigious pianist (who, by the way, makes no claim as a jazzman) interpreting such respectable songs as "I Can't Get Started" in the manner of Rachmaninoff, "My Funny Valentine" in the manner of Debussy, and "Water Boy" in the style of Negro gospel song. Since it lacks the overt camp of Liberace, Don Shirley's may be the ultimate in cocktail piano vulgarity.

A final note: an album called *Heavy Heads* (Chess LPs-1522) collects some good blues music by singers with colorful professional names like Muddy Waters, Howlin' Wolf, Bo Diddley, Little Walter, and Washboard Sam. They are "heavy" as opposed to lightweights, and "heads" for originators, not for acid.

Here is source material for fans of Elvis Presley, the Rolling Stones, the Animals, and the rest, to hear and ponder. Their bewildered parents and teachers might do the same. And if John Lee Hooker's "Let's Go Out Tonight" or Little Milton's "I Feel So Bad" doesn't get to you, well, as the old joke has it, check with your doctor: you may be dead.

The New York Times, September 15, 1968
Copyright © 1968/1969 by the New York Times Company.
Reprinted by permisson.

Poems among the Super Oldies

A recent Capitol release called *Super Oldies/Vol. 3* (STBB 2910) is a two-record set offering eleven popular selections. Some are genuine "hits," some are "cover versions" for other people's hits, and some are merely padding. Few are over a year or so old, which goes to show that a pop hit in the limelight these days ages faster than a raisin in the sun. But "oldies" or not (and "super" or not), these performances probably represent the state of our popular music—or that kind of popular music most favored by our young people. There is much to yawn at, something to enjoy, a couple of things to ponder, and at least one thing that might be viewed with alarm. Then, in at least two selections, there is something to be grateful for and to treasure.

The Beatles, although they are Capitol contractees, are present only by proxy or by influence. By proxy (their "Michelle" is done by a pair called David and Jonathan) presumably because they are too important to be caught slumming in such a catch-all set. By influence because (in case the old folks don't know it yet) Paul McCartney (may he continue to develop) is an exceptional popular-song writer.

Otherwise, to take a random sample, we have "Dead End Street," a quasi-blues that sounds as though it were put together by a committee of show-biz wise guys, with an element of self-pity unknown to the blues; it is sung by Lou Rawles, who is surely a phenomenon of the late 1960s, a youthful, handsome, middlebrow, Negro bluesman. And, we have ersatz rock (Chad and Jeremy do Rodgers and Hammerstein's "If I Loved You" with a pointless *ostinato* bass figure—it is pretty funny). We have black-face rock ("Nobody But Me" by—gasp!—the Human Beinz). We have country-and-western rock, I suppose you would call it ("Elvira" by Dallas Frazier). We have such examples of good songwriting as "Goin' Out of My Head" (but not done by Antony and the Imperials, who did it so well). Et cetera.

We have a disturbing ten-minute incantation called "Get That Feeling" that is grinding, relentless, loud, almost hysterical, and I might suggest that our musically aware anthropologists and psychologists turn their attention to it before it is too late.

Then we have John Hartford's "Gentle on My Mind" sung by Glen Campbell; we have Jim Webb's "By the Time I Get to Phoenix," by the same singer; and we have Bobbie Gentry doing her own "Ode to Billie Joe." These are exceptional "folk" poems, appropriately set to simple melodies, and very well performed.

There is an opinion abroad in the land that the true poet of our current pop music is Bob Dylan. I cannot agree. He has an exceptional talent with words; he knows a lot about what's wrong with *other* people; and he is properly "liberal" in the manner of the swinging sixties —which is to say, in the manner of the Depression thirties, made hip.

But the three ballads I have cited above are about believable people in dramatic situations. "Gentle on My Mind" is perhaps a bit too self-conscious in its evocative imagery (imagine, a 1960s pop hit that fails because its lyric is *pretentiously* poetic!). "By the Time I Get to Phoenix" gives the comments of a young man hitchhiking his way away from a girl whom, it is revealed, he doesn't really want to leave. The images are very good; the structure, the gradually built irony, is exceptional; the performance is just right, if perhaps just a touch over-acted.

"Ode to Billie Joe" is superb—so much so that it could withstand the most meticulous kind of classroom scrutiny and exegesis. It uses the same device as the often anthologized Scottish border ballad "Lord Randal," the gradual revelation of a tragic situation through an exchange dialogue. But in "Billie Joe," both the revelation and the situation are more complex, more filled with human ironies small and large, ultimately more tragic—and more mysterious (Was it a stillbirth? A miscarriage? A deliberate abortion?).

I could say more about it. As a performance, for example: Whoever decided to use Miss Gentry's guitar on the recording should be commended, as should whoever decided to use a string section so discreetly and effectively—and whoever decided to record this unlikely pop record.

I obviously consider "Ode to Billie Joe" something of an event in American popular music. It is also something of an event in American poetry, and I wonder how long it will take us to realize it.

Saturday Review, September 28, 1968
Copyright © 1968 Saturday Review, Inc.

Still Chasing the Advance Guard

The title *Sun Ra and His Arkestra—Sun Song* (Delmark DL 411, mono only) is perhaps a portentous, or at least curious, billing for a jazz LP, particularly when one is reminded that it was originally recorded (and obscurely released) over ten years ago. Titles of selections, such as "Call for All Demons," "Transition," "Future," "New Horizons," affirm the impression. But the style and content of the music is anything but advanced, even for ten years ago; it is indeed quite conservative and suggests that Sun Ra, in the phrase Stanley Dance used in these pages recently, is somewhat miscast as a leader in the avant-garde. For me, the music is not only conservative, it is professional—and, that being granted, frequently glib, not to say frequently shallow and rather dull.

Something of the same impression continues in the two volumes of *The Heliocentric Worlds of Sun Ra* on ESP-Disk 1014 and 1017, which offer somewhat more recent manifestations of the pianist-composer's work. Again, the titles refer vaguely to affairs of space and things cosmic ("Outer Nothingness," "Other Worlds," "Nebulae"), but this time a great deal of the music is self-consciously "weird," with lots of eerie tympani, echoing bells, and low-pitched sounds from bass clarinet and bass trombone.

On other numbers, such effects are larded around soloists who exhibit their fondness for some of the better-known players of the new jazz. The result is rather like encountering Ornette Coleman's cousin, wandering around in next week's reruns on the *Science Fiction Theater*.

Indeed, I suspect that if Sun Ra were to cool it on the cosmos and the fourth dimension, and to turn his hand to studio and sound-track work, his talent, his considerable skill, and his professionalism would flourish.

An LP called *Until* on the new Atlantic subsidiary label, Vortex (2005, stereo only), is the very interesting debut, as leader, of alto saxophonist Robin Kenyatta. For the timid, the program offers a whimsical, conservative waltz called, after Paul Klee, "Little Blue Devil," and there is a more or less traditional ballad in the title piece, "Until."

There are also a couple of free-form improvisations. On "This Year," Kenyatta exchanges comments with trumpeter Mike Lawrence and pianist Fred Simmons. "You Know How We Do" is a more ambitious undertaking, with an augmented rhythm section and with Roswell Rudd's trombone. Compositionally, both pieces are indebted to Ornette Coleman, as is Kenyatta's own playing. (I am sorry to keep mentioning Coleman this way, but considering the subject under discussion, I see no way of avoiding it.)

Kenyatta's phrasing has an appealing rhythmic variety, and, more important, he shows a capacity to alter tempo, to swing us along compellingly at one speed, then shift momentarily to another, and somehow make the shift seem welcome. I also admire, in "You Know How We Do," the terseness with which the leader makes his own statements, and the varied textures evoked in the simultaneously improvised ensembles

—ensembles in which Rudd's trombone, in his essentially revivalist-1930s style, makes its points.

Admittedly, it is possible to suspect a kind of something-for-everyone opportunism in the programming here, but I don't think so. Kenyatta's own words, quoted in the liner notes, are, "I'm not trying to put people on by saying I'm playing space music. I'm just trying to play music the way I think it's supposed to be played—honestly. A lot of people use a lot of words to describe what the've done, but I've never been able to; with me it's all emotional. Whatever a person *can* play, that's what he *should* play." I believe him.

Kenyatta is also a functional participant in *Intents and Purposes* (RCA Victor stereo, LSP-3844; mono, LPM-3844), a collection of four performances by a small ensemble under the leadership of composer-trumpeter Bill Dixon, most of which was originally conceived for dancers of a more or less "modern" persuasion.

Setting aside the question of improvisation for the moment (after all, Lukas Foss's "classical" ensemble *does* improvise), I suppose a listener's first question on hearing music like this might be, "But is it jazz?" One answer is that only jazz musicians would be willing to use their instruments with the sonorous freedom sometimes required here.

Another answer is that Dixon's use of jazz rhythms, both in phrasing and in some of the percussion, goes beyond what any mere borrowers from jazz are likely to come up with.

There were, for me, a couple of rather static, almost monotonous moments on the piece called "Metamorphoses 1962-1966," both from the strings (a cello and two basses) and from the leader's trumpet. But I much admire Dixon's more mobile textures on these four manifestations of his essentially romantic talent. I shall not soon forget the quiet ironies of these two "Nightfall" pieces. And I commend RCA Victor and producer Brad McCuen for having recorded this music.

The Don Ellis band has packed up its truckloads of electronic equipment, its acres of percussion, its odd (but sometimes monotonous) time-signature (would you believe $3\frac{1}{2}$ over 5?), its massive sounds, and its *au fond* be-bopish phrasing, and moved over to Columbia records. The first results are on *Electric Bath* (stereo, CS 9598; mono, CL 2785). The music is still tricky, skillful, enjoyable, and, I think, quite light-weight. May Euterpe protect Ellis from pretense.

Saturday Review, October 12, 1968
Copyright © 1968 Saturday Review, Inc.

New Jazz / Big Band / But . . .

If you are thinking that the big band of the new jazz of the 1960s is the Don Ellis orchestra, you are wrong, for strange time-signatures do not an *avant* make nor electronic equipment a *garde.* There is, however, a New York ensemble called the Jazz Composers Orchestra which is sustained largely by its two chief composers, trumpeter Mike Mantler and pianist Carla Bley, and assembled whenever possible from the musicians available. It made its first recording in 1964 for Fontana, *Communication* (stereo, 881-011-ZY), when that European label was willing to take a chance on a series of LPs by younger American jazzmen.

It has now made a recording of its own, a boxed set of two LPs called simply *The Jazz Composers Orchestra* (stereo, JCOA, 1001/2, available only from the Jazz Composers Orchestra Association, 261 Broadway, New York, N.Y. 10007, $12), which offers four works by Mantler, each featuring one or two soloists.

Mantler's compositional roots too frequently lie, it seems to me, in twentieth-century "classical" soil, and, like many a composer who admires modern classicists without consciously wanting to be one, he sometimes siphons off the sound of the music without its substance, somewhat in the deadpan manner of (I regret to say) a Hollywood hack.

But there is more to Mantler's music than that, to be sure. On *Communication #8*, he masses his sounds and textures in frequently exhilarating ways. But he presents his soloists—trumpeter Don Cherry, a relatively delicate player, and tenor saxophonist Gato Barbieri—with the problem of battling the mass. Cherry gets some licks in, however. On *Communication #9*, Mantler offers a rather barren landscape featuring Larry Coryell's guitar with some electronic twanging of which, I confess, I can make very little. On *#10*, trombonist Roswell Rudd gets a chance to do his thing. I like his thing (I like his humor!), and I like some of the sounds Mantler has used to complement it. On *#11*, tenor saxophonist Pharoah Sanders howls, cries, and screams. It is sincere; it is absolutely real; it is, in its way, effective. But in my opinion it is not very musical.

On *Communication #12*, Mantler's soloist is pianist Cecil Taylor, and Mantler pays tribute to Taylor in his own writing—which is not, let us face it, quite the same as getting Taylor to write something. Taylor does play something—he's all over the place at breakneck speed. Sometimes you might call it an avant-gardist's version of tickling the ivories. But at several moments when he has juxtaposed solo with the bass players and drums, there is no call for levity.

In a booklet that offers a kind of history and credo of the Jazz Composers Orchestra, its leadership explains that the new jazz offers a "loosening of melodic, melodic-rhythmic, harmonic, and harmonic-rhythmic dogmas" in both improvisation and composition; that it involves a modification in the ways of phrasing and the spectrum of sounds formerly used; and a "dissolution of the steady rhythm into its basic purpose: propulsion, now achieved by various means of a tension-release nature."

Clear enough, and informative. Nevertheless, the work of the soloists and the sometimes arresting percussive lines of drummers Andrew Cyrille and Beaver Harris being granted, this music frequently doesn't *sound* like jazz—or it sounds like a little jazz and a lot of something else. (The music of Ornette Coleman's small ensembles and the textures of Don Cherry's longer pieces sound like jazz to the squarest head in the house.) Also, the tension-release patterns of the Jazz Composers Orchestra don't always propel. But the more important aspect of its not sounding and moving like jazz is that the music lacks the emotional paradox of the best jazz, a paradox wherein joy and anguish may be momentarily resolved—a quality that has been uniquely and profoundly a part of the music at least since King Oliver.

A slightly cut-down version of the Jazz Composers Orchestra appears with the Gary Burton Quartet on a large company's release of *A Genuine Tong Funeral* (RCA Victor stereo, LSP 3988), written by Carla Bley. At her best, Bley is an unpretentious miniaturist, and I think she knows it. Her piece (the programmatic content of which I think it best to ignore) is a suite in ten parts. She does tend to substitute a kind of sustained but static moodiness for substance and movement in a couple of her slow sections. Also her "Morning" and "Funeral March" seem surprisingly old hat. But her "Lament" comes to life with some of the best sustained improvising I have yet heard from vibist Burton, beautifully accompanied by bassist Steve Swallow. Also, the degree of cooperation between composer and players achieved on "Some Dirge" is impressive. And in the swift "Epilogue" she gets some high effects from Burton's virtuosity.

In 1962, at the First International Jazz Festival that was held in Washington, D.C., the trio of John Benson Brooks, which featured alto saxophonist critic Don Heckman, performed a piece called "The Twelves," which undertook jazz improvisation using twelve-tone rows. Such things have been tried by others, with frequently stilted, dig-what-I-learned-in-music-school results. The Brooks ensemble not only played more interestingly, it performed with some humor, fire, conviction, and swing.

The results were recorded, and they now appear—well, sort of. A Decca album called *Avant Slant* (stereo, DL 75018) intercuts bits of the original music with stilted, unfunny verbal gaggery, sound effects, snippets of other music, quasi-poetry, "mod" verbiage, and a few conventionally conceived pop tunes ("Cover Me with Kisses," yet). The notes say something about this mess being for "Right Now." What I want from an LP is to be able to listen to it tomorrow.

Saturday Review, December 28, 1968
Copyright © 1968 Saturday Review, Inc.

Evans at Montreux

The information that the music in *Bill Evans at the Montreux Jazz Festival* (Verve stereo V6-8762) was the hit of the event may set up the wrong kind of expectation. What usually brings out the bravos at jazz festivals is a stomping, shouting kind of grandstanding that may not stand up too well on a record. Well, not always. Lionel Hampton was a smash at the 1967 Newport Festival, and the recorded evidence (on RCA Victor stereo LSP-3891) turns out to be enthusiastic big band jazz that is rousing without being banal.

Anyway, pianist Bill Evans' trio brought forth the cheers and played the encores last summer at the modest festival at Montreux, Switzerland, and they did it with musicianship and with conspicuously quiet but communicated emotion, which, as any booking agent will tell you, is not the sort of thing that is supposed to bring them to their feet at jazz festivals. Credit the Swiss, perhaps. And credit Bill Evans.

No, best to credit all three players here. It is immediately evident from the intricate, free, but never intrusive drummer's counterpoint of

Jack de Johnette on "One for Helen," and from the interplay with Evans of bassist Eddie Gomez on "A Sleeping Bee" that this is a trio of virtual equals, not a piano soloist with a couple of accompanists, and the best ensemble Evans has had in some time.

At the risk of bringing up the lazy reviewer's cliché, I would say that Evans' problem has been one of communication: on occasion the extreme introspection, even introversion of his style has made his work seem almost a private matter, and one in which a listener just might be intruding. Not here. It may have been the occasion, or the impetus provided by the current trio. But I prefer to think it is also a matter of Bill Evans' coming to terms with his one remaining problem as a musician, for he has a beautifully explored, unaccompanied version of Gershwin's "I Love You, Porgy" that might easily be his masterpiece on LP.

About four years ago, the public statements and interviews given out by a group of younger New York jazzmen indicated that they saw their own plight as avant-gardists as an aspect of the struggles of American black men in general. The implication was that anyone who did not like their music was a racist. One of the more vocal members of the group was essayist, playwright, and tenor saxophonist Archie Shepp, and for a while it appeared that Shepp was ready to employ a kind of verbal and musical chauvinism at the expense of his developing talents as a musician.

Archie Shepp in Europe (Delmark stereo DS-9409) comes from Copenhagen, circa 1963, and is now released here for the first time. It is actually the work of an interesting group called the New York Contemporary Five of which Shepp was a member. The leading talent and musical guiding light of the group was cornetist Don Cherry. The general approach and part of the repertory come from Cherry's former mentor Ornette Coleman. And, although alto saxophonist John Tchicai does not like to be compared to Coleman, his solos here invite it. Into this "free" atmosphere, however, are thrust some older and perhaps safer ideas, with rather incongruous results. For one, during Cherry's very good solo on "When Will the Blues Leave?" we are treated to a conventionally tonal background riff out of 1954 Miles Davis. Shepp generally lets us know he has been practicing his Sonny Rollins, and on "Mik" that he could make something out of it.

He did. But the pendulum seems to swing rapidly for Archie Shepp. For example, his 1966 *On this Night* (Impulse stereo 99) was the work of a maturing musician for much of its length. But Shepp's new *The*

Way Ahead (Impulse stereo A 9170), with a sextet (and with a cover design that is clever enough to be illegible) is a mixed bag.

A couple of the selections ("The Stroller," "Fiesta") throw together conventions from contemporary barroom blues with some of the procedures of "free form" jazz. In his solos, Shepp, in effect, comments on the proceedings from the sidelines—approving, disapproving, saying something perhaps, always there, but only occasionally involved with the others, and more inclined, I think, to demonstrate his wounds than tell us about them. "Frankenstein" echoes the kind of incantatory, simultaneous improvisation of John Coltrane's later work, a bit more orderly perhaps but a lot less forceful—sort of humorless Herman Munster rather than Karloff's monster.

Finally, Shepp, with superb assistance from bassist Ron Carter, reads "Sophisticated Lady" with a combination of gruffness, tenderness, and alarm that sounds bizarre in the telling but is largely cohesive in the listening, and may well demonstrate what a complex musician Shepp may become.

The New York Times, January 5, 1969
Copyright © 1968/1969 by the New York Times Company.
Reprinted by permisson.

Recording Miles Davis

The administrative offices of Columbia Records are now located in the parent company's externally handsome new CBS Building on New York's Avenue of the Americas. But for the purposes of recording, the old, reliable Columbia studios still seem to serve best. Thus, on a morning last winter, a Miles Davis recording session was set for the venerable Studio B, on East 52nd Street near Madison.

The date was called for 10:00, but by 9:40, Davis was there, his thin, broad-shouldered frame comfortably dressed in a long-sleeved, knit sport shirt and a pair of corduroy trousers. He was lounging casually on a chair in the control room, but he was obviously anxious to get to work. The day before he had not been so optimistic. "We may just end up rehearsing, or sitting around looking at each other," he had commented with a not unusual edge of humor in his voice.

Davis is notoriously taciturn on the bandstand, disinclined to announce his numbers or to acknowledge applause. But the more private Miles Davis is a talkative man whose conversation is a stream of anecdotes, free-associated reminiscences, and outspoken reactions and opinions, most of which are delivered with a kind of shared, ironic wit that tempers an occasional bitterness.

Columbia's engineer Frank Laico, with two assistants, was threading tapes, adjusting dials, and visually checking the placement of the battery of microphones on view through a glass panel in the large rectangular studio directly ahead. Davis meanwhile was commenting to guitarist George Benson: "When whites play with Negroes and can't play the music, it's a form of Jim Crow to me. Studio musicians—they're supposed to be able to play all kinds of music. So they should know what's going on in our music, too. One, two, three, four—anybody can do that. And if you don't do it, they don't believe the beat is still there." Davis was still smarting from the experiences of a previous session when an otherwise capable studio guitarist had failed him miserably. "I was so mad, they gave me a royalty check and I didn't even look at it."

This date, therefore, with Benson on guitar, was a kind of make-up for the previous session. Columbia is willing to devote much time and money to Davis' recorded output, and Miles Davis, for all the casual air with which he goes about it, is a careful craftsman. He has been with the company for over ten years now. His first popularity depended on a passionate, lyric interpretation of standard ballads and traditional blues, and there was a time when it seemed that Davis might be content with a safe repetition of that formula. But, from time to time, he has undertaken more experimental fare. The *Kind of Blue* session of 1959 used highly unorthodox procedures for improvisation and influenced the subsequent development of jazz. And recently, the more exploratory sessions such as *E.S.P.*, *Miles Smiles*, and *Sorcerer*, have virtually become the rule.

For the work in progress, Miles has augmented his regular quintet with a guitar and has invited pianist Herbie Hancock to try celeste, electronic piano, and electric harpsichord ("I woke up in the middle of the night last night hearing that sound," Miles remarked about the latter instrument). One piece already completed for the album is Davis' "Burlena," which involves the bass and guitar playing one melody line, the horns (Davis and tenor saxophonist Wayne Shorter) another, and drummer Tony Williams improvising an interplaying, percussive third part.

Davis was now in the studio, still chatting with Benson as he picked up and quietly strummed the guitarist's instrument. In the booth, the engineering staff was openly airing its pessimism.

"I kind of knew we wouldn't have to rush into this thing this morning."

"Yeah, I'm sort of surprised *he's* here."

But by 10:05, Davis was in place in the studio, running down one of the pieces on his horn. Teo Macero, Columbia's A & R man, had arrived and was immediately talking on the telephone. Tony Williams and his drums were making their way through the tangle of mike booms, wires, and baffle boards. And within a few minutes, Wayne Shorter, bassist Ron Carter and Herbie Hancock had entered, removed their coats, taken their places, and were beginning to examine the music on the racks before them.

Macero walked into the studio and embraced Davis. Almost on his heels arrived orchestrator Gil Evans, a thin, gray, sympathetic, and authoritative presence. "Hey, Gil! You got me some music?" Davis said as a greeting, and the two embraced as Evans answered, "Yes."

"I midwifed a couple of these pieces," Evans continued, referring to the fact that Hancock, Shorter, and Davis wrote most of the numbers to be used, but that he had helped lay a couple of them out for performance.

George Benson was quietly reading and strumming his part. Hancock sat surrounded by his four keyboards, trying out the electric harpsichord. "Which piece shall we work on, Miles?" he asked.

"I don't know," said Davis off-handedly, although he was clearly considering the matter. "Try yours," he said, after a pause—and suddenly Shorter and Davis began phrasing a rolling melody together—a single, casual foot pat from Davis had set the tempo and started them off.

A moment later, Benson and Hancock consulted. "Some of these are chords. Some are just sounds," the pianist-composer explained.

"Hey, Herbie, don't play that one," Davis remarked, indicating the harpsichord. "Play the black one," the electronic piano.

Ron Carter, surrounded chest high by baffle boards to isolate the sound of his instrument, surveyed the scene through wire-rimmed glasses, pipe in mouth. Dressed in a dark cardigan sweater, he looked rather like a retired druggist.

As they continued to run down the piece, it became evident that Tony Williams, Davis' young drummer, was feeling his way into it in a highly personal manner. He began with a bit of history, an old-fashioned, regular *ching-de-ching* cymbal beat. By the second or third run-through, he was trying a conservative Latin rhythm, executed chiefly with wire brushes on his snare drum. But within a few more tries, his part had become a complex whirl of cymbal, snare, and tom-tom patterns and accents, although there was no question of where the beat, the basic 1-2-3-4, was falling.

They began on the piece again. Davis counted, "One, two, three, four," but until the music began, he might almost have been tossing off random numbers rather than establishing a strict tempo.

Inside the engineering booth, Macero shuffled through some American Federation of Musicians contracts as he remarked, "That line is hard. It reminds me of those things Miles did for Capitol. Remember them? But this is much freer, of course." He was referring to some recordings by a nine-piece group with Gil Evans, Gerry Mulligan, and others, which started a fad called "cool jazz," and which were imitated in everything from big-band arrangements to cigarette jingles on TV.

Suddenly Davis, whose mike position in the studio had him sitting with his back to the control room, turned and said with a cheerful half-smile, "I want to hear this." In a moment, Macero was reading a complex number, followed by "take one," onto the tape. A run-down of the piece had begun, with Davis and Shorter phrasing together almost as one man.

At the end of a playback Macero got up and, singing and almost dancing his way into the studio, made a quiet point to Davis in the manner of a man telling a casual joke. He was obviously very happy to have started to work.

Davis worked out a couple of bent notes with Ron Carter and then Davis called Gil Evans over to clear up a point in the score, while in the background Carter and Benson ran through a portion of the piece. They were accompanied by impeccable finger-snapping from Tony Williams, who was pacing around the studio, rather like an athlete loosening up after a foot race. By 11:30, the musicians had run through the theme several times more, and it was beginning to swing hard. It was time to take it from the top, including a try at the improvised portions. "Okay, here we go," Davis announced, calling for the intro. "Tony's got two bars."

Halfway through his solo, Davis stopped and turned to Macero, who had reentered the booth. "Hey, Teo, can you make it so it doesn't sound so dull when I hear myself in here? Because what I hear, I don't like."

"I can put a little echo on it, but I'd rather do that when I have more control over it later on."

"Well, if I like it, I can play better."

Macero nodded an unspoken assent, while Laico made an appropriate adjustment among his switches and dials.

A moment later, when an engineer entered the studio during the run-through, Davis was highly annoyed and he let Macero know it. During an ensuing pause, Shorter tried out a new reed.

A minute later they were trying the solos again, and Davis was dissatisfied with his background. "Can we change that chord? I don't like that A Minor. Hey, Herbie, play a C Major." Hancock subjected his C Major to various augmentations and substitutions, interpolating various passing chords along the way. Davis was still dissatisfied. "Play a C chord all through there but put all that other stuff in it," he said tartly.

"Oh, I see what you mean," said Hancock and he tried out the sequence again.

As they ran through Davis' solo, he glanced at the revised chord changes on the music sheet in front of him. And somehow he managed to look up at his music from under his eyebrows, although it was well below eye-level.

It was 11:45, and Miles said, "Hey, Teo!"

He was immediately understood. "You want to record this next time." Laico started the tapes rolling.

During the take, Hancock executed a quiet dance with his shoulders, head, and feet as he played; the rest of him was almost immobile. Tony Williams' dance was broader than Hancock's and centered in his elbows. Davis, now satisfied with his chords, did his dancing with his horn.

During the playback, quiet settled on the studio. Macero entered unobtrusively with the income tax withholding forms for the players to fill out, a sure sign that the session was well under way. Davis leaned over a low table, bending from the waist, listening. Shorter munched on a snack he had brought along, but he was listening. As the last notes echoed through the studio, Miles made an inaudible comment, gave Macero a glance that indicated he wanted another take, and then said aloud to his side-man, "Make it tighter."

Hancock: "You want me to stay out of there more?"

Davis: "Yessir!"

Hancock: "But you want me to hit that B-flat chord."

Davis: "Yeah."

Macero (onto the rolling tape): "Take fifteen."

Davis (stopping the take in the middle): "Teo, I sound like I'm playing to the wall."

Macero: "Try it with the earphones on."

They were into another take. Davis, sitting on the edge of his stool, was so involved in his solo that he somehow managed to raise both feet off the ground.

At the end of the take, he looked dissatisfied. But Macero announced, "Martin liked it."

"What the—has Martin got to do with it?"

During the playback, Shorter ducked his head and pulled up his coat collar at something he didn't like in his own solo. But at the end, Davis announced, "That's all right, Teo."

It was 12:30, and by mutual unspoken agreement there was time to try another piece. "This is the one—'Paraphernalia,' " said Hancock, selecting a music sheet from the pile in front of him. He turned to the celeste and began running through his part, but after a few of its tinkling notes, Davis asked him to go back to the piano.

There was some discussion of a tricky portion of the piece during which Carter and Hancock are to hold certain chords as long as the soloist wants them, repeat them until the improviser is clearly ready for the next one. Davis sat quietly as the other musicians explained things and worked them out. His presence is authoritative and puts his side-men on their mettle, and he knows it. But when the moment is right for a decision, he makes one. "Wayne, you don't play the 3/4 bars, and the last 4/4 bar is cut out."

As they ran the piece down, the art of it began to emerge; it didn't sound difficult or complex. Shorter's solo seemed to float, suspended above the rhythm section. For his part, Davis was still instructing as he played. At the end, he crossed to Hancock's keyboard to demonstrate a point, and advised, "It sounds good. But Herbie, don't play all over the piano. Don't go up there," gesturing at the top third of the keyboard. And then he announced to the room in general, "Let's record it. Come on, this is simple."

After a couple of false starts they were into a take. Again Hancock's shoulders danced. During his solo, Davis looked as if half a dozen impressions were attacking his mind at once, but he played as if he were able to condense them all into brief, smoldering, allusive phrases. Shorter built his portion out of ingenious fragments of the main theme. Hancock echoed the theme in his section too, but quite differently. During Tony Williams' spot, Davis' expression showed his approval, and he signaled to Benson to take a solo as the tape was still rolling.

"Let's hear some of that, Teo," Miles requested at the end. As the playback began to fill the studio, he executed a quick sideways step across the floor in time to the music, then paused and said quietly, "That's hard work—making records."

Stereo Review, February, 1969
Copyright © 1969 by *Stereo Review*
Reprinted by permission.

Coleman's Raw Emotion

Ornette Coleman's new LP, *New York Is Now!* (Blue Note stereo BST 84287), is a general delight. It is also the kind of recital that can enlighten people as to what the new jazz is all about.

Of course the most authoritative instruction is the raw, untrammeled emotion in Coleman's own alto saxophone solos. But the new jazz also means that, since improvised variation is, after all, the main attraction in the music, a solo need not be obeisant—in structure, in harmony, or in tempo—to an opening theme.

Similar assumptions are fairly commonplace in other musics, to be sure, but they have only recently appeared in jazz.

The new LP has Coleman in the company of bassist Jimmy Garrison, with whom he has worked before, and with drummer Elvin Jones. Except for a relatively brief and only partly successful spoof, "We Now Interrupt for a Commercial," on which he plays chattering violin, Coleman confines himself to alto saxophone. As the other horn he introduces Dewey Redman on tenor, and Redman proves to be a good foil to the leader. He is a rich, adept, relatively cool saxophonist who does not posture, and in his solos, traditional ways of playing jazz are more dancingly apparent than in Coleman's. Redman may be a man to turn on many of those who are still unconverted to the idiom.

The stereo separation of the horns is particularly valuable here, for it lets one hear clearly how Coleman's music allows for individual interpretation and embellishment, even in an opening "unison" statement.

"Garden of Souls" sets the tone of the recital. It is serious, pensive, declamatory, and almost lightheartedly humorous in turn. It moves in mood and tempo with a logic of both human feeling and of sequential musical motive.

Humor and good spirits are more overt in "Toy Dance." "Broadway Blues" begins with Coleman's extension of a traditional lick and freshly explores the variety of moods possible in that venerable and basic music form. On "Round Trip" there is a delightful lesson to be learned in noticing how differently Garrison and Jones work with each of the two saxophonists, and there is a closing episode in which the horns improvise simultaneously in a kind of atonal counterpoint, or, if you will, new-thing Dixieland.

If a listener, nevertheless, does have problems with Coleman's music, I think it is probably because his ear unconsciously expects certain conventional harmonic cadences and resolutions simply by habit, and he may be bothered at first when he does not hear them. He may also be initially taken aback by the unorthodox sounds some of the players make, and by the obliquely intoned bursts of melody from Coleman's saxophone (some musicians *still* believe he can't play in tune!). But these, after all, are simply extensions of the tradition of individual instrumental sound, and of the blue notes and "vocal" inflections that jazzmen have always used. More important, the new jazz involves new rhythms, new accents, new ways of phrasing. If one is at first bothered by them (as many were at first bothered by Charlie Parker's fresh rhythmic attack), the answer may be simply in listening and getting used to them. The rewards are sizable. And *New York Is Now!* is a very good place to start.

The New York Times, February 23, 1969
Copyright © 1968/1969 by the New York Times Company.
Reprinted by permission.

Getting Along with Lunceford

The first billing was the "Chickasaw Syncopaters," and the band came out of Memphis in the late 1920s. By 1930, the group had made its first recordings, and five years later it had become one of the most successful swing bands in the country. Along the way, it had been decided that "Jimmy Lunceford and his Orchestra" would be the name, and it was a much more appropriate billing than the former, for the group was not a cooperative of instrumentalists but very much a leader's band.

Lunceford's recording career began at Victor, with two titles in 1930. Beginning in late 1934, there were five years at Decca. Following came a couple of years at Vocalion and Columbia. These latter are well, but not ideally, represented on Columbia's *Lunceford Special* (Stereo, CS 9515).

There are two new Decca releases, *Jimmy Lunceford Vol. 1 "Rhythm Is Our Business"* (*1934–1935*) (enhanced for stereo, DL 79237) and *Jimmy Lunceford Vol. 2 "Harlem Shout"* (*1935–1936*), (DL 79238), and these present the first two years with the company very well or rather badly. Very well, if the plan were to offer an average of what Lunceford actually recorded and played for the crowds. Rather badly, if the idea were to offer the best of Lunceford recordings from those years that are apt to be the most interesting thirty-plus years later.

The first set begins with some versions of Ellington pieces ("Mood Indigo," "Black and Tan Fantasy," and a tune, "Rose Room," Ellington had adopted) in versions that are deplorably lightweight, almost deliberately "cute." Before long, we encounter the kind of good lightweight material that was more appropriate to the Lunceford showmanship, vocals, and solos on a piece like "Rhythm Is Our Business." What we do not encounter often enough is the kind of rousing, powerhouse instrumental best represented by a piece like "White Heat" (which was not done for Decca), but well represented by "Oh Boy" and "Runnin' Wild." Meanwhile, we hear far too many deadpan ballads, too many vocal trios and the like, some of which are really dreadful.

One thing that was clear at the time is clearer still in retrospect: With rare exceptions, Lunceford was not interested in his soloists for the best that soloists can contribute, but only as pieces in a pattern of ensemble discipline and showmanship. Solos were effects to this band, effects among all the other effects it could achieve, and not the chief effects.

Not that Lunceford didn't have some good improvisers, and even some very good ones. Indeed, alto saxophonist Willie Smith was, at the time, one of the five or six best men on his instrument in jazz. But, whereas one might listen to Ellington for ten minutes and know what an exceptional alto soloist Johnny Hodges was, for knowledge of Smith's abilities, he might have to listen to Lunceford long and hard.

One might therefore expect, as I imply above, that the arrangements would be exceptional. Some few are. And others have good moments. (It's interesting, in rehearing this chart on "Avalon," to realize how many of its effects were borrowed by others.) But by and large, it was a general attitude that sustained this band, a kind of good time, stomping shout, or easy, middle-tempo swing that can be heard on "Bird of Paradise," "Stomp It Off," "Organ Grinder's Swing" (probably the best), "Sewanee River," or "Harlem Shout." These moods were quite genuine while they lasted (and this ensemble could swing a "two-beat" accented arrangement as none other).

Fletcher Henderson's best recordings survive their time because he showed what big-band jazz might be, showed that the individual improviser and the composer-arranger might work together, and often enough showed they might work together with excellence. Ellington, simultaneously both earthier and more sophisticated than Henderson, showed that the individual player and the composer-orchestrater might both be brilliant and yet produce a whole greater than the sum of its parts. The Count Basie band gave spirited reaffirmation to the role of the soloist in episodes that both opened up the future for the individual improviser and survive on their own as spontaneous melody in an appropriate context. But Lunceford, I fear, the pleasures of his music being granted, was much more of his time. His music would therefore have been better served, in my opinion, by a carefully selected LP or two than by the series that these two new Decca albums inaugurate.

Saturday Review, March 15, 1969
Copyright © 1969 Saturday Review, Inc.

Quartets and Cannonballs

The "modern" jazz of the mid-1940s had to wait until the mid-1950s to find its largest audience. When it did, the ensemble called the Modern Jazz Quartet, and the groups led by Miles Davis, regularly filled the night clubs, sold the records, and won the popularity polls. Each has maintained it popularity; the Quartet, partly by perfecting what it already did, and Davis, partly by finding some new things to do.

Under the Jasmin Tree (Apple stereo ST 3353) is the Modern Jazz

Quartet's first release under its new alliance with the Beatles' company, distributed here by Capitol. It has four pieces, two of them (as the strange liner notes do not point out) from a film score, and one of them a three-part suite. That latter, *Three Little Feelings*, was originally composed by the group's pianist John Lewis for a brass orchestra and Miles Davis, and is one of Lewis' best pieces. It translates very well in this Quartet version, due in no small part to the resourcefulness of vibraphonist Milt Jackson, who brings a crystalline buoyancy to the first part, an intricate lyricism to the second and straight-ahead swing to the third. The paradox of melodic delicacy and rhythmic force in this man's work continues to be a major marvel.

"The Blue Necklace" and "The Jasmin Tree" are from Lewis' score for a USIA documentary on Morocco. Both pieces (the former with the help of some unbilled wind chimes) manage to employ musical effects local to the area with minimal gimmickry. "The Blue Necklace" is, of course, the blues, and Jackson is a bluesman. "The Jasmin Tree" has some very good Jackson-Lewis counterpoint. But portions of the set's other piece, "Exposure," seem ponderously overwritten to me.

All in all, however, the MJQ's best set in several years.

Although John Lewis' own music remains relatively conservative, he is sympathetic to some of the more recent developments—he was for example, one of Ornette Coleman's earliest champions. Miles Davis, although he has declared himself out of sympathy with most avant-gardists, has become one himself and *Miles in the Sky* (Columbia stereo CS 9628) is one of several recent albums that prove it winningly.

The effort to continue a rock-blues accompaniment idea throughout "Stuff" becomes monotonous to me, and on "Paraphanalia" I keep being reminded of the structural premise rather than of what is being built on it. But "Black Comedy" has exciting textures, meaty solos, and some fine rhythmic retards to which drummer Tony Williams manages to add both suspense and momentum. And Davis's piece "Country Son" comes off as a particularly exciting, varied, "extended" jazz piece in both composition and performance.

Cannonball Adderley was an associate of Miles Davis in some of the early "experimental" work. But his own inclinations usually keep him in the modern mainstream, and his great success as a leader has often seemed to me more interesting sociologically than musically.

The Cannonball Adderley Quintet "In Person" (Capitol stereo ST 162) is the latest of a series of albums his group has recorded before night club audiences. It comes complete with applause, cheers, hoots, and announcements from Adderley—a former Florida schoolteacher—that feature of a few "ain'ts" and lots of down-home jive. The recital has "guest" appearances by Nancy Wilson, a sort of schoolgirl Dinah Washington, and by Lou Rawls, a handsome, middle-brow blues singer. It also has instrumentals in which there are more blue notes per four-bar phrase than you might have believed possible. Indeed, to me the whole occasion has the air of a communal celebration in which a black middle class determinedly seeks out its musical roots. Whereas one may welcome the quest, and hope it is a real one, one may also hope that Adderley's considerable talents will one day lead himself and his following to level on (let us say) that exceptional variation of "Autumn Leaves" which he recorded eleven years ago for Blue Note.

The New York Times, March 23, 1969
Copyright © 1968/1969 by the New York Times Company.
Reprinted by permission.

Ornette Coleman in Concert

The occasion was a reunion. Cherry and Haden were in the first group that Ornette Coleman brought to the old Five Spot in New York in the late fall of 1959 (was it really *that* long ago?). But the program featured seven new compositions by Coleman, and one by Charlie Haden.

Beginning with the first piece, "Broken Shadows," with Coleman and Redman in dirge tempo and Cherry playing an obbligato, it was evident that I was going to have a problem throughout the evening. When I first heard Denny Coleman on a record a couple of years ago, I was happy to take at face value the attitude that, whereas there was obviously much he didn't know about drums, he played what he played with a promising naturalness, good spirit, and personal feeling. Those things are not enough, to be sure, but they are the right beginning.

Something has gone awry. Young Coleman was loud at this concert (he was also amplified—more on that in a moment), and he was, it seemed to me, insensitive in his loudness. He was careless in what he played behind the soloists. For example, he missed Don Cherry's dynamics and tempo alterations of "Who Do You Work For?" and he didn't hear the quality of Haden's solos. In this music one mustn't miss such things. Swing is becoming a problem. Tempo is becoming a problem. The time has come, I think, when Denny Coleman's technical short-comings are beginning to stand in the way of what he wants to express and causing him to push. I'd suggest that the moment has arrived for a teacher—and, no, nobody asked me.

Charlie Haden. Well, Charlie Haden was also wired into the huge rock-type amplifier at the back of the stage. The result was to buzz and blur of one of the most precise and buoyant bass sounds I know of. During the second half of the program, Haden removed the small mike from inside his bass strings and put it on a low stand on the floor. It helped—some.

Cherry is a better, more confident trumpeter than he was nine years ago; he has ideas and approaches of his own in this music now. And Redman's relative conservatism seems to me a very good contrast in the group.

Beginning with the second number, "The Anthem," Coleman picked up piece after piece and made it soar. And for the record, I will also mention his solo on "Comme Il Faut," which was exceptional. His musical energy and grasp of tempo were wonderful. More important, of course, is his ability to sustain, develop, and vary an idea—this is the most orderly of players. But Coleman does, on occasion, keep an idea going somewhat past the point of inspiration and deep interest, and into the point of simple ingenuity.

Also for the record, I will mention "Space Jungle," a relatively light-weight piece for which each man brought out the alternate instruments listed above, because Cherry's Indian flute gave a lovely sound.

Still, I did feel the program lacked variety. There was a sameness about several of the pieces, a sameness of approach perhaps, for concert listening. Maybe the evening should have been shorter by a piece or two.

As I sat in the hall thinking about all of the above, and wondering if there was any way I could sum up my varied and sometimes dissatis-fied impressions of the evening, came the last piece, "Trouble in the East." It was contrapuntally written and collectively improvised by all the horns, but it was like no other collective improvisation ever under-taken in this idiom, or any other. It felt spontaneously ordered in all its aspects, and had the timeless joy and melancholy of the blues running through it. It had its feet planted on the earth and it spoke of the gods. It was one of the most exciting, beautiful, and satisfying musical per-formances I have ever heard.

Yes, it got recorded.

Boogie Woogie Goes Latin

One of the most singular record hits of recent months is an item called "Cow Cow Boogaloo" by pianist Ray Meriwether (it can be heard on Capitol stereo ST 102 along with eleven other short selections). The initiate will immediately recognize it as an up-to-date, Latinate version of one of the earliest recorded examples of the boogie woogie piano style, the "Cow Cow Blues" of Charles Davenport. The "cow cow" of the title is actually the cow catcher and the piece is, like many another boogie woogie piece, a train blues, an impression of a train ride.

Boogie woogie is a highly percussive style of piano blues, which juxtaposes a repeated bass figure a couple of beats or a bar or two long with a succession of improvised right-hand figures. With a little coordination, the style is easy enough to play. But without the right rhythmic touch and imagination (a quite individual matter) it is very difficult to play well. In the proper hands and in small doses, it can be fascinating. One of its greatest players, Jimmy Yancey, was a rudimentary pianist by other standards. But José Iturbi, in undertaking boogie woogie, failed miserably.

There was a boogie woogie craze of sorts in the 1940s, almost at the tail end of the swing era, during which the public was treated to such amiable but hardly authentic nonsense as "Scrub Me, Mama, With a Boogie Beat." Indeed, at the time, Davenport's piece was honored (if that is the word) in something called "Cow Cow Boogie," which turned out to be a pseudo-boogie song about a cowboy. Boogie's rhythm adapts readily to permutations of Caribbean and Latin American patterns, and current rock music and rhythm-and-blues abound in boogie devices.

The occasion for the foregoing exposition is the appearance of an LP called *Boogie Woogie Rarities, 1927–1932* (Milestone mono only, MLP 2009). Not all the contents are rarities. Indeed not all the selections are really boogie woogie, and some that are boogie are given not as solos but as accompaniments to blues singing. But there are a few gems and there is one masterpiece of the idiom, and I suppose that is a lot to get from an LP.

Davenport's piece is heard in its first (1927) recorded version, billed as "New Cow Cow Blues" because it is played in duet with B. T. Wingfield's plaintive cornet. It and several other selections (Jabo Williams's

"Jab Blues," Blind Leroy Garnet's "Chain Em Down," and Cripple Clarence Lofton's "On the Wall," for examples) represent, regardless of date, the blues finding its way, rhythmically, out of ragtime. Henry Brown's "Deep Morgan" shares Yancey's style. Wesley Wallace's train blues, "Number 29," by skipping a couple of beats in the bass, comes out as a waltz! And on "Hastings Street," the interplay of Charlie Spand's two hands is further complemented by Blind Blake's guitar figures.

The "Honky Tonk Train Blues" of Meade "Lux" Lewis, here offered in its first (1927) version, is an extraordinary piece, entirely consistent and sustained, and, within its limited means, full of variety. Other pianists who have undertaken it have missed its rhythmic subtleties almost to a man and have even omitted one of its best figures. Lewis, himself, rediscovered in the late 1930s, rerecorded "Honky Tonk Train" excellently a couple of times, but then began treating it as a "showpiece," speeding it up until it became an avalanche of jerky noise. So this version is invaluable—a masterpiece in a fragile genre that has all but disappeared.

Guitar by Charlie Christian

Charlie Christian was not, as some commentators have contended, the first important jazz guitar soloist. Anyone who has heard Lonnie Johnson, with Louis Armstrong or with Duke Ellington or on his own, will know that he was not. Then there was Eddie Lang, an influence and object of respect in the 1920s and early 1930s, but whose work does not, in my opinion, survive its time. And there was—astonishing cultural development!—the Belgian-French gypsy, Django Reinhardt. Christian even had a predecessor on amplified guitar in Eddie Durham, who was otherwise a well-known trombonist and composer-arranger.

But Christian was, in his brief career, not a major guitarist; he was *the* major guitarist and a major soloist regardless of instrument. Was and still is, for we have had several first-rate jazz guitarists since Christian, but none, I think, his equal. Anyone interested in jazz, the guitar, or the real achievements of American music should know his recordings.

Christian found a special style and special role for his special instrument, the amplified guitar. He knew the work of his predecessors, to be sure, but his major influences were the horn men, more specifically the saxophonists, and most specifically Lester Young. He translated their influence into a single-string melodic technique—despite his rhythmic sureness and superb swing, he was not much of a chord-and-rhythm man, and, indeed, his best accompaniments were buoyant riffs of which he seemed to have an unending supply. His guitar style was, however, far from being merely imitative of a saxophone style, and his sound was a careful amplification of a personal guitar sound.

Christian was (according to a cliché of jazz history) a transitional figure between the jazz of the 1930s and the innovations of the 1940s. True, he was more harmonically exact and sophisticated than Lester Young, but, like Young, he remained as much a linear melodist. He was a great soloist by any standard; and in his short time before the public (Christian joined the Benny Goodman Sextet in late 1939 as an unknown, and died a mere eighteen months later), he left a rich recorded heritage, not merely of excellent playing but of exceptional solos.

The typical Christian solo is organized in contrasts of brief, tight, riff figures and long, flowing bursts of lyric melody; and in his best improvisations these elements not only contrast effectively but also, paradoxically, lead one to another.

Christian's recorded heritage is not ideally served on current LP. About eleven years ago, Columbia reissued some of the Goodman performances (mono only, CL 652), which in a couple of cases were expanded by splicing in Christian solos from alternate, unused "takes." The Schwann catalogue still lists the album, so perhaps one can find it. One of Christian's masterpieces with Goodman, "I've Found a New Baby," has never been on LP in the United States, but it is available on a CBS-Disque Christian album issued in Europe, *Solo Flight* (62-581). which is worth obtaining. There are still available the invaluable jam sessions recordings, the only ones we have (Archive of Folk and Jazz Music 219), which feature Christian's chorus-after-chorus inventiveness on several pieces.

The foregoing words are prompted by the appearnce of a Blue Note album, *Celestial Express* (B-6505), which reissues two sessions from the 1940s led by clarinetist Edmond Hall.

The second comes from 1944 and is, in a sense, an ersatz Goodman small-group date, with generally good work from Red Norvo, a very good solo by Teddy Wilson on "Smooth Sailin'," and, on the slow "Blue Interval," excellent work by Wilson and two superb improvisations by Hall.

The earlier session represented on *Celestial Express* comes from 1941 and is a quartet with an unusual instrumentation, in which Hall's clarinet is joined by Meade "Lux" Lewis on celeste, Charlie Christian on unamplified guitar, and Israel Crosby on bass for a program of blues at various tempos.

Individually, the players do well. However, on the faster pieces, the instrumentation itself risks a kind of thumping, stringed heaviness in the rhythm section which the high, belled tones of the celeste could not temper as a piano would. Still, Christian has a good solo on "Jammin' in Four," and the take-your-turn, solo-and-accompaniment counterpoint of Lewis and Hall on "Edmond Hall Blues" is very good.

However, everything—instrumentation, sonorities, style, players— comes together on "Profoundly Blue." It opens with three superb Christian choruses, with Crosby in a true countermelody behind him, and with a few gently rendered comments from Lewis as well. It is a performance of such exceptional musical and emotional quality as to produce a sense of sustained wonder, both the first time one hears it and the hundredth. There is even a second "take" of "Profoundly Blue" included, but its excellences only serve to dramatize the magic quality of the first.

Happily, the LP transfer of this Blue Note reissue has been done without phony electronic stereo, but there is a bit of surface noise that was not audible on an early ten-inch LP issue of some of this material.

Saturday Review, May 17, 1969
Copyright © 1969 Saturday Review, Inc.

New Adventures of the Jazz Guitar

I was last saying in this space that although the jazz guitar has had many very good players since Charlie Christian, including some who have supplied a lyricism that he lacked, it has had none who was his equal.

It has also had a few public successes, and the latest is a Hungarian-

288   JAZZ MASTERS IN TRANSITION, *1957–69*

born guitarist named Gabor Szabo. Szabo, whose style is a singular amalgam of Mississippi, Mersey, Madras, and Magyar, well marinated in Mediterranean chicken fat and garnished with marzipan, has declared that jazz as we know it is dead (as *who* knows it?), but he makes it at the festivals and with the record-buyers, nevertheless.

Szabo has three virtually simultaneous current releases. *More Sorcery* (Impulse stereo, A-9167) contains Gabor originals, a Beatles ditty, a recent show tune, a bossa nova, etc., played by two quintets. It seems to be made up of the leftovers of previous LPs. *Bacchanal* (Skye stereo, SK-3) is more recent quintet stuff, with more Szabo originals, two Donovan tunes, a movie theme, a recent hit ("Love Is Blue"), etc. *Dreams* (Skye stereo, SK-7) has Szabo with a medium-sized ensemble (a couple of strings, some French horns, and lots of clicking, scraping, rattling, popping percussion) and arrangements by Gary McFarland.

One of the most interesting aspects of this music, evident in the quintet LPs especially, is the very different sound and effect that Szabo and his second-stringer, Jim Stewart, get from their guitars. Otherwise, Szabo's stock-in-trade would seem to be a kind of genteel, world-weary version of the modal, around-the-drone, incantatory improvising that in John Coltrane's music had a quite different force and import.

Blues-rock guitarist and singer Johnny Winter has two current releases—not to mention a ream or two of current publicity—*The Progressive Blues Experiment* on Imperial stereo, LP-12431, and just plain *Johnny Winter* on Columbia stereo, CS 9862.

Winter seems ready to out-twang everybody with his guitar and eager to out-muddy everybody with his rather weak and somewhat misused voice. He seems to me an embarrassingly sincere, derivative performer who will probably have all the success that Columbia Records expects of him. His press releases make much of the fact that he is an albino (otherwise I would make nothing of it).

Winter's work couldn't stand much comparison with that of literally hundreds of black blues guitarists. Take Albert Collins, out of Texas, on *Love Can Be Found Anywhere (Even in a Guitar)* (Imperial stereo, 12428). Collins, leading a little organ-tenor sax-brass blues band, carries his musical idiom as naturally as his personality and his gait; he is a pleasure to listen to and, I would imagine, a joy to dance to. He is a man, playing a man's music. Winter, by contrast, is a boy sheep in wolf's clothing—Howlin' Wolf's clothing.

Saturday Review, July 26, 1969
Copyright © 1969 Saturday Review, Inc.

Related Quality Paperback Books from Da Capo Press